Date Due

MAY 16 '73			
AUG 2 0 '74			
JAN 2 0 75			
MAR 1 8 '75			
APR 1 '76			
APR 2 3 1976			
JUN 8 '76			
JAN 2 4 1979			
JAN 0 3 1983			

Psyche & Symbol

IN

Shakespeare

ALEX ARONSON

Psyche & Symbol

IN

Shakespeare

Indiana University Press

<small>Bloomington / London</small>

93971

Contents

Acknowledgments

I AM GRATEFUL to the University of Tel-Aviv for having enabled me to spend my sabbatical at the Folger Shakespeare Library, Washington, D.C., where this study was begun under the pleasantest auspices.

I would also like to thank the Committee for Research in the Humanities at the University of Tel-Aviv for a grant toward the publication of this book.

I have received much encouragement and helpful advice from Dr. James Kirsch of Los Angeles and Professor Merritt Lawlis of the Department of English, Indiana University, which should not go unacknowledged.

Special thanks are due to Mrs. Dorothy Wikelund, Associate Editor, Indiana University Press, for having read through the manuscript with so much patience and understanding.

The greatest debt, however, I owe to my students, both past and present, without whose inspiration and love this adventure into the as yet unexplored relation between psyche and symbol would never have come into being.

A.A.

Tel-Aviv University

June 1971

The Shakespearean quotations are from the Oxford edition (in one volume) edited by W. J. Craig and first published in 1892.

All line numbering is based on the 1945 edition published by the Oxford University Press.

Unless stated otherwise all quotations from C. G. Jung's COLLECTED WORKS (C.W.) refer to the edition published by Routledge & Kegan Paul, Ltd., in England, and for the Bollingen Foundation by Pantheon Books, Inc., (1953–67) in the United States. The translator is R. F. C. Hull.

INTRODUCTION

Shakespeare and the Study of the Unconscious

[I]

ANYONE WHOSE APPROACH TO SHAKESPEARE is determined by psychological preoccupations commits himself to a set of attitudes and evaluations which have not infrequently been dismissed by the academic establishment as lacking a valid literary frame of reference. This is in part due to the ever-present suspicion that to apply the results of psychological research to the study of literature is to distort the meaning of the play, poem or novel with a technique of an antiseptic nature, which originated in the psychoanalyst's consulting room rather than in the reader's or spectator's imaginative response to the work in question.

Yet any study of response presupposes an understanding of the interplay of various forms of imagination on the part of the writer and the reader, or of the actor and spectator. Such an inquiry into the interdependence of literary creation and response assumes that a reader's or spectator's willing suspension of disbelief mainly relies on what can be apprehended in terms of a psychic heritage common to all men.

What this book, then, attempts to do is to interpret an archetype of response as it applies to the reading and staging of Shakespeare's plays. It is therefore claimed that the effect they have upon a spectator's sensibility has undergone no basic change since they were first staged. Historically considered there have been obvious shifts in emphasis in the producing or the acting of any given play—inevitably leading to a temporary distortion of response. Also, changing stage conventions or the rise of a new class of spectators bringing with them to the theatre their political ideologies, moral assumptions, or religious beliefs, have often introduced new intellectual attitudes and principles of evaluation. But the spontaneous response to laughter or to tears, to the wedding feast that concludes the comedy, and the funeral march with which the tragedy ends, continues to be determined by emotions that are shared by all men.

It is with these basic emotions, then, that this book is concerned. What it sets out to do is to reinforce the claim made by Dryden and Dr. Johnson that Shakespeare had "the largest and most comprehensive soul" and that his characters are "the genuine progeny of common humanity." Coleridge, going still further, calls these characters "ideal realities." It is this visionary formula that will provide a principle of integration for this inquiry into the transcendental nature of Shakespeare's characters as they appear before the spectator on the stage or stimulate the reader's responsive imagination.

That such an emphasis on Shakespeare's universality is still, or rather again, called for is illustrated by the multitude of literary and other cross references in the ever-expanding Shakespeare bibliography that bear little, if any, relation to the life of the play or the response that the play evokes. Yet these plays continue to live, be it as stage representations in the theatre or as re-creations in readers' echoing minds, and this in spite of the academic emphasis on the remote and the irrelevant. Their extraordinary vitality has, indeed, never been questioned. But except for a few remarkable though idiosyncratic instances, such as in the work of G. Wilson Knight, there has been no sustained inquiry into what constitutes "the life of the play." Even in those cases where comment was informed by a desire to provide the reader with new imaginative insights, the speaker's voice frequently lacked conviction. Being uncertain of his bearings, he could merely hint at some new though not yet clearly definable vision.

What all these voices share is an insistence on total rather than partial commitment, involving the imaginative participation of the reader or spectator on the multiple and at times contradictory levels of the play. This in turn implies an equal responsiveness to what the text communicates and the stage represents, as well as to what is not necessarily found on the surface of speech or action, but occurs on a less obvious plane of meaning, not directly communicable through words or through stage performance.

Shakespearean scholarship has, at all times, assumed that communication between the figure on the stage and the spectator takes place in terms of a universally acknowledged mode of consciousness, without which no communication at all is possible. However ambiguous Shakespeare's metaphorical language and the interpretation of character given by individual actors, the scholar remains committed to the principle of conscious communication as the only valid criterion of intelligibility. Whenever inconsistencies or contradictions in structure, characterization, or use of language become evident, the reader is asked to refer to background studies, to Shakespeare's sources, or, if everything else fails, to accept the assumption of a momentary fit of Shakespearean absent-mindedness. The meaning a Shakespeare play conveys may, indeed, change from generation to generation. Such changes, then, reflect the reader's or spectator's understanding of it insofar as it functions on a level of consciousness. This alone, it is claimed, determines what any given play "means" at a particular time, the assumption being that literary fashion and taste are dictated by modes of response consciously entertained.

It is this undisputed level of consciousness that has, during the last half century, been increasingly put to the test. Psychological inquiry into the act of creation has, for quite some time, pointed the way toward a liberation from the control of the conscious mind. It has also made the reader and spectator aware of possibilities of interpretation that would increase the range of their response and thereby add a new dimension to the meaning of a Shakespeare play far beyond what language and stage performance had accustomed them to assume in the past.

The literary critic finds himself placed in a position where traditional forms of comment and evaluation need no longer apply. Once he acknowledges the existence of unconscious motivations in the writing of the play, in its staging, and even in the response such a dramatic performance evokes, a multitude of psychic phenomena call for investigation which for lack of the required equipment the literary critic has always hesitated to undertake. Distrusting the fashionable invasion of literature by a confusing plethora of psychological and anthropological schools, all he can do is to clothe his newly acquired insights in metaphoric or semantic ambiguity. For no critical vocabulary exists as yet to define the function of the unconscious as it affects the writing, the reading, and the staging of a Shakespeare play.

This uncertainty as regards an objectively valid terminology which would do justice to the impact of the unconscious on a literary work is reflected in a variety of ways in the writings of contemporary Shakespeare commentators. Aware of the tenuous borderline that separates the real from the unreal, and therefore the communicable from the uncommunicable, one of them would like "the critic to be able to determine by some scientific process the exact course of this borderline." [1] There is little or no attempt made, apart from Freudian interpretations of Shakespeare's life and work (as will be seen later on), to apply any inductive scientific method to the elucidation of contents apparently placed below the level of consciousness. Analyzing the "miracle" of the writing of the plays, one of the critics visualizes Shakespeare's mind "flung open to the widest and deepest possible range of unconscious suggestion." [2] Another, at a loss to define what constitutes unconscious motivation in one's understanding of a Shakespeare play, uses a similar metaphor of depth to indicate what he thinks to be "some awareness of the motives lying deeper down." [3] He evidently aims at that level of communication where the "deep and sensitive anatomy of the hidden man" [4] stands revealed. This "superior reality exposing the deepest springs" [5] of action or inaction is, conceivably, more persuasive than the pale surface objectivity of textual criticism or character analysis.

What puzzled the literary critic was not so much the ubiquitous presence of nonrational impulses in the human psyche as their metamorphosis into poetry. The very concept of the artist as a bearer of civilization was found to be based on doubtful premises. Past aesthetic and literary theories were revealed as lofty superstructures hiding the uncontrolled instinctual drives deep below the level of civilized thought and disciplined emotion. The literary critic whose eyes had been opened, at the beginning of this century, to what was concealed beneath the surface of Symbolist poetry, was quick to grasp the significance of this revelation for *all* poetry. For in a wider and more all inclusive sense all poetry speaks through symbols. Eventually, the critic argued, it is the symbol that would perform the function of bridging the gap between the nonrational and the civilized.

T. S. Eliot's various pronouncements on this theme are of the greatest interest. For since he spoke with two voices, that of poet and that of critic, his insights may be assumed to have been the result of close self-analysis and a discriminating reading of other poets. Already in 1918 Eliot is quoted as having said that "the artist is more primitive, as well as more civilized, than his contemporaries." [6] Some fifteen years later, speaking of the musical qualities of verse which, he says in an essay on Matthew Arnold, is an essential virtue of poetic style, he defines the "auditory imagination" as "the feeling for syllable and rhythm, penetrating far below the conscious levels of thought and feeling, invigorating every word; sinking to the most primitive and forgotten. . . ." [7] A total response to poetry, he implies, can thus be achieved through a kind of musical empathy which depends neither on training in musical disciplines nor even on an emotional predisposition. Instead, Eliot refers the reader to contemporary anthropological research among primitives and concludes: "The pre-logical mentality persists in civilized man, but becomes available only to or through the poet." [8] His conclusion at that time left the main difficulty, that of an adequate critical vocabulary, unsolved. The most he could say was that poetry, by leading us back into the primitive and forgotten, also makes us aware "of the deeper, unnamed feelings which form the substratum of our being." [9]

What is true of poetry in general, is even more palpably relevant to the writing and speaking of dramatic verse. While the former supplies the reader with a two-dimensional image of the soul impinging directly upon his imagination without the assistance of any intermediary, the latter projects a "character," both in isolation and interacting with other characters, upon a three-dimensional stage. The poet's vision of reality acquires body and voice, personal gesture and intonation. Poetry, from being a still voice in the privacy of one's study, has now been transformed into a public utterance addressing itself not to the solitary reader but to an anonymous and ever-present audience. Eliot, in his essays on the Elizabethan dramatists, already realized that the figures on the stage suggest complexities of thought and emotion that transcend the range of mere poetic communication. Once again deprived of a meaningful critical vocabulary, Eliot at this point invokes those "unnamed feelings" which are, he implies, aroused in the spectator while watching the frequently incomprehensible demeanor of Shakespeare's characters on the stage. His final statement on the function of dramatic poetry does not throw any more light on the origin and meaning of these complexities. What he *does* say (and he says it better than anyone else) is that the verse drama must "somehow disclose . . . a deeper reality than that of the plane of most of our conscious living." It is, finally, the verse play that "must reveal, underneath the vacillating and infirm character, the indomitable unconscious will." [10]

Once more, it is the looseness of the critical terminology that calls for closer examination. Is this indefiniteness in the choice of words due, perhaps, to Eliot's acquaintance with contemporary psychoanalytical literature and its confusing metaphorical descriptions of the unconscious as being located somewhere "underground"? Literary criticism may then, indeed, be forgiven for employing equally ambiguous language whenever it attempts to convey the meaning of what is felt to be a level of experience deeper than is ordinarily accessible to daylight consciousness.

Sigmund Freud who, within the context of his analysis of the human psyche, was the first to describe the conflict between consciousness and the unconscious in the life of the individual, repeatedly uses a metaphor taken from archaeology with which the analytical method is compared. In one of his early works the unconscious is identified with the ruins of a buried edifice, possibly, though not necessarily, a temple, where fragments of pillars and of tablets with obliterated and illegible inscriptions are being unearthed by an archaeologist who, equipped with pick, shovel, and spade, "brings to light what is buried" and "clears away the rubbish." [11] In one of his last papers, again, the work of the analyst is depicted as resembling "an archaeologist's excavation of some dwelling-place that has been destroyed and buried." [12]

While the literary critic could only *evoke* a deeper layer of reality, the psychoanalyst felt no compunction about applying the "archaeologist's" cruder implements to literature. The unconscious was not to be approached, as it were, on tiptoe, in fear and trembling, but in conditions of unprejudiced objectivity which alone the scientist's laboratory setting could provide. Shakespeare's plays, when subjected to analysis, supplied the analyst with ready-made case histories. The beginning of this century saw a number of clinically trained psychoanalysts "clearing away the rubbish" in order to reveal Shakespeare's unconscious underneath.

[II]

THE LITERARY CRITIC who had been looking for instruments of analysis outside literature and the humanist disciplines was fascinated by the assumptions upon which psychoanalysis was founded, and which he now believed were going to vindicate the biographer's approach to literary creation.

Shakespeare's private and public life had been the subject of numerous and eccentric books even before the psychoanalyst started digging "below" the printed page. A biographical exegesis had haunted the literary critic ever since it was suggested that some of Shakespeare's plays had been written under evident mental stress, while others reflected what could easily be interpreted as the dramatist's personal moods varying from cheerful affirmation to rebellious anger. Even before the impact of psychoanalysis was felt, the sonnets had been ransacked for evidence of Shakespeare's homosexual inclinations. Plays such as *Troilus and Cressida, Hamlet,* and *King Lear* were claimed to be expressions of sex-nausea, possibly the result of intimate and frustrating experiences in the dramatist's own life. Prior to the rise of Sigmund Freud's reputation among literary critics certain outstanding characters on the Shakespearean stage had been identified as self-portraits, so that the inquisitive reader could, if he so wished, follow Shakespeare's spiritual progress from early manhood to middle-aged maturity merely by a close study of the characters of Hamlet, Timon, and Prospero.

The psychoanalyst attacked the riddle of Shakespeare's

fragmentary life history with considerably more self-assurance than the literary critic. From the very start he made full use of his medical training. This freed him of the humanist inhibitions that had till then prevented any unbiassed discussion of Shakespeare's hypothetical sex life. Thus he, at the very outset, introduced a startlingly explicit nonliterary terminology into Shakespearean research. Psychoanalytically oriented papers on individual plays abound with such terms as anxiety-neurosis, penis envy, anal-erotic character traits, to which were added a considerable variety of phobias and compulsions.

Sigmund Freud's frequent references to *Hamlet* are particularly relevant in this context, not only because of what they presume to tell us about the inner life of the Prince of Denmark, but because of the naive assumption that "it can, of course, only be the poet's mind which confronts us in Hamlet." [13] On another occasion (in 1907) Freud stated that the play is a reaction to the deaths of the dramatist's father and son, and that the origin of Hamlet's Oedipus complex must be looked for in Shakespeare's own unconscious. Shakespeare's use of the Oedipus complex in *Hamlet,* Freud said at a later date, is additional evidence for the general principle that poets are more sensitive to unconscious attitudes than most people.[14]

It is never altogether clear whether, by subjecting the play *Hamlet* to analysis, Freud wished to unravel Shakespeare's or Hamlet's unconscious, or the way the former is reflected in the latter. At times it may even appear as though Freud's constant preoccupation with this play indicates an involvement with the submerged contents of his own ego. He admits as much in the same letter in which he burdens Hamlet with the Oedipus complex, "I have found love of mother and jealousy of the father in my own case too," [15] he writes, implying that the reading of Shakespeare's play had a therapeutic effect on him and assisted him in his own self-analysis. As Freud's main concern was with psychotherapy, its application to literature was meant to provide additional evidence for what his medical practice had long ago revealed in abundance. Shakespeare and his creations lent themselves singularly well to clinical analysis since it was always within the range of a physician's acquaintance with an artist's deviations from the normal to indicate the way the artist's unconscious operates under certain conditions. If indeed it is assumed that Shakespeare, as so many others, suffered from an unresolved Oedipus complex, then the spectator's own unavowed attachment to his mother, and his unconscious, though murderous, intentions toward his father may be found reflected in himself as well. For, adds Freud in that same letter, "every member of the audience was once a budding Oedipus in phantasy." Even assuming that Hamlet's "disease" originates in his (and not Shakespeare's) unconscious, it could with equal justice be attributed to Freud's own patients. Thus, an analogy between Hamlet's sickness (or what Freud considered to be such) and the compulsion neurosis of his "hysterics" was easily established. Do they not, asks Freud, bring down their punishment on themselves and suffer the same fate as Hamlet when they are defeated by their inability to cope with life rather than by any external human or nonhuman agency? [16]

Sigmund Freud's seminal influence can be discerned in all succeeding psychoanalytical writings on Shakespeare. It is through analysis of the text of a play, illustrating a particular aspect of Shakespeare's life, that the hidden layers of his mind were brought to light. This same sort of revelation is also Ernest Jones's primary aim in his study on Hamlet and Oedipus. At the very beginning of his inquiry he states: "So far shall I be from forgetting that [Hamlet] was a figment of Shakespeare's mind that I shall then go on to consider the relation of his particular imaginative creation to the personality of Shakespeare himself." [17] In Kris's psychoanalytical study of the father-son conflict, as represented in *Henry IV,* the son's attempt to escape from an intolerable psychological dilemma is described as being "well known from the clinical study of male youths" while the final "parricide" of Falstaff "can only have been conceived by one who in creating had access to his own unconscious impulses." [18]

The method used by professional psychiatrists in their reading of Shakespeare applies not only to Hamlet's compulsion neurosis and the escape mechanism operating in Prince Hal's unconscious, but to any major or minor figure in Shakespeare insofar as emotional disturbance or pathological disposition is evident. The spiritual scale of Shakespeare's universe is thus reduced to the four walls of a psychiatrist's consulting room into which are led, one by one, first Shakespeare himself out of whose unconscious, after all, this universe sprang, and, following him, the characters that people his stage. Last of all, the spectators themselves have to undergo a similar method of clinical inquiry. The conclusions arrived at are, thus, compounded of similar elements when applied to the playwright, the figures on the stage, and the audience in the theatre.

What strikes the reader most in such professionally informed diagnosis, is the conspicuous emphasis on some intrinsic sickness of the human soul. As the classification used is psychopathological, each of the characters, described in isolation or as related to other characters, fits into a given psychological framework of severe mental disorder. Thus Antonio, in the *Merchant of Venice,* has been diagnosed as an endogenous depressive, Don John in *Much Ado,* as a psychopath, Jaques, in *As You Like It,* as an involutional, Hamlet, as a manic-depressive, Timon as a general paralytic, Pericles as a schizophrenic, and, finally, Leontes as a paranoiac.[19]

In its final analysis such a description of the play and its characters may well reveal them to be a sublimated mirror-image of Shakespeare's own neurosis. The assumption that Shakespeare's complex and equivocal personality must have "gone into his introverted characters" [20] shifts the critical emphasis from the original text of the play to the clinical interpretation, from Shakespeare to the analyst, and, finally, from the living character on the stage to a reassessment of psychopathology in action. It is the same basic neurosis, the same deficiency in psychic adaptation that, at the very moment of dramatic performance, links Shakespeare to the characters he created, and his characters to the spectator. The conclusion is difficult to escape that, according to this approach, it is a particular neurotic disposition common to all men (though affecting different disguises) that alone vindicates the artistic experience.

[III]

WITHIN THIS Freudian context of clinical emphasis on the sickness of the soul Jung's consistently affirmative attitude to literature and art provides a healthy counterpoint. In one of his earliest writings on art he rejects the paradox which identifies the artistic process with disease: "If a work of art is explained in the same way as a neurosis, then the work of art is a neurosis or a neurosis is a work of art." [21] Jung's repeated insistence on dream analysis rather than on clinical diagnosis in his approach to art and literature constitutes a breaking away from the consulting room and a frank admission that the unconscious is not as readily available as orthodox psychoanalysis had made it out to be. When, however, Jung writes that "a great work of art is like a dream" and therefore contains as much ambiguity and multiplicity of meaning as a dream, he does not imply that every dream is, therefore, a work of art.[22] On the contrary, Jung characterizes the nature of dreams as intrinsically opposed to everything one is accustomed to associate with the creative work of the artist. Thus, he insists on the absurdity, the terror, and the formlessness of dreams. They rarely constitute a logically, morally, or aesthetically satisfying whole. What distinguish the dream from the consciously created values of the human mind are "lack of logic, questionable morality, uncouth form, and apparent absurdity or nonsense." [23]

Prospero's despondent thought "We are such stuff as dreams are made on" gently hints at the inconsistencies and equivocations, dark forebodings and questionings, which human consciousness, when wide awake, discovers in the stuff of which dreams are made. Jung's Prospero-like pronouncements on the morally oblique content of man's unconscious raise still more alarming questions. How can we reconcile these two apparently contradictory views that a work of art is "like" a dream, while the dream itself is revealed to be a communication from beyond the border of consciousness, a mirror of the moral chaos and the intellectual incoherence that slumber within each one of us?

Some of Jung's basic psychological concepts are founded upon assumptions that establish a close and meaningful connection between the act of dreaming and the act of literary creation. His threefold division of the human personality into consciousness, the personal unconscious, and the collective unconscious, is a fundamental postulate in all his psychological investigations. Jung's limiting definition of the ego as the center of the field of consciousness indicates that the totality of the psyche cannot be restricted to consciousness alone, but outgrows it both in width and in depth. Thus, the ego is subordinated to a variety of less visible psychic contents which Jung calls the unconscious. The conscious ego never forms a whole, but constitutes a part, and not necessarily the most valuable part, of the psyche. Even the most developed mental capacity contains within itself only a fragment of psychic completeness— the ideal that man strives to achieve throughout his life.

The ego can be fundamentally altered only by an assimilation of the unconscious components of the personality. Thus an expansion of consciousness takes place whenever it integrates those images that arise from the depths of the psyche. Such images may be the result of childhood experiences remembered at a later date, the repressed contents of a personal unconscious which both Freud and Jung accept as an essential part of their therapeutic practice. The other kind of images which Jung calls archetypes arise from an equally "extra-conscious" psyche whose contents, however, are impersonal and collective. Jung defines this "collective unconscious" as "an omnipresent, unchanging, and everywhere identical condition or substratum of the psyche *per se.*" Such a condition is shared by all human beings, whether mentally healthy or neurotic, creative or noncreative, in infancy or old age. It is, in Jung's scheme of psychic contents, the most characteristic feature of the human condition. It is that which counterbalances consciousness and which has to be assimilated in order to channel these psychic contents in the direction of wholeness.

Jung's theory of archetypes can, thus, be understood only if his assumption of a collective unconscious is accepted. His investigations into the legacy of ancestral life revealed to him mythological images which awaken whenever psychic energy regresses, going back even beyond the period of early infancy. Jung calls these images archetypes because they reveal to the investigator the remotest beginnings of human consciousness, where they served the purpose of supplying a meaning to what appeared to the archaic mind the mystery of all living processes, leading from birth to death and back again, across the darkness of nonbeing to rebirth. These archetypes are not disseminated by migration or tradition. No outside influence can be held responsible for their amazing renewal in time and space. Jung calls the totality of these archetypes "the deposit of all human experience" reaching back into a nonhistoric past. But, he adds, "not, indeed, a dead deposit, a sort of abandoned rubbish-heap, but a living system of reactions and aptitudes that determine the individual's life in invisible ways—all the more effective because invisible. It is not just a gigantic historical prejudice, so to speak, an *a priori* historical condition; it is also the source of the instincts, for the archetypes are simply the forms which the instincts assume." [24]

In Jung's creative vision of the psyche the archetype is the most effective symbol for the inner structure of the personality. As no names were available, Jung invented them for those archetypes that can be made conscious after they appear in dreams, fantasy formations, or in art. Thus we have the *anima* and *animus* archetypes, the *Shadow,* the *Wise Old Man,* the *Great Mother,* the *Self.* Myth supplies many of the names symbolizing the heroic life, such as the Quest for Salvation, the Fight with the Dragon, the Search for the Hidden Treasure. Archetypes, if perceived at all by consciousness, are seen as dual beings, and are therefore described in terms of natural processes related to the polarity of Birth and Death, Light and Darkness, Summer and Winter, Warmth and Cold, Dryness and Moisture.

It is only within the framework of Jung's theory of archetypes that the affinity of creative writing with the act of dreaming can be understood. Frequently, when writing about dreams, Jung employs a literary vocabulary. This is especially true of his description of what, in the English translation of his works, are called "big" dreams. They are distinguished from ordinary everyday dreams which can be interpreted through an analysis of personal memories, of desires and fears such as everyone experiences. The context of such dreams is the individual. Their interpretation requires a certain "intelligence du coeur," as Jung calls it, a combination of empathy, ability to coordinate, and a down-to-earth understanding of the ways of the world. The "big" dreams originate in the deeper layers of the unconscious, the "objective psyche" which contains symbolic images relating the individual to an archaic past of the existence of which he is entirely unaware in his waking life. Any attempt at interpreting such a dream involves a descent into the "universal human being" in us. In our conscious life these images and motifs will be revealed as pertaining to a mythological and transpersonal past. To interpret them is to relate them to the living present of the dreamer. When describing these dreams Jung recapitulates many of the well-known features of myth

such as those "that characterize the life of the hero, of that
greater man who is semi-divine by nature. Here we find the
dangerous adventures and ordeals such as occur in initiations.
We meet dragons, helpful animals, and demons; also the Wise
Old Man, the animal-man, the wishing-tree, the hidden treasure,
the well, the cave, the walled garden, the transformative processes and substances of alchemy." [25]

The same distinction between "ordinary" and "big" dreams
is carried over into Jung's analysis of creative writing. One mode
of artistic creation he calls "psychological" because it "deals with
material drawn from the realm of human consciousness," which
of course also includes the artist's emotional life insofar as his
emotions have been assimilated by his consciousness. Such literary work illumines and interprets all that lies on the surface
of conscious life, while the dark and invisible contents of the
psyche are dismissed as irrelevant or evaded. Jung calls the
second mode of writing "visionary." It derives its existence "from
the hinterland of man's mind." In connection with this visionary mode of artistic creation Jung mentions, among others, the
writings of Dante, the second part of Goethe's *Faust*, Wagner's
Nibelungenring, Nietzsche's "Dionysian exuberance," the poetry of William Blake, and Jacob Boehme's "philosophical and
poetic stammerings."

When Jung attempts an analysis of the visionary mode he,
characteristically, falls back upon the language used in his
description of dreams: "Sublime, pregnant with meaning, yet
chilling the blood with its strangeness, it arises from timeless
depth. . . . This disturbing spectacle of some tremendous process that in every way transcends our human feeling and understanding makes quite other demands upon the powers of the
artist than do the experiences of the foreground of life. . . . But
the primordial experiences rend from top to bottom the curtain upon which is painted the picture of an ordered world
and allow a glimpse into the unfathomable abysm of the un-
born and of things yet to be." [26]

Shakespeare's plays conform only in part to the two definitions on the nature of dreams and on the nature of the "visionary mode" in literature. An illustration of what Jung might
have had in mind when he drew his distinction between what
is psychologically intelligible and what is not may be found in
the enacting of the two king-murders, in *Julius Caesar* and in
Macbeth. In the former the murder forms part of the murderer's
consciousness, where it is debated and analysed. When it is
finally executed, it is in fulfillment of a clearly intelligible political ideology. In the latter, the murder, rooted in Macbeth's
unconscious, is only feebly resisted in a moment of clarity when
the consequences and the intrinsic evil of the action become
manifest to the conscious mind. At last it is carried out in all
the emotional incoherence and fury arising from obedience to
blind fate. Brutus' knowledge of what he has done never leaves
him. Macbeth's most characteristic exclamation after the murder
is "To know my deed 'twere best not know myself."

These are extreme instances of the "psychological" and the
"visionary" mode translated for the stage into human terms.
The Shakespeare who concerns us here frequently combines the
two, though as a rule one remembers him as being gentle
rather than demonic, serene rather than grotesque, warmly
human rather than cold and alien. If in spite of these reserva-
tions Jung's preoccupation with the psychological and the visionary mode in literature appears to furnish deeper insights into
Shakespeare's work than any previously available, it is because
somewhere in between these extremes of self-knowledge and
negation of self Shakespeare's universe can be found. Jung
himself admits that there is something darkly "inhuman" (a
word that he uses in this context) about the submission of the
individual will to forms of experience which transcend the
artist's and the dreamer's own sense of being. It is in the very
nature of such a vision that it should be beyond their intellectual
grasp. For the artist confronting his own creation in retrospect,
is no longer "on the other side." In this again he resembles the

dreamer confounded by the apparent meaninglessness of his own dreams. They may, at best, catch a glimpse of that encounter between the primitive and civilized, the timeless and the timebound, the unconscious and the conscious, that characterizes both the "visionary" work of art and the dream in which the "objective psyche" is reflected.

[IV]

JUNG'S INTERPRETATION of the work of art and the dream concentrates on the analysis of their symbolic content. According to him, both speak through symbols which are a kind of primordial language and, therefore, are communicable only through man's image-making power. This, he says, is a gift that the savage mind and the mature intellect have in common. The latter, however, has first to divest itself of the inhibitions that an overdeveloped consciousness has imposed upon it. Insofar as dreams are concerned, the unconscious is at all times "free" to create images. Jung assumes that, except for those dream images that grow out of repressed personal contents, the more significant images are rooted in a common store of experience shared by all men. If this is taken for granted (and Jung's own dream interpretations may be accepted as sufficient evidence), then the dreams of a man of genius, such as Shakespeare, stand for primordial experiences similar to the dreams of the savage. Considered as symbols of a reality "beyond," neither dream explains itself in a simple and direct way. Any attempt at interpreting its symbolic content rationally is bound to fail unless these symbols are seen to be related to a multiplicity of meanings, only remotely connected to the dreamer's conscious experience of life.

In a recent study of the literary use of symbols and metaphors a relevant distinction is drawn between what the writer calls the "stenosymbol" (which is open to logical or scientific interpretation) and the organic symbol, also called expressive or depth symbol, which is found most commonly in poetically charged language. The meaning inherent in the first kind of symbol is "monosignative," while the latter tends to be "pluri-signative," the former supplying direct and immediate analogy for something that cannot be otherwise expressed, while the depth symbol produces, in the words of the same writer, "an integral meaning that radically transcends the sum of the in-gredient meanings." [27]

Jung calls such an integral meaning primordial or arche-typal, for its symbolic content points away from the personal and the historical toward the universal and mythological. Al-though the relation of such depth symbols to myth may not be immediately manifest, Jung's inquiry into the structure of dreams provides, once more, the missing link. For if, as he claims, the symbolic content of both poem and dream is rooted in a collective unconscious, it therefore pertains to man's pri-mordial existence as portrayed in myth. Thus the integral meaning of Jung's depth symbol is related to the dark back-ward and abysm of time where the "personal" dream is fused with the "collective" myth: "In view of the close connection between mythological symbols and dream symbols, and the fact that the dream is *'le lieu des sauvages,'* it is more than probable that most historical symbols derive directly from dreams or are at least influenced by them." [28]

The symbol, then, stands for something which may appear incomprehensible when tested by present time and circum-stances because the mythological past is no longer readily avail-able to modern man's restricted consciousness. This explains why Jung, speaking of symbols, so frequently despairs of ever being able to find a linguistic equivalent for their "meaning." It can only be "darkly divined," but never "adequately expressed in the familiar words of our language." [29] In his essay on the relation of analytical psychology to poetry this difficulty of inter-preting symbols in conventional terms is repeatedly insisted

upon. Thus the symbol is called there "an expression of an
intuitive idea that cannot be formulated in any other or better
way . . . something for which no verbal concept yet exists,"
and finally, "the intimation of a meaning beyond the level of
our present power of comprehension."

Contemporary theories about the origin, growth, and function of myths have many affinities with literary theories as embodied in criticism. For myth speaks with the voices of numberless poets. Its anonymity relates it to a common past shared
by the poet and the people among whom he lived. Its stories
are made of the stuff of which their dreams, their aspirations,
and their fears are constituted. Its gods and goddesses are
immortal because the stories in which they play their parts are
without a beginning and without an end. For myth is the sim-
plest of all patterns in time in which man can reflect himself
simultaneously on the highest and the lowest level; in terms
of his physical substance, forever doomed to die; and as spirit,
eternally reborn. The heroes and heroines of myth accomplish
their superhuman task by always conforming to the dictates
of a spiritual essence within them which gives them a strength
above mortals though less than that of the gods. Thus the
storyteller—whoever he might have been—is dwarfed by the
myth he narrates. His anonymity is due neither to humility
nor to the neglect of time. He lives in the shadow of his art.
He, like the story he tells, is eternally renewed in the stories
told by others, long after the initial *raison d'être* of the original
myth has been forgotten.

The literary critic, looking for the timeless pattern of myth
in non-mythological literature, such as in Shakespeare, will have
to distinguish between what Shakespeare knew of myths from
his reading of books and what lived within him as part of a
common human heritage of which he was as little conscious
as were the people that came to see his plays. Much has been
written on Shakespeare's learning. This is not the place to
enlarge upon it. He knew and loved Ovid. He must have read

Virgil. But most of his knowledge of classical mythology (the only one of which he was consciously aware) he derived from medieval or contemporary sources. His blunders, anachronisms, misspellings may have been due to faulty translation, carelessness (his own, his copier's, the printer's), or because the original sources were no longer available. He adapted classical mythology to his plots and characters with the same natural ease as he adapted other historical or literary sources.

If, as Jung claims, the symbolism of archetypes originates in the unconscious, it may be studied in both the primeval language of myth and the creation of individual artists. In both instances alike the symbol will convey an unconscious core of meaning which refuses to be translated into the language of logic or science, because such a meaning remains unrelated to any historical form of conceptual knowledge. The artist, then, draws his strength from the primeval patterns of myth although he himself is entirely unaware of the original source of the symbols he uses.

Throughout this book mythological figures are referred to, not as consciously present in Shakespeare's associative memory, but rather as illustrations of the way in which the "objective psyche" operates through him. Nor do we wish to insist on such mythological parallels in order to establish farfetched analogies between Shakespeare's dramatic universe and some remote nonhistorical past. For what these two share is not a common "interest in human nature," but psychic constellations altogether independent of sources and backgrounds. It is, therefore, not "what really happens" in the myth or on the stage that accounts for such psychic correspondences. They originate in the universal identity of unconscious contents whenever and wherever they rise to the surface, either in the anonymity of myth or in Shakespeare's creative work.

The very diversity of such correspondences fills one with wonder. And if this book refers to such disparate mythological figures as Hecate, Prometheus, or Asklepios, it is not because they explain or even help the reader to interpret "characters," but because they reflect, as it were in a dimension of the infinite, a universally valid psychic constellation which the stage represents at a particular moment in the play. Similarly, such mythological pairs of opposites as Eros and Psyche, Silenos and Dionysos, Hermes and Aphrodite, Zeus and Ganymede symbolize archetypes of human encounter which demand recognition in depth if the universality of Shakespeare's art is to be acknowledged.

[V]

IN ONE OF HIS RARE attempts to give a personalized definition of archetypes Jung illumines a singularly disconcerting aspect of Shakespearean tragedy, the ominous encounter between man and his unconscious. Using the term "archetypal personalities," Jung draws a picture of them as "masklike, wraithlike, without problems, lacking self-reflection, with no conflicts, no doubts, no sufferings. . . . Unlike other contents, they always remain strangers in the world of consciousness, unwelcome intruders saturating the atmosphere with uncanny forebodings or even with fear of madness." [30]

Such an anthropomorphic description of archetypes is, of course, not meant to be taken literally. Archetypes are neither "personalities" nor "images" unless they are rendered visible through art or dreams or spontaneous hallucination. They can be known only through an effort of the conscious mind. It is, indeed, part of their paradoxical nature that they remain invisible until, quite literally, they are "brought to light" by consciousness. These psychic phenomena point to a range of experience embracing all that is accessible to conscious thought and, in addition to this, suggesting varieties of knowing no longer dependent on images formed in the mind alone, but on modes of awareness originating in the collective unconscious. We cannot apprehend the existence of such a transpersonal form of the unconscious except by looking for it within ourselves. There we may discover the archetypes in a multiplicity of shapes. Once such an archetype has been encountered, it can no longer be dismissed by putting up an intellectual resistance against it. It is there to be integrated. If this proves to be too difficult an undertaking, it will draw its subject under its spell. One of Shakespeare's most revealing metaphors, that of the "ocular proof," relating the need for increased spiritual insight to the inadequacy of mere visual perception illustrates the conflict originating in the encounter between ego-consciousness and archetype.

"Consciousness," says Jung, "has always been described in terms derived from the behaviour of light." [31] One of the characteristics of light is that it can only be realized through perceptual vision. Darkness, on the other hand, requires no such proof of visibility. The unconscious exists on its own terms, impervious to eyesight. Consciousness, then, may be defined as a process which works both ways, i.e. while it "sees," it is also "seen." Or, like the sun (another one of Jung's favorite metaphors), it renders visible and constitutes a visual proof of its own existence. In this sense consciousness, like the eye or the sun, is the focal point of individual discrimination.

If then, "by reason of its solar nature, the eye is a symbol of consciousness," [32] it is also a precondition for all forms of knowledge directed outward, away from the unfathomable darkness of the inner self. Although its scope is severely limited by its constant and necessary reference to the ego (which here is the opposite of man's inner self), it is the only instrument available to man to draw the unconscious out of its depth, to make it "visible," as it were, and finally, to submit it to analysis.

As far as the Shakespearean stage is concerned, consciousness functions on two levels, that of spectator and that of the figure in the play. What the latter "sees" or believes he sees, is meant to be perceived by the spectator as well. The illusion of conscious seeing must be kept up throughout the play, even if the character's reaction to what he believes to be "real" may remain, very largely, incomprehensible to the spectator.

Shakespeare's dramatic art resembles Jung's conclusions in that it assumes the existence of a dualism in the human personality which is frequently expressed in terms of symbols derived from light and darkness. Whenever ego-consciousness, symbolized by the light of the eye, is shown to be in conflict with some form of the transpersonal unconscious, symbolized by an emanation "from beyond," the phenomenon of weakened sense perception becomes the focus of dramatic action. What then is represented on the stage is an apparent shrinking of the visible universe into threatening nothingness as the unconscious in the shape of an "archetypal personality" increases its domination over the ego. The borderline between the real and the imaginary is shown to have shifted from daylight perception to the darkness of some primeval chaos. What the figures on the stage "see" no longer pertains to visual experience. The encounter between the eye and the archetype depersonalizes the character. Instead of a process of recognition leading from seeing to thinking, and from thought to knowledge—the kind of process to which our consciousness has accustomed us—the figure on the stage is faced by a sudden irruption of the invisible *per se*. Confronting the archetype he becomes aware of the insecurity of the human condition symbolized by his blurred vision of what, in truth, is physically nonexistent. Though he "perceives" the invisible, he cannot name it.

Thus, at the end of *Julius Caesar*, Brutus, becoming aware of the presence of his "evil spirit" in the semidarkness of his tent, blames "the weakness of mine eyes" which, he believes, have given shape to "this monstrous apparition" (IV, 3, 275). Again, in *Hamlet*, the young prince, remembering his own "weakness" and "melancholy," doubts whether the spirit that he has seen is indeed his murdered father, for "the devil hath power / To assume a pleasing shape" (II, 2, 636). Lastly, a few

minutes before murdering Duncan, Macbeth distrusts his eyesight which shows him a floating dagger he cannot touch because his eyes "are made the fools o' the other senses." Yet
he knows, because his consciousness tells him so, that "it is the
bloody business which informs / Thus to mine eyes" (II, 1, 48).

These three instances are Shakespeare's most notable drama-
tizations of the unconscious, achieving an autonomous existence
as "perceived" in the light of an increasingly blurred consciousness. Indeed, as far as the spectator in the theatre is concerned,
watching the figures on the stage as he had always wanted to
look on life itself, dispassionately and cultivating an attitude
of philosophical detachment, the existential autonomy of these
monstrous apparitions is a harrowing experience. They may
well be assumed to live a life of their own, long before and
after they have been "seen." The dramatic impact of these
scenes arises from the spectator's awareness that what *he* has
seen cannot be explained away by the weakness of *his* eyes.
The spectator is, indeed, in a privileged position. He, at least, can
afford, in the security that his own consciousness as mere on-
looker provides, to look at that which, in Macbeth's words,
"might appall the devil" himself.

There can be no fully satisfactory "ocular proof" of the
archetype. Those that are made to "see" the invisible are spe-
cially predestined to suffer through the "weakness" of their eyes.
For the more developed the consciousness of the figure on the
stage, and Brutus, Hamlet, and Macbeth are among the most
"perceptive" of Shakespeare's mature heroes, the greater the
likelihood that their overdeveloped consciousness will be tested
by psychic phenomena which, because of their archetypal nature, elude logical analysis. The distinction drawn by Jung,
between sense perception and apperception corresponds to the
basic dualism of sight and insight in Shakespeare's plays. For
sense perception tells the hero that something *is*, it does not
provide information *what* it is that he is seeing, hearing, or
touching. "Directed" apperception is the name Jung gives to

the process of thinking which follows seeing and leads to recognition. "Undirected" apperception which is also called "apprehension," Jung defines as unconscious psychic processes obtruding themselves upon consciousness. The hero's inability to integrate this process provides the key for an understanding of his downfall and final extinction. Any explanation basing itself upon prevailing superstitious beliefs in Shakespeare's age which Shakespeare himself might have shared evades recognition of man's essentially dual nature.

The spectator in the theatre might find the paradox of the "invisible" archetype confusing in the extreme. If the motive and the cue for passion is the amorphous content of the unconscious, the stage must needs supply an equivalent "dramatic" symbol which would not merely hold up a mirror to conscious life, but reflect processes not subject to cognitive or visual perception. Spirit, ghost, and dagger are such symbols. Their visibility cannot be tested by any "ocular proof." Yet consciousness, that of the figure on the stage and spectator in the theatre, claims them for its own.

In Jung's hierarchy of archetypes the *anima* figure, whether in dream or in art or in the fantasy formation of the insane, is an "embodiment of this omnipresent and ageless image (of woman) which corresponds to the deepest reality in man." Whenever this archetype appears in personalized form, such as in a Shakespeare play, woman is revealed as "the great illusionist, the seductress who draws him into life—not only into its reasonable and useful aspects but into its frightful paradoxes and ambivalences where good and evil, success and ruin, hope and despair counterbalance one another." [33]

The *anima*-archetype is equally impervious to the ocular proof. When Troilus watches Cressida in Diomedes' arms he wishes to "swagger himself out on's own eyes" because he quite rightly distrusts the limited knowledge which his eyes supply to his consciousness. His refusal to believe the evidence of his eyes "as if those organs had deceptious functions / Created only to calumniate" (V, 3, 120) agrees with Jung's description of such an encounter with an archetype as "a vision seen 'as in a glass darkly'." Yet what Troilus sees when he watches Cressida's equivocal conduct in Diomedes' tent is "real" enough when judged by the standards of visual perception. But his eyes show him only a partial truth, the one that his consciousness can grasp. Jung, describing a universally valid dilemma rather than making a statement of psychopathology, analyses the Troilus situation which Shakespeare merely hints at: "Consciousness is fascinated by it (the *anima*-archetype), held captive, as if hypnotized. Very often the ego experiences a vague feeling of moral defeat and then behaves defensively, defiantly, and self-righteously." [34] This is an exact description of Troilus' conduct in the scenes following this encounter.

When Othello asks Iago to supply the "ocular proof" of Desdemona's unfaithfulness, he compels his imagination to enact, as if in a dream, the same experience that had defeated Troilus. In the simplicity of his soul, Othello believes that visual evidence is all that is required to prove Desdemona's disloyalty—"I'll see before I doubt, when I doubt, prove" (III, 3, 190). When the imaginary confrontation takes place (for it matters very little that Othello never actually sees Desdemona in Cassio's arms), his conscious mind disintegrates. A victim of the archetype, he is defeated by his distorted eyesight which reveals to him the image of his *anima* compulsively intent on annihilating his consciousness. For this reason, if not for any other, Othello is the more tragic figure of the two. What Troilus sees is believable and, therefore, though causing intense anguish, it can still be integrated. What Othello does *not* see because it is beyond the reach of perception, is unbelievable. When his consciousness finally breaks to pieces, "chaos is come again."

The "ocular proof" is Shakespeare's metaphor for ego-consciousness attempting to achieve self-knowledge by the use of eyesight only. Gloucester's blindness is the other side of the metaphor. In the dim light of their consciousness Troilus and

Othello "see" what their psychic instability predestined them
to perceive and what they most feared to look upon. Gloucester,
in the darkness of his blinded eyes, acquires an imaginative
awareness which Shakespeare calls "feeling" and which corresponds to Jung's undirected apperception. When Gloucester
remembers the kind of "superfluous and lust-dieted" man that
he used to be before his blindness, he describes himself as one
"that will not see / Because he does not feel" (IV, 1, 70). And
as he finds himself in a world inhabited by men that trust their
eyes more than their feelings, he, blind Gloucester, alone can
tell Lear that he sees "feelingly" how this world goes.

This feeling awareness of a reality beyond the range of
visual experience is the first step in the transformation of the
individual from fragmentary ego-consciousness to a realization
of the self. If the ego succeeds in assimilating the contents of
the unconscious, the ideal of completeness becomes an attain-
able aim. For the self, according to the empirical findings of
psychology, "is an ever-present archetype of wholeness which may
easily disappear from the purview of consciousness." [35] As Gloucester's consciousness lacks substance, his physical blindness is
merely a hint at some deeper insight into his former ignorance
of his own self. Yet it also reflects a more mature awareness
of what, in effect, constituted the "weakness" of his eyes before
he learned to see. "I stumbled when I saw," provides the finish-
ing touch to this evolution from spiritual blindness to, at least,
a beginning of self-knowledge.

[VI]

JUNG DISMISSES the artificial division of consciousness into higher and lower, superior and inferior, ego and id,
as contrary to the underlying unity of all psychic processes.
The attempt to establish an absolute opposition between mind
and body, spirit and matter, the rational and the irrational, is,

according to him, the result of a conscious device intended to relate man's outer and inner life in a meaningful way. He calls this process of rationalization "an intellectually necessary separation of one and the same fact into two aspects, to which we then illegitimately attribute an independent existence." [36] The hypothetically perfect personality would be one that has successfully resisted the threat of a corrosive dualism which is frequently due to individual or social maladaptation. Jung, in his therapeutic practice, must have been fully aware of the destructiveness of such unresolved psychic conflicts. Yet without a willing confrontation with such conflicts no cure could be accomplished.

The psychic energy required for the development of a complete personality derives from this awareness of inner polarity. The growth of personality which Jung calls a "centering" or "equilibrating" process leads from threatened division to unity, finally establishing a balance of energy. It is the only way open to man to attain completeness. Such an equilibrium between opposing forces gives rise to an integrated consciousness in which the body-mind antithesis is no longer allowed to function. Consciousness is, then, seen to slide "upward" or "downward" along an imaginary scale at one end of which reason predominates, while at the other end instinct prevails. Those instinctual processes most opposed to consciousness are gradually assimilated by it. The artificial distinction between matter and spirit, science and art, physical and spiritual aspirations, is no more felt to be valid. Jung calls this growth from a split to a unified consciousness individuation.[37]

Shakespeare's concern with this process of self-realization will be studied on many different levels. The dividing line between comedy and tragedy will matter less than what separates the fragmentary ego from the potential wholeness of the self. Incompleteness need not be experienced as tragic, it may just as well make one laugh. In Jung's psychotherapeutic practice, for instance, an unconscious search for wholeness was frequently revealed in his patients' dreams. No definitions of comedy or tragedy apply to dream symbols of completeness. Jung, actually, derives the meaning of the word "whole" or "wholeness" from "to make holy" or to "heal," in German *heilen* and *heilig.* Dream interpretation, then, may reveal "the way to the total being" and bring about healing and redemption. The analogy between dream and the Shakespearean stage reveals an identical concern with one's own true image in terms of visual or verbal symbolism. Whether in dream symbolism or on the stage, "the ego cannot help discovering that the afflux of unconscious contents has vitalized the personality, enriched it and created a figure that somehow dwarfs the ego in scope and intensity. . . . In this way the will, as disposable energy, gradually subordinates itself to the stronger factor, namely to the new totality figure I call the self. . . ."[38]

The process of individuation takes place in a Shakespeare play within a context of generally accepted customs, moral prescriptions, and religious observances which form the social framework the individual may either acknowledge or reject. As individuation leads to a highly differentiated personality, difficulties of adaptation to a still higher norm in collective standards of thinking, feeling, and acting may arise. On the stage an actual conflict with a collective mode of values takes place whenever an individual way is raised to a norm. This may lead to individual dissociation as in many of Shakespeare's tragedies. It may equally occur in comedy, where it is, with the approval of everyone concerned, quickly suppressed. "Extreme individualism" (as Jung calls such social maladaptation) may indeed evoke a response of either anguish or laughter, according as to whether it causes pain or amusement to others. We may laugh at Malvolio's puritanism: it does not hurt anybody. We cannot afford such an easy-going acceptance of individual waywardness when we witness Angelo imposing his twisted, ego-oriented asceticism on the society of Vienna, in the first two "tragic" acts of *Measure for Measure.*

On the Shakespearean stage the balance between individual and social norms is tenuous and at all times vulnerable. Yet on this balance depends the outcome of the process of individuation. For what has to be assimilated is of twofold significance: ego and self must preserve their intrinsic qualities if the union between them is to create wholeness, while at the same time this new and enlarged identity of the self must be related to modes of social solidarity which alone will make it grow. Jung's botanical metaphor illustrates this relationship between individual growth and social adaptability: "A plant which is to be brought to the fullest possible unfolding of its particular character must first of all be able to grow in the soil wherein it is planted." [39]

Frequently social maladjustment and unresolved individual conflicts evoke a similar response. For both have in common a concern with the individual in his search for a regulating principle of unity. Individuation which in Jung's description of psychological growth is the aim of the individual's progress from a divided to a harmonious personality may more easily be achieved in comedy. Such ideal perfection is rendered possible within the dream context of a utopian society which furnishes a particularly fruitful soil for successful individual and social adjustment. Shakespearean comedy, then, places the individual in unreal surroundings which are characterized by a perfect balance between individual and social norms. There alone, and with no more effort than is required to interpret a dream, he will find his true self in terms of the new synthesis between antagonistic forces within his personality.

The analogy with dream interpretation points to the need of integrating the unconscious. Only by withdrawing into the forest and by losing their former incomplete identity in the darkness of the night, are the four lovers in *Midsummer Night's Dream* enabled to discover the principle of harmony and love when they awaken. What the forest "near Athens" reveals to them is experienced by Orlando, in an equally dreamlike manner, in the Forest of Arden. Only in terms of the unreality of the setting

can Orlando's growth from personal insecurity to quite unbelievable human perfection be explained. Claudio, in *Much
Ado*, undergoes an even more astonishing metamorphosis from
petty egocentricity to willing repentance when he realizes the
anguish and ignominy his thoughtlessness has caused. His "conversion" is a form of personal commitment, a profound psychic
change brought about by what we are made to understand is a
conscious effort. Also the "landscape" in which his transformation takes place is not a perplexing and inhospitable forest, but
"a study of imagination." Friar Laurence, assuming the role of
an analyst and a healer of souls, compels Claudio to interpret his
own "dream" without the helpful intervention of a darkened
wood. Shakespeare's comic context does not permit us to be present at this spectacle of enforced self-analysis. We merely witness
the result, a "new" Claudio discovering what he thinks to be
a "new" Hero—followed by the long awaited wedding feast.

The sense of wholeness in Shakespeare's comedy, of dangers
overcome and darkness conquered, is never the result of a mature longing for self-realization. The hero is still in his early
manhood, quite unaware of the need to strive towards completeness. Individuation is, as it were, forced upon the dreamer. He
seems to endure this process of growth without ever becoming
fully conscious of the direction his dream takes. Only when he
"awakens" does he realize that he has fulfilled himself through
forest-anguish and isolation, through mistaken identity and self-
deception. Shakespeare's dramatic art makes his individuation
seem real because his metaphor of light growing out of darkness, or, in Jungian terms, of wholeness growing out of fragmen-
tation, is the spectator's own favorite metaphor when *he* dreams
of a paradise of completeness. The archetype of the harmonious
self is within each one of us. Shakespeare's comic universe is,
then, a mirror held up to our own longing for a conflictless, care-
free, and undivided existence.

The words *tragic* and *tragedy* do not occur in the very detailed index to Jung's *Collected Works*. This omission is typical

of Jung's generally affirmative attitude to life. Deviations from the norm do not seem to him either comic or tragic. Whenever they interfere with the goal of individual or social integration, they constitute obstacles to healthy psychic growth. As a healer of souls Jung rejected the ultimate despair that yearns for liberation from suffering through self-destruction. In all his writings death is described as a counterpoint to birth, indicative of renewal, a symbol for the exuberance of all life-processes regardless as to whether they constitute a beginning or an end. The following remarks, chosen at random, illustrate this point of view:

"The negation of life's fulfilment is synonymous with the refusal to accept its ending. Both mean not wanting to live, and not wanting to live is identical with not wanting to die. Waxing and waning make one curve." [40]

"I am convinced that it is hygienic—if I may use the word—to discover in death a goal towards which one can strive, and that shrinking away from it is something unhealthy and abnormal which robs the second half of life of its purpose." [41]

"That the highest summit of life can be expressed through the symbolism of death, for any growing beyond oneself means death, is a well known fact." [42]

Most literary attempts at defining the tragic emotion as experienced by the hero on the stage fail when measured by the effect that his suffering and death have upon the spectator. The disaster that pursues the tragic protagonist and draws him on to its final and seemingly inevitable conclusion is not rationally determined. No logical explanation is available or even anticipated. Our pity and fear are not evoked because we understand and therefore identify with the hero's anguish, but rather because we do *not* understand and frequently find it difficult to identify. Our sense of compassion is, thus, directed toward what, in its final analysis, must remain incomprehensible. No wonder, then, that many a spectator is tempted to approve of Bradley's noncommittal definition of Shakespearean tragedy as "a painful mystery." For what could be more mystifying, Bradley thought, than the fortuitous sacrifice of the virtuous and the wise by the side of the vicious and the foolish?

A reassessment of the tragic experience in Jungian terms reveals a somewhat different emphasis. As a psychiatrist he deleted the words *tragic* and *tragedy* from his terminology because he consistently believed in the possibility of eventually resolving the inner polarity which leads to instability, conflict, and the longing for death. Within this context of professional concern for the well-being of his patients, there can be no tragic experience in the Aristotelian sense of the term, with its stress on "a destructive or painful action, such as death on the stage, bodily agony, wounds and the like" (*Poetics*, XI, 6). In Jungian therapeutic work the process of healing includes an acceptance of the phenomenon of dying as part of the process of living. If death is found to be the sole remedy—not as an escape from but as a fulfillment of self—then it is the physician's task to help the patient in facing his death as he has helped him in his daily confrontation with life. The traditional prejudice regarding premeditated suicide is thus meaningless, for neither religious nor moral prohibitions take into account the autonomous functions of the psyche when it aspires toward fullest and most intense self-realization either in life or in death.

In accordance with such a view all psychic change is a form of dying. The greater the required change, the more violent will be the struggle between the old and the new, the moribund and the not-yet-born. The diseased, uprooted, divided life must be allowed to die its predestined death if death is the only cure. Not to be afraid of dying and therefore no longer to resist the impulse toward extinction, is to have acquired, in the very midst of life, the knowledge of the cathartic power of death. In the tragedies written during Shakespeare's greatest maturity, his heroes share this recognition of fulfillment at the very moment of their deepest anguish.

Edgar, in *King Lear,* is Shakespeare's most accomplished portrayal of a man who, having taken upon himself

> the basest and most poorest shape
> That ever penury, in contempt of man,
> Brought near to beast . . . (ii, 3, 7)

is raised to the highest level of individuation. This is rendered possible through suffering inflicted upon him by others, through compassion with the suffering of others, and, finally, through recognition of a way of life which accepts this "little world of man" where birth and death, youth and old age, are equally binding obligations. Whatever ripeness Edgar ultimately achieves originates in his descent to the level of "unaccommodated man" who is no more than "a bare poor forked animal" (III, 4, 110). The spiritual and physical decline from man to beast is deliberate and self-imposed. The apparent irony of his description of himself as "Hog in sloth, fox in stealth, wolf in greediness, dog in madness, lion in prey" (III, 4, 94) has a sharper edge of bitterness and alienation than is apparent at first sight. Having brought about what Jung calls "a collapse of the conscious attitude," Edgar cannot be altogether certain of his own bearings. For such a disintegration of all human values, indeed of all those values that make a civilization possible, may well appear to him a cataclysmic upheaval followed by the final descent of man from the height of his pretended spiritual excellence to the authentic level of the beast. His self-abasement reflects a sense of his own unworthiness. This is also the moment when Edgar, implicitly, is most closely committed to upholding his human dignity.

The point to be stressed is that Edgar's survival as a human being depends on his awareness of chaos and on his ability to integrate the darkness that threatens him with annihilation. The man-beast antithesis is therefore vital for his survival. This is why Shakespeare constantly reminds us of Edgar's bodily suffering, his nakedness in the storm, which opens our eyes to the relevance of the question— "Is man no more than this?" Shakespeare's answer can be found in the process of gradual recognition which takes place in Edgar's mind. For Edgar realizes that mental suffering pertains to man, not beast, and that it must first be grasped by consciousness before it can be overcome. "Who alone suffers suffers most i'the mind" (III, 6, 113) is the foundation upon which his individuation is built. It reaches its culminating point in the humility of self-knowledge which makes Edgar finally describe himself as

> "A most poor man, made tame to fortune's blows,
> Who, by the art of known and feeling sorrows,
> Am pregnant to good pity." (IV, 6, 226)

To him also may be applied Jung's realization that "only the complete person knows how unbearable man is to himself."

Edgar is not allowed to die. He must carry the burden of his human awareness some time longer. Shakespeare wrote *King Lear* in the overwhelming knowledge that tragedy was not enough. For what remains to be shown was man in possession of his self, after his descent into the chaos of the unconscious, acting in the hard-won freedom of his newly gained insight. Edgar's return from his pilgrimage into the depths of primeval darkness might be described in such words as these of Jung's:

> In this way there arises a consciousness which is no longer imprisoned in the petty, over-sensitive, personal world of the ego, but participates freely in the wider world of objective interests. This widened consciousness is no longer that touchy, egotistical bundle of personal wishes, fears, hopes, and ambitions which always has to be compensated or corrected by unconscious counter-tendencies; instead, it is a function of relationship to the world of objects, bringing the individual into absolute, binding, and indissoluble communion with the world at large.[43]

Though Jung's *Collected Works* abound with references to writers and their art, his main concern was not with literature but with life. He never presumed to establish criteria by which to judge the value of any literary creation. His research into the depths of the human soul claims validity only when measured by psychological, not literary, standards. Jung made use of books as he made use of dreams, of myths, of the fantasy formations of the mentally healthy or the emotionally disturbed. Never once does he refer to a work of literary criticism. In all likelihood he would have applied the same criteria, derived from the compensatory function of the unconscious, to the literary critic's psychic constellation. For obvious reasons he was more interested in the creative than in the derivative mind.

This book aims at establishing a meaningful relation between Jung's inquiry into the unconscious and Shakespeare's dramatic work—without unduly insisting on the consulting-room quality of the former or diminishing the creative wisdom of the latter. For what these two share, in a pre-eminent degree, is a living concern with man's psychic heritage. Nothing, indeed, is too foreign to be translated into human terms by their inquiring minds, nothing too high or too low to find a place in their ever-expanding vision of the encounter between man and his unconscious. But what made the writing of this book necessary was the realization that playwright and healer, separated though they are by 350 years of human history, by temperament and language, background and learning, reached such startlingly similar conclusions regarding the degree of human excellence that man must achieve if he wishes to survive.

Throughout the writing of this book the problems posed by the need to divide the material into clearly defined and comprehensive units of intelligibility have appeared almost insuperable. A play-by-play interpretation would have put a misleading emphasis on what might appear to be Shakespeare's growing awareness of archetypes. Though an increasing responsiveness to archetypes can be observed in the mature Shakespeare, a division of this book into "early," "middle," and "late" plays would have shifted the focus of attention from what is at any period of his life of universal validity, to an analysis of his hypothetical spiritual biography.

As Shakespeare grows older the emphasis admittedly falls more heavily on the archetype of self and therefore on the need to free the ego of its uncontrolled appetites, its possessiveness, its greed, its love for power. For this reason Prospero is a more convincing figure than Theseus or Vincentio. Similarly, with growing maturity, projections of the unconscious are felt to be more threatening, and therefore they are given a more complex character. Iago is a more demonic figure than Don John, and Antonio, Prospero's brother, more subtly "machiavellian" than any one of Shakespeare's earlier villains. Likewise Shakespeare's *anima*-figures acquire greater depth and credibility as he grows into middle age. Cressida and Cleopatra conform more closely to an archetypal pattern of femininity than any of Shakespeare's earlier heroines. They are more uncompromisingly, and therefore more destructively, the *anima* that deprives man of his reasoning power.

Jung's method of analysis in depth rather than in historical perspective committed this writer to an emphasis on psychic content rather than on character development. The application of such a method makes no claim to absolute validity. Conceivably it reflects the author's own preoccupation with what lies below the surface of the spoken word, the actor's gesture, and the conventionalities of the stage.

Although the development of Shakespeare's art has been kept in mind throughout this book, it could not provide the frame of reference for a discussion in depth of his plays. It is, very largely, left to the reader to supply the historical continuity, though as far as possible plays are discussed within an accepted chronological framework. Occasionally it was found to be more relevant to join two plays or a group of plays because of intrinsic similarities in psychic structure even though they belong to different periods in Shakespeare's life. Frequently it was the symbol that the unconscious projects into nature or into man that was used as a connecting link for plays which, then, are seen to share, not a philosophy or an outlook on life, but a common psychic structure.

The reader whose interest in Shakespeare grew out of his love for the theatre need not be intimidated by this approach. For as all drama originates in psychic polarity, the dualism and conflicting nature of ego and self, the conscious and the unconscious, *anima* and *animus,* mask and face, are the very stuff of which all great drama is made.

Thus the three parts of the book came into existence. The first, THE EGO, defines the Shakespearean hero in terms of his conscious mind only. The symbols most prevalent are those of the *mask,* especially with reference to kingly power, of *appetite* in its multiple shapes, of the *shadow* thrown by the hero's persona, and, finally, of the *inner voice* that tempts the ego away from its restricted and restricting consciousness into doing evil, and thereby prepares the way toward individuation. It is the individual, not as "a centre of balance," but as an ego-oriented bundle of idiosyncrasies that stands at the core of the first part of the book.

ANIMA, the name given to the second part, indicates the shift from the personal to the transpersonal, from the prevalence of the conscious mind to the gradual domination of the ego by unconscious forces over which it has only partial control. The opposing psychic elements that are at work in Shakespeare's plays here appear as archetypes of integration or division, as paternal or maternal figures which, whether actually present on the stage or not, promote or prevent individuation. The chapter, entitled "Hecate" provides an extreme instance of the maternal archetype in its most destructive aspect.

The third and last part, THE SELF, leads from conflict to resolution. What has been merely hinted at in previous chapters, namely the need to integrate the disparate elements of the human personality, is here finally given a local habitation and a name. The process of individuation, however, is never more

than a remote possibility. No Shakespearean hero ever fully conforms to this ideal of full integration of ego and self. Mythological figures, standing somewhere midway between gods and
men, furnish the symbolic equivalent for the psychological process that Shakespeare himself suggests in some of his plays. For
the three figures from myth share one quality with Shakespeare's
seeker of self: they bring light to others though they are themselves destined to suffer the agony of darkness and isolation.
Thus Prometheus is chained to the cliffs of the Caucasus, Orpheus is torn to pieces, Asklepios must first be wounded that he
may be able to cure the wounds of others. This constant interplay of darkness and light, disorder and harmony, sickness and
health, are the steps leading from denial of self to final, though
still distant, self-realization.

PART ONE

The Ego

1

The Mask

An individual's persona, says Jung, is his "system of adaptation, or the manner he assumes in dealing with the world." It resembles the mask of the actor in ancient times insofar as it is meant to hide a man's true face while it exhibits to the world that "which one as well as others think one is." [1] Everyone, continues Jung, develops in his public or professional life such a persona in order to come to terms with social reality; everyone, that is, except the actor. His ability to assume different and even contradictory roles, and to do so in public, prevents him from ever acquiring an individual persona of his own. He may thus play the part of a lawyer, a merchant, or a policeman—he will never *be* one. This is why, in all likelihood, Jung never mentions acting as a profession in need of a specific persona. The actor in order to face the audience on the other side of the footlights will not have to be encumbered by any personal mask.

Shakespeare's concern with the actor is twofold: on the one hand it reflects his interest in acting as a professional skill which requires considerable training, discipline and what Hamlet calls "discretion." On the other hand nowhere in his plays does Shakespeare indicate a preoccupation with the actor's ego; holding the mirror up to nature implies an absence of personal identity.

Conceivably Shakespeare thought a good actor to be one who readily surrenders whatever personality he possesses in order to impersonate the better the mask that his role has compelled him to wear.

Shakespeare's fascination with complex personalities, split by opposing psychic tendencies, repeatedly led to the creation of actor-figures whose "acting," however, was determined by a deep psychological need. Their personae, then, served as much-desired screens behind which their divided natures could be concealed. They, indeed, are "actors" who play at being kings or beggars, wise men or fools, friends or foes.

Both Shakespeare and Jung thought of man's divided nature as akin to that of the actor compelled to play a part not necessarily of his own free choice. Thus he is invariably tempted to adjust his ego to the mask he is wearing rather than to make the mask conform to his self. Some of Shakespeare's most intriguing plays represent the tension arising from the unresolved conflict between man's unconscious and his persona, between the opposing demands made upon him by his psyche and the public role he is made to play. In such figures as these no self-realization is possible until the true face beneath the assumed mask has been revealed. The image of the mirror which Jung uses to describe this process is peculiarly fitting; for "the mirror does not flatter, it faithfully shows whatever looks into it, namely the face we never show to the world because we cover it with the persona, the mask of the actor." [2]

In both Jung and Shakespeare the static and passive nature of the mask is opposed to the psychic phenomenon of dynamic participation in the life of man and society. To *act* and to *be* are irreconcilables in their spiritual universe. The creation of a healthy balance between art and nature, mask and face, civilization and barbarism, is an integral part of their way of looking at life. The true "self," they both suggest, is the result of a compromise between persona and personality.

Jung's frequent digressions into an analysis of the relationship between persona and the ego in terms of an individual's consciousness of his own self indicates a more than passing interest in the mask as a "secondary reality," at times also called "a two-dimensional reality" or "a semblance." [3] What must have alarmed Jung, as a healer of souls, and what so powerfully attracted Shakespeare to the mask as a form of pretended individuality, was the element of unpredictable personal risk and fortuitous drama involved in a "player's" existence. For both were aware of the fact that there can be no aspirations toward achieving an integrated personality if the ego identifies itself with the persona to such an extent that man is no longer capable of distinguishing between the outer pressures emanating from his public life and the inner truth which resides in his unconscious.

One of Jung's favorite metaphors refers to the ego as an island "which floats upon the ocean of the dark things." [4] The "dark things" are the contents of man's unconscious which never cease to threaten to flood and engulf the island. For "while the island is small and narrow, the ocean is immensely wide and deep and contains a life which is far greater in every way than that of the island." [5] Whenever Shakespeare's kings claim our attention because of their compulsive need to "act," we may assume that what they had to hide beneath their masks was some intrinsic ego-disability preventing them from exercising their kingly power in a meaningful way.

[I]

SHAKESPEARE'S HISTORY plays develop the theme of the king as player whose mask alone determines his fitness for kingship. The three kings that concern us here, Richard II, Henry IV, and his son, Prince Hal, later Henry V, are larger than life-size examples of persona applied to the exercise of political power in a society undermined by moral corruption and spiritual doubts. Jung defined persona with reference to the individual's standing within a professional group: the king whose divine right to kingship is being questioned and who has to uphold its validity before himself and before his people, may be compelled to wear a mask of majesty, if not as an individual, at least as a public figure. That is why all Shakespeare's kings complain, in moments of political emergency, and always in solitude, of their "hard condition," the "ceremony" that attends them in peace or in war, the hollowness of "place, degree, and form," the abstract mask behind which the personal face shrinks into insignificance. Each one of them is a "player-king" and therefore not always certain of the true relationship of his consciousness as an individual and his consciousness as a king.

Having to play the part of a king without an adequate mask is Richard's predicament. It is the dilemma of the actor whose part has ceased to carry conviction. For when the persona begins to crumble, the true face reappears. But by that time there is little enough left of the human countenance to be shown in public. Once the mask is off, all that remains is "the hollow crown," a player-king's "golden round" which impels him to continue playing on a gradually darkening stage, "allowing him a breath, a little scene / To monarchize, be fear'd, and kill with looks" (*Richard II*, III, 2, 164). Richard's own realization that his maskless face reduces his former majesty to the level of a common player who in his complete identification with his mask has forgotten that he is no longer on the stage, is matched by the indifference of the people who—after having applauded Bolingbroke's stage-appearance—now find Richard's vain attempts at "playing the king" unconvincing. For this is the way they see him now:

> As in a theatre the eyes of men,
> After a well-grac'd actor leaves the stage,
> Are idly bent on him that enters next,
> Thinking his prattle to be tedious;

> Even so, or with much more contempt, men's eyes
> Did scowl on Richard. (v, 2, 23)

At one point in the play Richard indeed asks for a mirror to discover therein the face he has never before shown to the world. That he himself, until that moment, has been unaware of the existence of that face, having taken his persona for a divine dispensation of which a symbolic reflection could be found in heaven but not in a looking-glass, is the measure of his essential innocence as man and as king: neither Bolingbroke, his successor on the throne of England, nor Prince Hal, ever expresses the need for a mirror in which to look for the hidden recesses of a face they have so successfully hidden behind their player-king's mask. When Richard asks Bolingbroke to provide him with a mirror, "That it may show me what a face I have / Since it is bankrupt of his majesty" (IV, 1, 266), he formulates the psychological dilemma to which Jung refers when he says that "the mirror lies behind the mask" and therefore reveals a truth which, in Richard's case, is identical with the bankruptcy of his persona. Looking into the mirror, this is what the king discovers:

> Was this the face
> That every day under his household roof
> Did keep ten thousand men? Was this the face
> That like the sun did make beholders wink?
> Is this the face which fac'd so many follies,
> That was at last out-faced by Bolingbroke?
> A brittle glory shineth in this face,
> As brittle as the glory is the face. (IV, 1, *281*)

Richard's recognition of a king's public role moves from the past to the present tense as he realizes the fundamental distinction between his persona which, in the past, was a symbol of majesty, and his face which now that it stares back at him from the mirror, is merely a reflection of himself as "unaccommodated man."

Bolingbroke, a worthy predecessor of Macbeth, wears his mask with a difference. Acknowledging the corrupt society for the sake of which he usurped the crown as the sole arbiter of right and wrong in political conduct, he intentionally deceives the people and, for a short time before his accession, even the nobles of the country, by a mask of humility, the reverse side of the king's persona: now that the argument is no longer centered in a king's divine right, majesty itself has become a matter of expediency and convincing play-acting. The mask to be worn is not that of the traditional king, an archetype of integrity and wholeness, but that of the actor "playing" at being a king and conforming to the idea that the people have of kingship in a society in which the inevitable distinction between persona and a man's true face, that is his soul, is in any case no longer perceived by either the high or the low. Their estimate of Bolingbroke is determined by practical, that is political, considerations only. As an ambitious young man who considers political power well worth fighting for, a Machiavellian of the deepest dye, an adventurer of much personal courage and little honesty, he cannot be judged by his invisible face, but by the mask he wears in public. Disguise itself becomes a "commodity" with which power can be bought. Therefore in order to "out-face" Richard he exhibits an exaggerated sense of unworthiness. In the same scene in which Richard's appearance evoked unqualified contempt from the people, Bolingbroke

> from one side to the other turning,
> Bare-headed, lower than this proud steed's neck,
> Bespake them thus, "I thank you, countrymen." (RII, v, 2, *18*)

What has been said before about the actor's double disguise in which he has to play both himself and the person he is supposed to represent, his real and his stage personality, applies to Bolingbroke's divided consciousness. There is never the slightest doubt in his mind as to the double role he is playing. Gradually his individual consciousness as Bolingbroke's is replaced by a "masked" consciousness which enables him to see his successful

usurpation, disguised as humility, as if it were his true self. Thus
when he, as Henry IV, tells his wayward son how he substituted
political cunning for "divine right," he emphasizes his persona
and thereby raises his status as player-king above that of "sunlike
majesty" which, as a primordial symbol, can be interpreted as
"a dominant of consciousness, such as a generally accepted principle of a collective conviction or a traditional view." [6] Instead of
assuming kingship by divine right, Bolingbroke says,

> [I] . . . stole all courtesy from heaven,
> And dress'd myself in such humility
> That I did pluck allegiance from men's hearts. (1HIV, III, 2, 50)

It is very much later, at the end of his life, that Henry IV
realizes in retrospect as it were, the implications of the deceit he
practised upon himself no less than upon others. His crown is
as "hollow" as Richard's. The "by-paths and indirect crooked
ways" by which he got it are those of the stage where a man's
mask, if well worn, enables him to acquire an artificial identity.
The old dying king says as much in his last conversation with his
son: "For all my reign hath been but a scene / Acting that argument" (2HIV, IV, 5, 197). Hotspur, who opposes the king almost
from the very moment of his accession, has seen through his
mask long ago, and violently denounces him as a mere player-
king. He calls him "this king of smiles" (1HIV, I, 3, 246) and
specifically refers to his face as "this seeming brow of justice"
(1HIV, IV, 3, 83) "angling" for the hearts of men "with tears of
innocency, and terms of zeal" (IV, 3, 63). The image that the king
creates of himself among his people is, with remarkable thorough-
ness, destroyed by Hotspur, whose persona as medieval knight
fighting a losing battle in the name of "honor" is, throughout
the play, opposed to the player-king's dishonor. Yet, Shakespeare
appears little moved by Hotspur's mask of honor. Here, indeed,
one mask cancels out the other, and the king's past evil is not
redeemed by the young man's violent "courtesy." When Hotspur
dies, his mask dies with him. His exaggerated sense of honor is

as hollow as the king's mask of majesty. The Prince who appears to stand somewhere midway between his father and Hotspur when the play opens, declares himself in favor of the player-king rather than the player-hero, kills Hotspur in battle, pays him the tribute that he believes is due to his nobility of mind, and, finally, "out-facing" both his real father and his substitute father, Falstaff, adopts the only persona worthy of a king when he puts the "hollow crown" on his head and decides to wear his mask with more conviction than any of his predecessors have done before him.

Throughout the two plays this young man's psychological make-up is determined by his concern for the "right" mask. There is no place for ambiguity so far as his "public" consciousness is concerned. The Prince never appears to be what he is. At the time of his own accession, illusion and reality achieve a more than questionable synthesis: to all practical intents and purposes, the actor's mask has become his face. Nowhere, in the course of the two plays, not even in that remarkable scene in 2 Henry IV where we find the Prince, in a moment of weariness, confessing to "obduracy, persistency, and hypocrisy," does he dispense with his mask. He always remains the player-prince, perfecting himself so well in the art of acting the role of a king that substance and shadow will be one, both being controlled by him for one and the same purpose—to hold up a mirror to others where they may view themselves as they really are. His mask will *be* the mirror. Thus, when in his first soliloquy he compares himself to the sun—for the time being hidden behind "contagious clouds"—and already then thinks of his future "reformation" as "glittering" and as "bright metal on a sullen ground," Shakespeare introduces to us the master-player whose persona alone will enable him to redeem time "when men think least I will" (1HIV, I, 2, 216–239).

Much can be and has been said about Prince Hal's remarkably self-controlled conduct. The conventional approach has been to study him as a "character." The nineteenth and early twentieth centuries were particularly rich in observations such as these:

> The truth is that we never could forgive the Prince's treatment of Falstaff . . . Falstaff is the better man of the two.[7]

> Prince Henry is not a hero, he is not a thinker, he is not even a friend; he is a common man whose incapacity for feeling enables him to change his habits whenever interest bids him.[8]

> Most of us can forgive youth, hot blood, riot: but a prig of a rake, rioting on a calculated scale, confesses that he does it coldly, intellectually and that he proposes to desert his comrades at the right moment to better his own repute—that kind of rake surely all honest men abhor. . . .[9]

The historical approach to Shakespeare's treatment of Prince Hal avoids the sentimental overemphasis on his despicable "character." Instead it attempts to find excuses in the historical setting or in popular dramatic tradition for the Prince's callous disloyalty and selfishness. Thus we have the following observation on his first soliloquy:

> We must not take the speech naturalistically at all, so as to accuse Henry of a deliberate plan to secure favourable publicity. . . . It is, rather, an objective statement of the facts, as they are, and as they will be (for it includes an element of prophecy). . . . The rejection of Falstaff is already anticipated, and we know that all will work out in accordance with the highest moral precepts.[10]

W. H. Auden, in his essay on Falstaff, looks upon the Prince as "the Worldly Man," an Elizabethan version of the success story *par excellence*. Conceivably, then, Prince Hal is the ideal Machiavellian who, dedicated to some public end, sacrifices whatever personal satisfaction may interfere with the achievement of such an end.[11] Emil Auerbach, from a similar historical angle, places the Prince within the humanist framework of changing moral and religious values and sees in him—as in other great Shake-

spearean characters—a symbol for "the dissolution of medieval
Christianity, running its course through a series of great crises"
and thence revealing "a dynamic need for self-orientation, a will
to trace the secret forces of life." [12]

The psychoanalytical approach forcibly limits the argument
to what is recognizably oedipal in the Prince's conduct. Freud
quotes a passage from *Henry IV*, Part II, as evidence for a son's
"natural resentment against the father" which expresses itself
through "the unimpeded train of thought in the unconscious"
and inevitably leads to "the idea, or rather the wish, that the
father (or his substitute) may disappear from the scene, i.e. that
he may die." [13] Ernst Kris, analysing "Prince Hal's Conflict"
shows how "the Prince tries to dissociate himself from the crime
his father had committed": consequently, "he can permit himself to share Falstaff's vices, but when finally he is in possession
of the crown, he turns against the father substitute" and opposes to both father and substitute his own ideals of "kingship,
royal duty, and chivalry." According to Kris these exalted ideals
"are with him when he first appears on the stage" and continue
growing within him "throughout the tragedy" [sic].[14] Sub-
stantially similar is Professor Alexander's observation about the
Prince's "deep infantile layers of personality" which the Prince
must master in himself before becoming a fully balanced adult.[15]
It is interesting to note that a very recent nonpsychological ap-
praisal of the Prince reaches precisely the opposite conclusion.
For according to this reading of Hal's rejection of Falstaff, we
have "instead of a synthesis in which an enlarged sense of human
possibility emerges from the dialectic between duty and holiday
. . . a forcible sundering of the two kinds of experience. . . .
[Prince Hal's] comprehensive nature is comprehensive no more,
but partial and exclusive." [16]

Judging by these various comments on Hal's "character"—
whether as a stage-figure or as an embodiment of a psychological
conflict-situation—the young Prince suffers from a dissociation
of personality which compels him to uphold a dual image of

himself, be it as a Prodigal Son or as a calculating follower of the traditional concept of kingship. Most commentators then assume that there are indeed two Henrys, the Prince who never for an instant forgets his future as a king that is in store for him, and the man whom Shakespeare must have imagined to be "common," unfeeling, and selfish. The dissociation sets in with his first soliloquy, for "it is true that the soliloquy is unlike Hal. . . . It is not Hal, primarily, who makes the speech at all. The Prince makes it. There are two Henrys. This is no quibble; it is the inmost heart of the matter. . . . Hal and the Prince, we shall never get anything straight about this story, if we confuse them or fail to mark the differences, the connections, and the interplay of the two." [17] Even more explicitly, another reader maintains "that there are two Prince Hals in the play, as there are two Falstaffs, the Hal of the stage, and the Hal of Shakespeare's mind who emerges as the contemplative reader puts together all the *disjecta membra* of the Prince." [18]

The mistaken assumption that Shakespeare created lifelike characters makes such conclusions almost inescapable. If there are two Henrys, how many Hamlets will the "contemplative reader" assemble at the end of the play? And does not the distinction between the Prince of the stage and the Prince in Shakespeare's mind raise a further and more awkward question as to Shakespeare's possible hypocrisy in creating such a Janus-like figure? Surely, the possibility of interpreting the Prince Hal-Falstaff relationship in terms of archetypal drama rather than as part of a historical setting or of Shakespeare's political biography, opens vistas far larger and less ambiguous than those quoted above. "For drama, like religious ritual, plays upon atavic impulses of the mind. All true drama penetrates through representative fiction to the condition of myth. And Falstaff is in the end the dethroned and sacrificed king, the scapegoat as well as the sweet beef." [19]

A detailed analysis of the myth of the hero leads one to conclude that a division of the central figure into two symbolic representations—that of the hero as a young man or even as a child, and his tutor in the guise of a paternal image, the former apparently sponging on the latter—is very common and can indeed be found in widely separate legends belonging to different ages, religions, and continents.[20] In some of the stories told about Dionysos, supposed to have been the son of Persephone and Hades, he either appears as a mask or is represented with a strange mask-like face. Various representations show him, still a suckling, surrounded by women, one of whom is giving suck to the child—"A male figure is also present, and is waiting to perform his duties by the child: this is Silenos, who in later, but not very late, tales was Dionysos' tutor. The expression 'male figure' is almost an over-statement. As the god's tutor, Silenos became very unlike the Silenoi who were the lovers of the nymphs (. . . creatures with pointed ears, hooves and horses' tails, but in other respects in human-phallic shape, with snub-nosed faces and unruly manners. . .) he is an aged, effeminate figure with a thick stomach and almost womanly breasts. . . ." It is, however, not without significance that this same Silenos, in tales told in Asia Minor, "when made drunk and taken captive, revealed deep truths." [21]

Though intellectually the Prince's equal, Falstaff with his constantly shifting masks lacks a unifying principle. There is no frame of reference within which his comic but self-defeating attempts at "counterfeiting" might acquire lasting significance. The Prince's persona, on the other hand, is and will remain his essential identity: the question is no longer whether he "knows himself" as an individual, but whether he experiences himself as a social being. Falstaff's "individuality" becomes increasingly ambiguous as the play progresses. As a Silenos-figure, he fulfills his function as a tutor by constant disguises. He finds it as little embarrassing to play the Prince's father as to change roles with the young man, and play the son—the Prince in the meantime acting his own father with characteristic self-assurance. It seems perfectly in keeping with Falstaff's singular talent as many-faced actor that the Prince should even desire him to take the part of a woman in an improvised play about Hotspur: "I prithee call in Falstaff: I'll play Percy, and that damned brawn shall play Dame Mortimer his wife" (1HIV, II, 4, 106).

As a Silenos-archetype who has at one time been a "lover of the nymphs" but now is an aged figure "with a thick stomach" who speaks "deep truths" when drunk, Falstaff, Shakespeare's most accomplished Trickster-figure, appears as what he really is, the "shadow" thrown by the Prince's persona, his unconscious projected outward and assuming the most obvious archetypal shape—that of the tutor misled by his pupil, old Silenos enslaved to young Dionysos, the many-faced in the service of the mask. Falstaff says as much on a number of occasions:

> "Thou hast done much harm upon me, Hal, God forgive thee for it: before I knew thee, Hal, I knew nothing, and now am I, if a man should speak truly, little better than one of the wicked."
> (1HIV, I, 2, *103*)

> "I have forsworn his company hourly any time this two and twenty years, and yet I am bewitched with the rogue's company."
> (1HIV, II, 2, *17*)

> *Chief Justice:* "You have misled the youthful Prince.
> *Falstaff:* The young Prince has misled me. I am the fellow with the great belly, and he my dog." (2HIV, I, 2, *166*)

> *Chief Justice:* "You follow the young Prince up and down, like his ill angel.
> *Falstaff:* Not so, my lord, your ill angel is light." (2HIV, I, 2, *187*)

> *Chief Justice:* "Well, God send the Prince a better companion!
> *Falstaff:* God send the companion a better prince! I cannot rid my hands of him." (2HIV, I, 2, *227*)

The rejection scene follows a similar pattern, only this time it is the Prince who calls Falstaff "a fool and jester / The tutor and the feeder of my riots" (2HIV, V, 5, 67). By banishing Falstaff he sends his unconscious into exile, frees himself of the burden of his maskless companions, and, finally, carries out a promise he had set himself when, in his first soliloquy, he decided to "falsify men's hopes" by offending so well that he will turn offence into a fine art. The emphasis on the social context which characterizes this soliloquy as well as anything the Prince does in the course of the two plays, is significant. Hal's existence as an individual and as future king of England is determined by the people among whom he lives. He is indeed, in spite of occasional fits of weariness and despondency, the least introspective of Shakespeare's young heroes. His persona is made to measure. Rarely has one of Jung's definitions been more fitting than the following when applied to Prince Hal:

> Through his more or less complete identification with the attitude of the moment, he at least deceives others and also often himself, as to his real character. He puts on a *mask,* which he knows corresponds with his conscious intentions, while it also meets with the requirements and opinions of his environment. This mask, viz. the ad hoc adopted attitude, I have called the *persona* which was the designation given to the mask worn by the actors of antiquity. A man who is identified with his mask I would call "personal" (as opposed to "individual"). . . . Thus the persona is a function-complex which has come into existence for reasons of adaptation or necessary conveniences, but by no means is it identical with the individuality.[22]

How "conscious" the Prince's intentions are is stated by the Earl of Warwick to the king who had just then complained of his son's "headstrong riot" and "hot blood":

> My gracious lord, you look beyond him quite.
> The Prince but studies his companions
> Like a strange tongue, wherein, to gain the language,
> 'Tis needful that the most immodest word
> Be look'd upon and learnt; which once attain'd,
> Your Highness knows, comes to no further use
> But to be known and hated. So, like gross terms,
> The Prince will, in the perfectness of time,

> Cast off his followers, and their memory
> Shall as a pattern or a measure live
> By which his grace must mete the lives of others,
> Turning past evils to advantages. (2HIV, IV, *4*, *67*)

By choosing the mask, Prince Hal cuts himself off from his fellow men and makes his unchanging persona the sole criterion by which he is to be judged. His is a new psychological dimension with which neither the nobility nor the common people are as yet acquainted. When the mask is no longer accidental, a convenient disguise for the moment, it may even raise the individual who wears it to the realm of the archetypal. In this sense, it may almost be said that Prince Hal's use of the mask re-establishes the divine right of kings that had been usurped by his father when he murdered Richard II. Prince Hal thus participates in a ritual of which he is the main protagonist and Falstaff his indispensable "tutor." Without Falstaff, the future "pattern" and "measure" of kingship would have been incomplete. But once the Prince has learnt the tongue that people speak when they are among themselves and think themselves unobserved, he dismisses the anarchy of their maskless existence, and chooses the life of conscious and purposeful disguise instead. Though his choice is dramatically and psychologically justified, he remains an alien on the stage, among his own people, and a stranger to himself. And as the ritual takes its inevitable course, and Falstaff, Hal's "offending Adam," is exorcised in the name of the Mask, we yearn for the Prince's past shadow which was more "real" than the king's present face.

[II]

WHATEVER ONE'S FINAL ESTIMATE of Prince Hal's "performance" may be, one is left with the disillusioning realization that the divine right of kings has been successfully disposed of by a rationalization of kingship. The perfect ruler will be one who will "out-face," not merely his competitors on the political stage, but the heavens themselves. Yet it is fairly obvious that Shakespeare's sympathy is not with the modern player-king and his puny attempts at justifying himself before God and man, but with kingship as "a psychic *a priori* which reaches far back into pre-history and comes very close to being a natural revelation of the psychic structure." [23] Whenever kingship forms part of Shakespeare's dramatic design, it is indeed assumed to be the fountainhead of all living processes, the final authority over right and wrong, the supreme symbolic representation of the principle of integration on earth.

The "face" of the king should be identical with the face of heaven. The earth is its mirror in which is reflected the kingly countenance. Obliterating the face of majesty is like darkening the universe and smiting men with blindness. When the king ceases to see, the stars go blind, the sun no longer rises, and even the moon suffers eclipse. The art of the actor will then be of no more avail. The player-king, reflected in the apocalyptic visions of his own tortured mind, will see himself as a "poor player / That struts and frets his hour upon the stage / And then is heard no more." This is what Macbeth realizes at the end of his life. Following Macbeth from the moment he meets the witches to his final awareness that his existence on earth has been but "a walking shadow," is like witnessing an actor's "stealthy pace," his "ravishing strides," from one form of darkness to another, from face to mask, and back again to final facelessness.

This is a different story from that of Prince Hal and his father, Shakespeare's archetype of the player-king. Prince Hal starts his career as the protagonist of a play of which he is the writer, the producer, and the chief actor, out-playing all the other actors on the stage. His consistently unequivocal aim has been to redeem the time. He indeed fulfills his promise—however crooked the ways he chooses to do so. Macbeth who at the beginning of the play seems to be quite incapable of any kind of crookedness redeems time by his death. "The time is free," Mal-

colm exclaims, when heaven and earth, once again, can reveal
their countenance in the redeeming light of the sun.

The significance of Shakespeare's symbolic use in *Macbeth*
of darkness and light, of sun and moon images, has frequently
been pointed out. What remains to be done is to relate these
symbols to Shakespeare's increasing preoccupation with the mask
and the invisible face of the player-king. In the earlier history-
plays the sun never sets, although it may at times be covered by
clouds. We watch the prince's antics, his progress from Eastcheap
to Whitehall, in broad daylight. Possibly Shakespeare wanted us
to admire the well-fitting mask in the light of common day. For
the young man is far from being common, and the setting in
which he experiments with his persona, either before Falstaff or
in front of his father, the king, is of the flesh-and-blood variety,
free of ghosts, apparitions, and boiling cauldrons.

The setting in which Macbeth and his wife strut and fret is
an exact replica of their own inner darkness. Whatever chaos
their unconscious creates, is immediately projected into a universe from which light and the light-receiving sense of sight are
banished. Therefore their prayers for darkness are in reality addressed to "heaven," to be blind to their desires and to their
deed:

> *Macbeth:* Stars, hide your fires!
> Let not light see my dark and deep desires.
> The eye wink at the hand . . . (I, 4, 50)

> *Lady Macbeth:* Come, thick Night,
> And pall thee in the dunnest smoke of hell,
> That my keen knife see not the wound it makes,
> Nor Heaven peep through the blanket of the dark
> To cry, "Hold, hold!" (I, 5, 51)

Their prayers are answered in a way which neither husband nor
wife ever anticipated. The "deed" having been committed and
the faces of the grooms smeared with blood ("for it must seem
their guilt"), the mask that Macbeth is now compelled to wear

is found to be much larger than his face. It covers not merely
his own guilty countenance but the face of the whole earth. The
"stage" on which the murder has been done, is darkened by the
over life-size persona of the murderer:

> Thou seest the heavens, as troubled with man's act
> Threaten his bloody stage: by th'clock 'tis day,
> And yet dark night strangles the travelling lamp.
> Is't night's predominance, or the day's shame,
> That darkness does the face of earth entomb,
> When living light should kiss it? (II, 4, 5)

Even if and when the sun does rise again, the "face" of heaven is
tormented by the echoing cries of widows and orphans. "Each
new morn / New sorrows strike heaven on the face" (IV, 3, 4).
Earth and heaven are endowed with eyesight and the sense of
hearing. They are menacingly present when the deed is being
committed. The darkness that "entombs" them both is no obstacle to seeing or to hearing. Rather on the contrary, what the
heavens see, the earth can hear. Therefore Macbeth must first
pray to the "sure and firmset earth"—

> Hear not my steps, which way they walk, for fear
> Thy very stones prate of my where-about (II, 1, 57)

before the murder can be committed.

To project his "personal" mask into nature, to blind the
stars and the eyes of men, so that *all* reflection, from below and
from above, would be safely disposed of, is Macbeth's most
wished-for consummation. "Masking the business from the common eye" (III, 1, 125) becomes a compulsive end in itself, not
necessarily even related to his appalling deed. The mask has to
be preserved at all cost. Without it, life would become unbearable. Macbeth does not know that his "borrow'd robes" do not
fit, and "hang loose about him, like a giant's robe / Upon a
dwarfish thief" (V, 2, 21). What he, intuitively, perceives after
the murder is that "to present an unequivocal face to the world
is a matter of practical importance" and that therefore "the con-

struction of an artificial personality becomes an unavoidable necessity." [24] What he does not and cannot know, is that "this painfully familiar division of consciousness into two figures, often preposterously different, is an incisive psychological operation that is bound to have repercussions on the unconscious" and may become "a very fruitful source of neuroses," because "a man cannot get rid of himself in favour of an artificial personality without punishment." [25] The most common punishment is a back-sliding into the collective unconscious flooding the personality, until the dividing line between the self and the archetype is abolished. What remains is no longer the individual but "only a mask for the collective psyche, a mask that *feigns individuality* and tries to make others and oneself believe that one is individual, whereas one is simply playing a part in which the collective psyche speaks." [26]

The difference in depth of psychological insight between Prince Hal and Macbeth as player-kings, is the measure of Shakespeare's growing awareness that what matters is not the "face" at all but the "heart." In *Macbeth* he seems to reject the adolescent Prince's adaptable persona, substituting for it the tragedy of "Bellona's bridegroom" and his futile attempts at concealing behind the mask of kingship his imperfect ego "tossed like a shuttlecock between the outer and inner demands" of his psyche. [27] That these attempts are defeated by a "darker purpose" which no mask could really hide, is one of the main themes of the play. And as Macbeth becomes increasingly entangled in the dualism of face and mask, the dichotomy is finally dissolved in the darkness that reflects nothing but its own ambiguity. Which was the face and which the mask, Duncan already wanted to know when he wondered at the treachery and malice of the first Thane of Cawdor who, at one time, was a man on whom he "built / An absolute trust." Cawdor, who is described as if he had been an actor on the stage and had many times before his death rehearsed the most impressive way of dying, exhibited a guiltless face to the world. Yet Duncan admits, "There's no art /

To find the mind's construction in the face" (I, 4, 12), a statement most forcefully disproved by Lady Macbeth who, looking
at her husband after his meeting with the witches, reveals to him
the need for disguise and darkness:

> Your face, my thane, is as a book, where men
> May read strange matters. To beguile the time,
> Look like the time. . . .
>   Look like the innocent flower
> But be the serpent under't. (I, 5, 63)

Lady Macbeth's own unconscious prevents her from ever fully
realizing the consequences of her "unsexed" condition. She
breaks down when the doctor cannot supply that "sweet obliv-
ous antidote" which would "cleanse the stuff'd bosom of that
perilous stuff / Which weighs upon the heart" (V, 3, 43). Macbeth, however, drinks his "poison'd chalice" to the lees. Already
before the murder he is aware of the intricate relationship between his ego and his self: "False face must hide what the false
heart doth know" (I, 7, 82). After the murder, and now in full
possession of the "golden round," he is compelled to mask his
guilt and "Make our faces vizards to our hearts / Disguising what
they are." (III, 2, 34)

Prince Hal started his self-revelation with the over-confident
exclamation, "I know you all." This is the kind of assumption
that may facilitate the transition from the knowledge of others to
self-knowledge. The question whether the Prince really knows
himself is never asked in explicit terms. By implication, however, one is made unpleasantly aware, in the course of the play,
that all the knowledge the future ruler of England requires is
symbolized by his masked face. He sees without being seen. He
studies others while he keeps himself withdrawn from observation. All the robes he wears are "borrowed." What he knows,
then, is not himself *as he is,* but rather as he wishes to appear to
others. His knowledge of the mask suffices to create for him that
artificial identity which will enable him to avoid the perils of a

"collective psyche" and remain, intrinsically, his own pliable and masked ego. Knowing himself through others, he is secretly pleased to observe the many artificial identities he is burdened with by them. He is authentic only as an actor: for he is essentially without heart.

Macbeth's mind is differently constituted. What he knows is that he has "murdered sleep" and that neither in sleeping nor in waking will his heart ever be at peace again. However much he may pray to "seeling Night" to "scarf up the tender eye of pitiful day" (III, 2, 47), no darkness on earth or in heaven will be dark enough to mask his heart from his own eye.

Yet beneath the mask the shadow continues to grow, while the substance shrinks into nothingness. At the moment of his dying, Macbeth *is* his own shadow.

2

Appetite

THE WAY TOWARD INDIVIDUATION is open only to those who
succeed in freeing their egos from the load of unconscious
content that has not been integrated. As the object of individuation is the achievement of psychic balance, the ego must come
to terms with the demands from without and from within, however incompatible they may appear to be in the light of consciousness. For though no other criteria but those established by consciousness are available by which these demands can be judged,
the conscious ego is only a part, and not necessarily the most
important part, of the total human personality. Whenever man
undervalues, neglects, or discards the unconscious as irrelevant,
the psychic balance suffers eclipse.

Troilus, Bertram, and Angelo are problem-heroes because of
their inability to achieve that emotional poise which alone might
counterbalance their over-inflated egos. Academic scholarship
rarely takes them seriously. For they lack the stark simplicity of
Othello's noble soul, of Macbeth's "vaulting ambition," or of
the doom that issues from Lear's "darker purpose." Their "heroism" wants the virtues of selflessness and devotion. Their love
does not aspire toward a marriage of true minds, but is a sterile
intoxication of the senses. Whenever the "heroic" attitude is

present, it appears as a pose or as inspired rhetoric, a mask that fails to hide the hollowness at the core of their beings. Each one of them, at the moment of crisis, reveals a spectacle of utter disorientation. He who should have acted "heroically" is "delivered up . . . like a rudderless ship that is abandoned to the moods of the elements." [1] Even when he chooses to die fighting, as Troilus does, his heroic pose serves only as a pretext for futile and morally equivocal sacrifice. For the heroic mask is valid only as long as there is some hope of attaining the desired aim. When, however, the problem-hero realizes that the demands made upon his ego outgrow his inner resources, he finds his goal no longer worth fighting for. And though "formerly perhaps he wanted more than he could accomplish, now he does not even dare to attempt what he has it in him to do." [2]

What these three problem figures, then, have in common is a refusal to confront adult living. This is in part due to an overdeveloped ego-consciousness leading to psychic difficulties of which they themselves are scarcely aware; in addition, they are placed in societies which themselves are problem-ridden because rooted in corrupt or decaying moral assumptions that make any adaptation to the prevailing moral tone of little benefit to themselves or to the community. Jung's definition of one specific psychic element, most frequently met with in adolescence, is partly applicable to Shakespeare's singularly ego-centered problem-heroes: ". . . a more or less patent clinging to the childhood level of consciousness, a resistance to the fateful forces in and around us which would involve us in the world." [3] Their "individualism" is merely a kind of oddity: it narrows down their consciousness and reduces their emotional range to the momentary flickering of lust. To judge these figures by their conduct, the attitude of singularity which distinguishes them from others as *individuals* is "nothing but an unnatural usurpation, a freakish, impertinent pose that proves its hollowness by crumpling up before the least obstacle." [4]

[I]

Troilus and Cressida DEVELOPS THE ANTITHESIS BE-
tween consciousness and the unconscious, the ego and the self,
simultaneously on an individual and a collective level. On both
these planes human frailty and its concomitant, excessive appetite, are found to be equally menacing: the individual, unable to
resist the instinctual drives originating in his unconscious, is torn
between a code of values, consciously entertained, and the anarchic self-expression that his instincts demand; [5] society, on the
other hand, by giving way to such "appetites" as exaggerated
national pride or compulsive aggressiveness for the sake of upholding some ambiguously defined "honor," is likely to destroy
itself in the process of preserving the very thing which—when
judged by rational standards of conduct—may scarcely seem
worth preserving.

This is the paradox as well as the central "problem" of this
exceedingly difficult play. What it appears to question is the
value of any human experience insofar as it is based upon appetite alone. On the other hand, conscious judgment of human
failings is too often put into the mouths of those whose own
ways are ego-dominated and who therefore lack the charity that
would provide their judgment with the emotional frame of reference by which to measure such failings. Uncontrolled appetite
and dispassionate reason are equally condemned in the course
of the play: there is no moral criterion to counterbalance the
equivocal emotionalism of the lovers or the shallow heroism of
the warriors. Twentieth-century critics find themselves in the un-
enviable position of having to reappraise a Shakespeare play
without any valid support from earlier critical assessments. For
no other play by Shakespeare has evoked so many extremes of
merely personal affirmation or rejection. Thus, at the beginning
of this century, Arthur Symons thought of *Troilus and Cressida*
as "laughter in the midst of storm; it has all the wisdom that

lies in the deepest irony," [6] while a decade later, in a comparative study of Chaucer's and Shakespeare's treatment of the Troilus and Cressida theme, another author wonders how "such a work should ever have proceeded from the great soul of Shakespeare." [7] In the opinion of quite a number of readers the play reads like the ravings of a madman, for one finds in it "the ghastly strength of mania, the awful lucid vision of the crazed who can see one thing and one thing only and that horrible. But the writing of it probably saved Shakespeare from going mad." [8] Others more tolerant among them saw a message in the play intended to warn against "the devastating consequences of unrestrained physical passion" [9] or against a surrender to "the dark night of the soul" and "the unilluminated wreckage of the universe of vision" [10] that the play symbolized for them. What made one critic laugh, evoked the strongest possible moral disapproval in another. What some of them called a "comedy of manners" was likely to arouse tragic emotions when individual conduct was measured by the elevated standards established by a medieval code of chivalry and honor. The dehumanizing effect of war and appetite was noted by all these critics alike: some indeed found the spectacle exhilarating, others found it nauseating.

What seems so profoundly unsatisfactory about much recent as well as nineteenth-century criticism of the play, is the confusion between what actually happens on the stage and the critics' own predisposition to judge both plot and characters by moral rather than psychological standards. That *Troilus and Cressida* may make the cynic laugh, the wise man speculate, the sensitive grieve, and the neurotic identify himself with it, seems to lie at the root of the critic's perplexity. The attempt to interpret the play "in depth" will not necessarily dissolve such critical ambiguity: it may, however, reveal aspects of the play that provide such ambiguity with a psychological *raison d'être*. Once the more obvious historical and dramatical cross-references are disposed of, Shakespeare's play can no longer be classified according to conventional literary terminology as being a tragedy, a comedy, or a satire: its insistence on the effect of appetite on man's search for individual fulfillment in a love-relationship, or on collective endeavors to establish the rule of law among nations, corresponds to Jung's emphasis on unconscious processes in the analysis of emotional difficulties arising from individual maladjustment and collective alienation.

Throughout this extraordinary play, the city of Troy is an anima-oriented symbol which may be likened to a maternal image harboring the inhabitants in herself like children. Her "sons" and "daughters" are Eros-dominated. Her "honor" is equally feminine: as it lacks the element of chastity it is constantly in peril of being "lost." Both Hector and Troilus, though starting from different premises, are conscious of the precarious nature of an honor which cannot be defined in absolute terms, but only with reference to sexual appetite, which steals Helena from Menelaus, or, with reference to national pride, which makes keeping her a matter of sound political judgment. In defending the adultery he committed, Paris, indeed, wants to have it both ways: why not, he asks, redeem one's appetite by submitting it to a political test which, actually, might even justify his deed and make appetite itself look "honorable"?

> But I would have the soil of her fair rape
> Wiped off in honourable keeping her. (II, 2, *158*)

The maternal city has indeed been "soiled" by the rape, adultery, and elopement which brought Helena to Troy. Paris and his paramour hide behind the walls of the city. Their love-making takes place in the darkness of the king's palace. Paris, the witless son of his soiled "mother," is not likely to stir anyone's sympathy: nor does either Trojan or Greek take him seriously. His love-making is a matter of public discussion. His father interrupts the impassioned defence of his amorous enterprise and rejects his claim to valor and heroism because he speaks "Like one besotted on your sweet delights" (II, 2, 143). Pandarus sees nothing but the bawdy side of their adulterous relationship. Re-

ferring jokingly to Cressida's infatuation for Troilus, he tells
Helena, in Paris' presence, "My niece is horribly in love with
a thing you have, sweet queen" (III, 1, 109). When, finally, Paris
himself asks Diomedes to confide to him "Who, in your thoughts,
merits fair Helen most, / Myself or Menelaus?" he gets a reply
from the Greek that no Trojan had dared as yet to give him,
though they all must have felt the strength of the argument
before Diomedes put it into words:

> Both alike.
> He merits well to have her that doth seek her,
> Not making any scruple of her soilure,
> With such a hell of pain and world of charge;
> And you as well to keep her that defend her,
> Not palating the taste of her dishonour. (IV, *1*, *54*)

This then, reduced to its crude essentials, in the manner of
Thersites, is the object of this war: a cuckolded husband defending his honor against a lecherous bachelor who seeks refuge behind the maternal walls of the city, believing that what has been
dishonor outside the protective enclosure will be transformed
into honor by merely withdrawing into the anonymity of the
"womb" where honor and dishonor, in any case, are shown to be
equally ambiguous concepts. Paris, an otherwise very insignificant
figure in the play, exhibits all the symptoms of a son who has
not yet freed himself of his maternal attachment and whose
infantile regression looks for rational justification in moral arguments. As his sexual involvement with Helena serves as a pretext
for aggressive war, there is little enough to choose between the
two kinds of appetite enacted on the stage.

Jung's definition of "libido" includes both these forms of
appetite, as well as many more. He sometimes calls it "life-urge"
or "a will to live" or simply "psychic energy." All of them alike
are what he calls energy-values capable of communicating themselves to any field of human activity "be it hunger, hatred, sexuality, or religion, without ever being itself a specific instinct." [11]
Jung's analysis of the libido concept, then, accepts the sexual

connotation which the Freudian term had previously established, but adds to it all those appetites and compulsions which
are themselves psychic phenomena emanating from the unconscious, and which frequently require a nonsexual interpretation.
It is not without relevance for our play that Jung should, among
others, quote Cicero's definition of "libido" with approval. According to the Stoics, says Cicero, "will is a rational desire, but
when it is divorced from reason and is too violently aroused, that
is 'libido' or unbridled desire, which is found in all fools." [12]

The two "fools" that provide Shakespeare with the initial
impetus in writing his play are Paris and Achilles, the former
exhibiting the regressive symptoms of an unregulated sexuality,
the latter cultivating a particularly infantile brand of insolence
and pride. While the "unbridled desire" of the one causes a
senseless war, Achilles' "psychic energy" withdraws into "seeded
pride," thereby preventing a successful prosecution of the war
which, with the peculiar logic inherent in appetite, both Trojans
and Greeks find equally "honorable." When Ulysses delivers his
great oration on "degree" before the assembled Greek generals,
he wishes to attack any form of disunity—in particular the one
caused by Achilles' childish display of hurt vanity—that stands
in the way of "victory." According to Ulysses, the discord following upon uncontrolled appetite, inevitably leads to ruin:

> Then everything includes itself in power,
> Power into will, will into appetite,
> And appetite, an universal wolf,
> So doubly seconded with will and power
> Must make perforce an universal prey
> And last eat up itself. (I, 3, 119)

The argument, within the total context of the play, is, however, fallacious. Had Achilles, and for that matter, Ajax and
many other Grecian generals, restrained their vanity and pride,
the war would have ended long ago, the walls around the city
would have been razed to the ground, the Trojans killed, their

wives taken into captivity, and Helen would, at last, have been restored to Menelaus. Psychologically speaking, then, Achilles' repressed aggressiveness, itself a compensation for an ambition that could not be realized in life and therefore looked for wish-fulfillment in childish day dreams, is to blame for the present "dishonor" of the Greeks. Troy, a maternal image for both Trojans and Greeks, is still unvanquished. The "soilure" of Helena's rape is being repeated nightly within her protective walls. Ulysses' eloquent defence of "degree" is therefore easily deflated when Thersites' corrosive mind reveals the ugly truth hidden behind this eloquence. Honor and degree are mere abstractions if "all the argument is a whore and a cuckold" (II, 3, 78). The honor that the "fools" on both sides of the fence are fighting for is evidently a foolish honor and the shaking of degree will harm no one except the fools.

When listening to Hector's equally impassioned censure of appetite before the Trojan council of war, which, incidentally, is also a family council, one realizes the hopelessness of his position as, in all sincerity, he defends the rule of "law" against uncontrolled instinctual drives. Both he and Ulysses start from the identical assumption that without subordination to degree no ordered social life is possible. While Ulysses speaks with an eye on Achilles and the threat that his suppressed appetite constitutes for the Grecian war-effort, Hector, more directly, refers to Paris and his "unbridled" lust that has led to moral laxity among Trojans, and the toleration of adultery as a publicly acknowledged extra-marital relationship. If, as Ulysses asserts, "degree, priority and place" ought to be observed for the sake of social unity in war, the "law" of which Hector speaks, is the one upholding the institution of monogamous marriage:

> If this law
> Of nature be corrupted through affection,
> And that great minds, of partial indulgence
> To their benumbed wills, resist the same,
> There is a law in each well-ordered nation

> To curb those raging appetites that are
> Most disobedient and refractory. (II, 2, *176*)

Troilus, more sincere than Ulysses but less mature than Hector, is hardly aware of the ambiguity of his position when he rises to the defence of adultery and turns Helena, who in the eyes of at least the more clearheaded Greeks, is no more than "a flat tamed piece," "a whore," and "a plaquet," into

> A theme of honour and renown;
> A spur to valiant and magnanimous deeds,
> Whose present courage may beat down our foes
> And Fame in time to come canonize us. (II, 2, *199*)

When Cressida proves unfaithful, following the dictates of her own wayward appetite, as Helena had previously done when she eloped with Paris, Troilus' own hurt vanity uses different language. He now is guided by his desire for vengeance rather than by abstract moral principles. Leaving to his brother Paris the doubtful honor of keeping Helena, he is suddenly faced by a world of appetites where cunning Greek is no longer clearly distinguishable from noble Trojan, for when Achilles, at last, satisfies his appetite by killing Hector against all rules of chivalry,[13] and Diomedes follows his own instincts by making love to Cressida, neither of the two requires honor or fame to justify his deeds. Troilus then adapts himself to the prevailing spirit of cynical opportunism in either camp and joins the battle in a last frantic attempt to recapture a lost appetite rather than a lost honor.

Shakespeare calls these self-destructive tendencies of undisciplined instinctual drives "appetite," while Jung defines them as psychic energy that has not been "canalized" in a more adequate form than the original one. Throughout the play this psychic energy is expressed through food-images and especially those referring to the tasting of food, to digestive processes, to over-eating and the physical nausea consequent upon it. Eating as an autonomous "psychic" function, no more related to physical hunger but a form of compulsive behavior independent of one's will-power, may, like any form of automatism, be taken as a symbol of self-destruction: it is then that, in the language of depth-psychology, the conscious is swallowed by the unconscious, and uncontrolled libido prevents rational conduct. And if, because of circumstances beyond conscious control, appetite is thwarted, it may, by a process of displacement common enough among mental patients, turn against itself. Ulysses already had spoken of appetite as an "universal wolf" that at last will "eat up itself" for want of any other diet. A more concise formula is used by him again when he directly addresses Achilles and attempts to arouse an appetite that might prove useful to the Greek war-effort:

> How one man eats into another's pride,
> While pride is fasting in his wantonness. (iii, 3, *145*)[14]

And since the two forms that appetite takes in this play, suppressed vanity and suppressed sexual lust, are linked by the destructive or death instinct common to both, Thersites' final observation—after witnessing the encounter between Troilus and Diomedes on the battlefield—sums up the questionable nature of the victory of one appetite over the other: "Yet, in a sort, lechery eats itself."

The warning that the two father-figures, Ulysses in the Greek and Hector in the Trojan camp, had pronounced against appetite, has gone unheeded. The killing of Hector is no longer a matter of either political or strategic expedience, but deliberate murder committed in cold blood to satisfy the appetite of one whom Cicero would have called a "fool." [15] Paris whose sexual vanity is a worthy counterpart to Achilles' pride continues in his public exhibition of adultery; and Troilus who, on a previous occasion, has disregarded the "law of a well-ordered nation" by defending adultery in terms of his own emotional involvement, but who in the meantime, assisted by the morally equivocal Pandarus, has "tasted" "Love's thrice repured nectar" (III, 2,

20), discovers that the eating has choked the eater. What he vomits up, soils him no less than her—

> orts of her love
> The fragments, scraps, the bits and greasy relics
> Of her o'ereaten faith. (v, 2, *193*)

Both Achilles the warrior and Troilus the lover choke on what they feed. They are left with their respective dishonors, "greasy relics" of their overeating. Their libido has regressed into what might be called a presexual stage, expressed by Shakespeare through constant use of nutritional images and symbols put in place of the sexual function. In Jungian terminology, as "the hero has fasted, his hunger becomes predominant. Fasting . . . is employed to silence sexuality; also it expresses symbolically the resistance against sexuality translated into the language of the presexual stage." [16] Thus Achilles calls Thersites "my cheese, my digestion" (II, 3, 44), while Ulysses describes Achilles' pride entirely in terms of undigestible fat that has accumulated around it. He calls him "The proud lord / That bastes his arrogance with his own seam . . ." and warns the Greek generals that "by going to Achilles / That were to enlard his fat-already pride" (II, 3, 205). Pandarus, who seems to derive a vicarious sexual enjoyment from the amorous encounter between Troilus and Cressida, is not just a lecherous and wicked old man but an adept in appetite who "panders" to the hunger induced by the "fasting" of the two lovers. He knows all about Troilus' emotional insecurity and the consequent regression of his libido. The language he uses is bawdy though nutritional, and ostensibly refers to the baking and eating of a cake:

P: He that will have a cake out of the wheat must needs tarry the grinding.
T: Have I not tarried?
P: Ay, the grinding, but you must tarry the bolting.
T: Have I not tarried?
P: Ay, the bolting; but you must tarry the leavening.

т: Still have I tarried.

р: Ay, to the leavening; but here's yet in the word "hereafter" the kneading, the making of the cake, the heating of the oven and the baking; nay, you must stay the cooling too, or you may chance to burn your lips. (I, *1*, *15*)

Pandarus' language is equally nutritional when he tries to convince Cressida, whose appetite craves for satisfaction and who is no less "starved" than Troilus. This remarkable uncle describes Troilus' social status and handsome appearance as "the spice and salt that season a man." Cressida who responds to bawdy talk with amazing alacrity prefers her meat unseasoned. "Ay, a minced man. And then to be baked with no date in the pie, for then the man's date is out" (I, 2, 277). These equivocal references to the preparation of food, followed by the "tasting" of it, and finally leading to vomiting and nausea, surely do not reflect the personal interest that Shakespeare began to take in various processes of nutrition as has been suggested,[17] nor need we assume that Shakespeare wished by these images to "throw . . . light on [Troilus] character [and] . . . make his thoughts more clear." [18]

Never minimizing the effect of powerful unconscious urges originating in undirected psychic energy, yet always aware of the comic implications of such repressed desires—especially as they cannot come to fruition except with the help of a third party, Pandarus, Shakespeare conveys the regression of their libido in the language of nutrition and digestion rather than of sex. Troilus' "hunger," however, can only be satisfied in a sexual encounter with Cressida. And just as Paris took the foreign-born Helena home to his "mother," so Troilus now yearns after Cressida, whose father, incidentally, had gone over to the Greeks and left her an orphan, committed to the questionable care of an uncle (maternal, in all likelihood) who "feeds" both her and Troilus' imagination with descriptions of "tasty" dishes out of a "mother's" kitchen. The "cake" and the "meat" are indeed nutritional, not intended for a love-feast, rather "devoured /

As fast as they are made, forgot as soon / As done" (III, 3, 148).

Is Pandarus aware of the possible consequence of what he is doing when he "panders" to their appetite? Can he at all realize the extent of suffering that Troilus has to undergo after Cressida's enforced departure to the exceedingly "masculine" Greek camp? Surely, whatever one may think of this maternal uncle, Troilus' genuine, though adolescent, search for fulfillment and self-knowledge in a society ruled over by chaos that "follows the choking," must have been quite beyond the range of Pandarus' cynical assessment of life. This encounter between the two lovers, Pandarus might have thought, could never have led to a marriage of true minds. Yet when Troilus asks his beloved to look into the "fountain" of the unconscious where both their appetites lie slumbering, she sees "more dregs than water," an ominous prediction of the "orts, fragments, and scraps" that will remain of this love a few hours later. It is at this moment that Troilus, identifying himself with his anima and losing "the immortal part" in him, suffers a division of his personality. Paralysed in both "will and power," he blindly follows his "raging appetite" until the "universal wolf," regardless of any obstacle that judgment may put in its way, "eats up itself."

[II]

TROILUS'S DIVIDED EGO deserves closer scrutiny than has generally been bestowed on it. He has little in common with Shakespeare's earlier lovers who had been placed in fairly homogeneous societies and could overcome whatever difficulties there were, guided either by the wisdom of a saintly old man (such as Friar Francis in *Much Ado*) or by the unswerving dedication of a girl (such as Helena in *All's Well*). The conflict situation, whether arising from within or from without, could be solved by the willingness of the girl to undergo a love-test and even to bear undeserved suffering in order to prove herself worthy of the love of one who was in constant need of emotional guidance and instruction. To win him over to her love she had to appeal to that core of integrity within him that was able to respond to the depth of her emotion. In all these earlier plays individual fulfillment achieved through marriage involved a return to a society that, at last, had rediscovered the benefits bestowed upon it by "order" and "degree."

Marriage between the two lovers meant integration on an individual level. Yet it could take place only against the background of an integrated society where, as in *As You Like It, All's Well,* or *Measure for Measure,* self-realization was rendered possible after a period of trial and error, of regression and exile. Marriage, then, stands for the return of the individual to the larger society of adult men and women. The perils of alienation—one of Shakespeare's main concerns at the time of his greatest maturity—have been successfully disposed of.

To measure the effect of *Troilus and Cressida* on us, we may have to discard most of the emotional criteria that former plays have so firmly established. Shakespeare, in this play, compels us to apply subtler standards of evaluation than those sanctioned by literary criticism. Even *Romeo and Juliet,* for all its superficial similarities to this play, scarcely provides us with valid criteria for comparison. For if in the earlier play the discord between the two families is an external impediment to happiness, in the later play the division involves a split between ego and self, leading to an increasing domination of the unconscious to which the two protagonists are exposed in the course of the play. Their divided personalities thus reflect a far more threatening psychic disunion between reason and unreason, conscious "judgment" and unconscious "blood." Their failure in love is, then, part of an inherent inability to "canalize" their psychic energy. Neither do they realize, being slaves of their appetite, to what extent the dictates of their blood are subject to social approval. As they are victims of an emotionally charged situation which not they but others control, theirs will be an unfulfilled love from the very outset, unsure of its own validity and strength and, therefore, lacking in artlessness and candor.

Neither the Greeks nor the Trojans, as Shakespeare portrays them, constitute homógeneous societies. Integrity having been "swallowed" by appetite and pride, the two lovers are indeed placed in a divided context within which the testimony of their love, and their sense of belonging to a given social community are being subjected to severe doubts and questioning. Yet they are not—like Romeo and Juliet—"star-crossed," for their fate lies within themselves, and Troilus' apologetic remark "But still sweet love is food for Fortune's teeth" (IV, 5, 293), is merely an excuse for his inability to keep Cressida, in the teeth of both Trojans and Greeks.

Troilus' repeated admissions of defeat, as well as his constant readiness to surrender to self-pity and self-blame, when all that is required is the controlling discipline of his consciousness, distinguish him from earlier lovers in Shakespeare. This peculiar form of self-abasement reveals symptoms of inner disunity that characterize the neurotic's frantic search for values in societies such as those portrayed in this play. He possesses a more finely organized sensibility, and a greater responsiveness to the conflict between what natural instincts, on the one hand, and culture, on the other, impose upon man. He therefore is at a permanent disadvantage when it comes to making moral decisions. Thus his split personality is revealed in terms of progressive psychic deterioration and a disastrous involvement in morally ambiguous situations, which he tries to solve without having the support of an integrated personality to guide him. When he is compelled to take sides, he consistently follows the dictates of his uncorrupted judgment and his candid belief in the integrity of others. At the same time, he is only partially, if at all, conscious of the disrupting effect of Cressida's powerful attraction upon him. His singular defense of "honor" (though he must know as well as his brother Hector that Helena is not worth the keeping) and his own surrender to appetite (though Cressida's moral standing must be no less questionable than Helena's), are both Eros-dominated, that is, guided by ingredients of his unconscious that symbolize an underlying anima-oriented disposition in his own psyche. This acceptance of Eros rather than of Logos leads to conflict-situations over which Troilus does not, and indeed cannot, have any control. Appetite and judgment are more than ever irreconcilables since there are no valid criteria to provide a bridge between the two.

According to the evidence supplied by analytical psychology, Troilus' emotional dilemma, beginning with the very first scene of the play, is due to neurosis, the origin of which Shakespeare leaves unexplained. Yet already in this scene he blames himself for not being "master of his heart." The dichotomy he hints at is the result of an imbalance of psychic forces, for "too much of the animal distorts the civilized man, [while] too much civilization makes sick animals. . . ." [19] If, as Troilus' case exemplifies, we identify the "animal in man" with the nonego, that is, the archetype, and "civilization" with the ego, that is the conscious individual, then the type that Troilus represents must inevitably suffer from dissociation, the more so as his mind (which is far superior to that of any other young lover we have met before in Shakespeare) will be constantly engaged in unprofitable self-analysis—itself a possible symptom of neurosis. In extreme cases we should have "on the outside . . . the differentiated ego, and on the other a sort of negroid culture, a very primitive state of affairs. We should have, in fact, what actually exists—namely, a veneer of civilization over a dark-skinned brute; and the cleavage would be clearly demonstrated before our eyes. But such a dissociation requires immediate synthesis and the development of what has remained under-developed. There must be a union of the two parts. . . ." [20]

Such a union, may, in all likelihood, be established with the help of an integrating process provided by some form of therapy. A cure may indeed be effected through a love-relationship, through dedication to an ideal, indeed through any involvement in a trans-personal cause. For the synthesis of which Jung speaks will be found in a point of new equilibrium, "a new centering of the total personality, a virtual center which, on account of its focal position between conscious and unconscious, ensures for the personality a new and more solid foundation." [21] Neither his love for Cressida nor his somewhat preposterous defense of honor provide Troilus with such a central focus of integration. Instead he plunges deeper and deeper into the vortex of self-division, and though he alone among all the other young lovers in Shakespeare seems to have the making of a potentially integrated personality, it eludes him.

The text of the play bears out the growth of this neurosis. The civilization of which Troilus is a part is indeed a mere veneer: to the oversensitive and the emotionally immature it constitutes a very real obstacle to the attainment of self-knowledge. It is therefore quite in keeping with such a setting that Shakespeare should introduce Troilus at the beginning of the play, hopelessly in need of guidance or emotional support. Pandarus who is the least likely to provide either of the two, is the recipient of Troilus' confused confidences. Troilus tells him in so many words that he is no longer capable of mastering his impulses, and that compared to the Greeks whom he is supposed to be fighting he is

> weaker than a woman's tears,
> Tamer than sleep, fonder than ignorance,
> Less valiant than the virgin in the night,
> And skill-less as unpracticed infancy. (I, *1*, *9*)

Shortly afterwards he admits that he is "mad in Cressida's love" and blames the gods for "plaguing" him so much. This exhibition of self-pity, far from arousing tragic emotions, is almost embarrassing. Pandarus seems to think so too. For, after having praised Cressida's beauty, he now pretends to be indifferent to Troilus' plea, and blames himself for having meddled in a matter far beyond his own limited scope, which is clearly of a sexual nature and does not involve "love" at all.

Though Pandarus seems, at first, at a loss how to control Troilus' emotion, he regains his self-possession when he praises Troilus to Cressida. Compared to Troilus, he tells her, Paris is "dirt" and the common soldiers of the Trojan army are like "porridge after meat." He almost seems as much enraptured by Troilus' beauty as Troilus himself is by Cressida's: "I could live and die in the eyes of Troilus" (I, 2, 261). A pandar's profession undoubtedly requires such emotional acrobatics.[22] Nor is Cressida taken in by his equivocal commendations. The "glass of Pandar's praise" shows her what she has known all along.

In admitting his love for Cressida to Pandarus, Troilus reveals symptoms of inner conflict that will eventually destroy the precarious balance of his psychic being.

> I cannot fight upon this argument:
> It is too starved a subject for my sword, (I, *1*, *97*)

he tells Cressida's uncle. Such an admission may not amount to much more than the simple realization that to fight for someone else's adulterous love (even if some kind of national "honor" may be involved) is no "argument" worthy of a soldier's heroism. On the other hand, within the context of the first hundred lines of the play, this admission reflects Troilus' emotional instability at this crucial moment in his life. As it so frequently happens with neurotically afflicted personalities, a sexual analogy is hinted at: what then actually prevents him from fighting may be his own repressed sexuality which requires an outlet very different from fighting the exceedingly masculine Greeks who, in Troilus' own words, are "strong and skilful to their strength / Fierce to their skill and to their fierceness valiant" (I, 1, 7).

Troilus then finds himself, at the beginning of the play, in the position of one who, because of intense regression of his libido, realizes that all his troubles "were due to a sexual wish that is unjustly denied fulfilment." Jung adds that "this reasoning is typical of the neurotic," and, to drive his point home, he relates the treatment a certain tribe of American Indians used to mete out to those who exhibited such deviations from "heroic" conduct at a time of national emergency: "It was the custom for the warriors, before setting out on the warpath, to move in a circle round a beautiful young girl standing naked in the centre. Whoever got an erection was disqualified as unfit for military operations." [23] Troilus, as it were, disqualifies himself when he realizes that his repressed sexual appetite might constitute a serious drawback to his "honor" as a soldier. Neurosis among primitives exhibits the same symptoms and produces the same results as among the civilized: an unfulfilled appetite is likely to become the center of far vaster disturbances than are indicated by the regression of the sexual instinct alone.

This characteristic mixture of unfulfilled sensuality and compulsive heroism, neither of which is provided with an adequate outlet, proves to be Troilus' undoing. Those whom he fights possess those very qualities he lacks. They are in control of the situation, be it erotic (as is shown in Diomedes' bantering love-talk with Cressida) or military (as is shown by Achilles' murder of Hector). Troilus reveals his own basic weakness when, before taking leave of Cressida, he compares himself to the Greeks once more:

> The Grecian youths are full of quality;
> They're loving, well composed with gifts of nature,
> And flowing o'er with arts and exercise . . .
>   I cannot sing,
> Nor heel the high lavolt, nor sweeten talk,
> Nor play at subtle games: fair virtues all,
> To which the Grecians are most prompt and pregnant. (IV, *4, 76*)

The possibility of defeat is constantly present in Troilus' tortured consciousness. Even the sex experience itself is related to a suppressed death wish. He visualizes his meeting with Cressida as a kind of

> Swooning destruction, or some joy too fine,
> Too subtle-potent, tuned too sharp in sweetness
> For the capacity of my ruder powers. (III, 2, 22)

He is afraid of this experience because it might deprive him of "distinction in my joys," and thus compares it to "a battle when they charge on heaps / The enemy flying" (III, 2, 27). A few lines later he is even more explicit in his description of his feverish anticipation of an experience that might, eventually, result in an increasing awareness of his own impotence:

> And all my powers do their bestowing lose,
> Like vassalage at unawares encount'ring
> The eye of majesty. (III, 2, 37)

Defeat, loss, and death, all of which are part of Troilus' love poetry, are given an added emphasis by his need of Pandarus to bring this so greatly desired and feared experience about. Not only does he depend on Pandarus' assistance (psychologically, a parody of the wise old man in earlier plays, such as Friar Lawrence, Friar Francis, Vincentio, the fathers of Portia and Helena, whose function it was to bring the two lovers together), but he also sees in him a figure symbolizing death, his "Charon" who will help him to cross "the Stygian banks,"

> And give me swift transportance to those fields
> Where I may wallow in the lily beds
> Proposed for the deservers. (III, 2, *11*)

In addition to all this, Troilus refers to his passion once more in terms of a nutritional image, the "tasting" of Cressida, and asks himself

> What will it be
> When that the wat'ry palate tastes indeed
> Love's thrice-repured nectar? (III, 2, *20*)

and himself supplies the answer, "Death, I fear me."

There is something abstract, intangible, unsubstantial in the love experience as anticipated by Troilus. To come to terms with his anima, the feminine archetype that is doomed to destroy or revitalize his psychic energy, requires a strength he does not possess. It alone would discipline his emotions, save them from the constant threat of morbid introspection, and finally enable him to absorb the archetype without ever completely identifying himself with it. In terms of character analysis, "the weakness of Troilus' passion . . . implies that it is patent of corruption; and that corruption . . . is the logical consequence of an effort to extract from the refinement of the sensual a substitute for spiritual experience." [24] The "corruption" of which Traversi speaks here is, of course, not due to Cressida's love for Troilus, nor is it an emanation of the breakdown in social values which the two lovers witness around them. The neurotic is, by definition, a bearer of "corruption": his intense, overwhelming desire to "wallow" and his own premonition of inadequacy in sexual matters or otherwise, inevitably lead to a division of the ego where what he himself calls the "monstrosity of love" becomes the focal point of all anticipation, "that the will is infinite and the execution confined; that the desire is boundless and the act a slave to limit" (III, 2, 87). This may be merely a reference to the transitory nature of all human love or, as seems more likely in the total context of the play, to the limitations imposed by a mind divided against itself upon all forms of psychic energy, possibly including the sexual act itself.

The very "purity" of Troilus' love, which, he says, is "simpler than the infancy of truth" strengthens the general impression of frailty and neurotic insecurity. It is, however, when Troilus is shown face to face with his real (as opposed to his imagined) defeat, in the person of Diomedes making love to Cressida, that one is made to realize the pathetic helplessness of his divided ego: for he now looks at Cressida through the distorted vision of two simultaneous perspectives, as if dream and reality, seeming and being, the eternal and the temporal, had become one.

[III]

IN THIS EXTRAORDINARY SCENE truth and untruth are indeed no longer distinguishable. The dividing line between what the eye sees and what the imagination remembers can no more separate judgment from appetite than man from beast. How many Cressidas does Troilus see? His sense of sight gives him the "ocular proof" that what he sees is "Diomed's Cressida" metamorphosed into "the devil Luxury" whom any man can have "if he can take her cliff." The purity of his own love for her, on the other hand, tells him that this cannot be, for "reason," Troilus still believes, cannot revolt against itself "without perdition." Which then is the "true" Cressida? How can there be "rule in unity itself" when the indivisible nature of his love suffers incomprehensible separation, while at the same time

> Within my soul there doth conduce a fight
> Of this strange nature, that a thing inseparate
> Divides more wider than the sky and earth;
> And yet the spacious breadth of this division
> Admits no orifex for a point as subtle
> As Ariachne's broken woof to enter. (v, 2, *144*)

Yet the germs of "perdition" were there, in their first meeting, under the watchful eye of Pandarus. Cressida never made any secret of her own divided self. Troilus had previously described her as "stubborn-chaste." Actually, her stubbornness is mere femininity, a kind of self-protective mask which she puts on to make herself the more desirable. There is little enough chastity in her reply to Pandarus' observation, "A man knows not at what ward you lie": "Upon my back, to defend my belly; upon my wit, to defend my wiles; upon my secrecy, to defend my honesty; my mask, to defend my beauty" (I, 2, 282). Cressida is, in effect, as "true" as Troilus in her love for him. She actually says so, and there is no reason to disbelieve her. As long as Troilus is around, she also behaves in a way that admits of no doubt. But she is not "simple," and she is no longer a child. Being guided by her feminine instinct she first misleads her eccentric uncle into believing in her innocence—as indeed she could not help doing considering her present orphaned condition, and exposed, as she must have been, to the amorous advances of more than one Trojan. Immediately afterward, having confessed her love to Troilus, she adds a piece of practical wisdom which shows her to be in complete control of this emotionally charged situation. Possibly, she hints,

> I show more craft than love
> And fell so roundly to a large confession
> To angle for your thought. (III, 2, *160*)

This evidently goes far beyond Troilus' "simplicity" and "truth." Equally incomprehensible—had Troilus known of it—would have been her reason for "holding off": it is due to neither stubbornness nor chastity. For she formulates her apparent timidity in psychological rather than sentimental terms: "Things won are done; joy's soul lies in the doing" (I, 2, 311).

Far from idealizing her love, she freely admits to a "divided" self, composed of both sincerity and insincerity, fidelity and infidelity, wisdom and folly:

> I have a kind of self resides with you,
> But an unkind self that itself will leave
> To be another's fool. (III, 2, *155*)

When, finally, Troilus receives the ocular proof of her "unkind" self and refuses to believe the "truth" of what he sees, Cressida, consistent to the last, expresses her inner division in terms, not of suffering, as might have been expected, but of a dichotomy that puts all the blame on the "eye" and hence seems to acknowledge her guilt as part of her feminine "heart":

> Troilus, farewell! one eye yet looks on thee,
> But with my heart the other eye doth see.
> Ah, poor our sex! this fault in us I find
> The error of our eye directs our mind. (V, 2, *104*)

That almost the very last words spoken by Cressida in the play should, once again, be a conscious formula, an attempt at rationalizing her weakness in terms of her "mind" is significant. For "mind makes up the 'soul,' or better, the 'animus' of women, and, just as the anima of the man consists of inferior relatedness, full of resentment, so the animus of woman consists of inferior judgment, or, better said, opinions." [25]

Most readers in the past, biased no doubt by the reputation that legend has woven around her, found Cressida repulsive, the archetype of feminine guile, temptation, and treachery.[26] They approved of Ulysses' "masculine" evaluation of her as a "daughter of the game," and, by escaping into moral judgment, they missed what is most striking in Shakespeare's treatment of the love theme in *Troilus and Cressida*. For Cressida as she appears on the stage combines elements of simplicity and complexity, of maturity and immaturity, that render any one-sided moral verdict a misrepresentation of Shakespeare's "divided" picture of her. For there is as much candor and nobility in her confession of love to Troilus as there is implied doubt as to the validity of this love. Her sincerity is never unmixed with baser matter. Contemporary critics have shown less prejudice. While one of them, with more than usual perceptiveness, speaks of "the humility of her opportunism," [27] another calls her "this young novice . . . an experimentalist in feelings, curious and sparing as a winetaster, though exuberant in expression." [28] A third, considering the human situation in which Cressida is placed, remarks that it is "impossible for her to be shown as really responsible for her actions, and without responsibility there can be no moral evaluation." [29]

No other figure among Shakespeare's young women has given rise to so much contradictory comment. It is only very recently that "a split of the higher personality from the lower" [30] is put forward in a serious attempt at interpreting Cressida's conduct. That Troilus should be—without his being aware of it—attracted to both these aspects of her psyche, her girlish artlessness and her cunning, and that the "sweetness" of her taste and the "choking" that followed the feasting were equally overwhelming, may explain the peculiarly self-destructive nature of Troilus' love for Cressida. Yet he must have felt, even though only indistinctly, and before he opened his tormented heart to Pandarus, that this "split" between higher and lower made her more desirable rather than less, that she indeed was the only woman that would complement his own divided self, because he mistakenly saw his own inner dualism reflected in her. That is why he, "in his love choice, is strongly tempted to win the woman who best corresponds to his own unconscious femininity—a woman, in short who can unhesitatingly receive the projection of his soul." And Jung—evidently not thinking of Shakespeare's play, but of the archetypal situation that may arise in the perilous encounter between anima and animus in general—adds: "Although such a choice is often regarded and felt as altogether ideal, it may turn out that the man has manifestly married his own worst weakness." [31]

It is Troilus' failure rather than Cressida's that Shakespeare portrays on the stage. For Cressida's two selves do not, in effect, contradict each other. When she finds that Troilus, in the "simplicity" and "truth" of his love, cannot hold her (and it matters little enough to her whether this is due to Trojan weakness or Greek strength) she, following her father, an unwilling yet passive victim of the incomprehensible exigencies of war, goes over to the enemy camp. That Diomedes proves to be Troilus' "shadow," refusing to idealize her and treating her as she had all along wanted to be treated, namely with the moral indifference of a soldier whose libido follows the dictates of momentary sexual arousal and is free from the perplexities of "winnowed purity in love," pleases her instinctual nature. Diomedes discovers her vulnerability by humiliating her. This is indeed what she has desired all along instead of "lily-beds proposed for the deserver." Troilus, then, fails when instead of subduing the threatening archetype, he projects his own anima on to her, and thereby gets entangled in a web of idealizations that can but falsify his love relationship and create an image of Cressida in his mind that in no way corresponds to the "real" Cressida. Yet neither her childlike naturalness nor her feminine wiles are beyond the range of psychological analysis: "There are certain types of women who seem to be made by nature to attract anima projections; indeed one could almost speak of a definite anima-type. The so-called sphinx-like character is an indispensable part of their equipment, also an equivocalness, an intriguing elusiveness—not an indefinite blur that offers nothing, but an indefiniteness that seems full of promises. . . . A woman of this kind is both old and young, mother and daughter, of more than doubtful chastity, childlike, and yet endowed with a naive cunning that is extremely disarming to men." [32]

And if, as has been said, the eye is the "organ" of consciousness, Troilus' blurred vision of Cressida in the arms of Diomedes is, in effect, symbolical of the final breakdown of his psyche. He never realizes that Cressida's "kind" and "unkind" selves constitute her psychic "unity" and that her behavior merely reflects his own divided self; she first "tastes" what he has to offer, "some joy too fine" and "tuned too sharp in sweetness," and then looks for less refined consummation with Diomedes whose "shadow" nature must have served as a kind of compensation for all that Troilus so evidently lacked. His inability to perceive all this illustrates a frailty which is, if anything, human. For the "defeat" at the hands of the goddess is a recurring theme in legends, in mythologies, and in dreams. What, ultimately, defeats Troilus is his own vision of woman. For, just as in a dream, this last encounter between anguished Troilus and lighthearted Cressida, reveals the hero looking at his beloved through the visual distortions of his own unconscious, while "behind" the mirror of Troilus' tortured dream, the nonhero Diomedes merely sees her as she is. Yet, what Troilus "dreams" (and he, not at all surprisingly, desires only to "swagger himself out on's own eyes") *is* reality, even though it has all the qualities of a nightmare. In the language of mythology, peculiarly applicable to Troilus' situation, "the mystical marriage with the queen goddess of the world represents the hero's total mastery of life; for the woman is life, the hero its knower and master. And the testings of the hero, which were preliminary to his ultimate experience and deed, were symbolical of those crises of realization by means of which his consciousness came to be amplified. . . ." [33]

Troilus' field of consciousness, however, is considerably diminished by his emotional defeat at the hands of Diomedes. The amazing speed with which his love for Cressida turns into hate for Diomedes (V, 2, 202), the senseless cry for "vengeance" that now is constantly on his lips, even the praise that Ulysses bestows on him in the middle of the battle when he describes Troilus as one

> who hath done today
> Mad and fantastic execution,
> Engaging and redeeming of himself,
> With such careless force and forceless care
> As if that luck, in very spite of cunning,
> Bade him win all (v, 5, 37),

point at a deepening of his neurosis. This escape into heroism, apparently in order to redeem his honor, is still qualified by the divided mind of this unregenerated dreamer who, tumbling headlong from one extreme of wish fulfillment to another, now, more than ever, seems bereft of any conscious guidance. Even his compensatory death wish appears more like a pose, a substitute for something unattainable in his love experience, rather than—as in the case of Shakespeare's tragic heroes—a form of self-realization. To a sensitive intelligence responding to these last scenes, this heroic emphasis may appear somewhat overarticulate. For Troilus at the end of the play does not really as has been said, "champion . . . the fine values of humanity, fighting against the demon powers of cynicism," [34] nor does he begin now "to find his true self"; [35] least of all, does he now "become what Shakespeare predicts, the pattern of the true man." [36]

Shakespeare's invariably penetrating curiosity regarding the pathology of heroism, his sometimes ironical, sometimes deeply moving treatment of the hero who has nothing more to fight for, though there is always something left to fight against, his recurrent insistence on the dehumanizing spectacle of the hero as a "hollow man," achieve a painful though anticipated climax in these last scenes of *Troilus and Cressida*. For when Troilus dismisses love in order to hate and to kill more wholeheartedly, his surface heroism does nothing to disprove Thersites' ironic comment on the less salubrious aspects of love and hate: "Lechery, lechery! Still wars and lechery! Nothing else holds fashion" (V, 2, 232). Troilus' heroic desire to kill Diomedes—even if judged by the standards of mere commonsense and not necessarily by those that Thersites' cynical view of life has established —"is an infantile defiance of a fate greater than [ordinary human beings] or else a pomposity meant to cover up some touchy inferiority." [37] For, adds Jung, in the "humdrum existence" of nonheroic life—and Shakespeare's portrayal of the Trojan war, with its petty squabbles, its misplaced idealism, and its twofold emphasis on appetite in love and war, scarcely deserves a better name—there is "not much room for conspicuous heroism."

How little room there is for heroic exploits is symbolized by the stealing of Troilus' horse. Diomedes, who steals it, sends it as a present to Cressida. Troilus, infuriated by the loss of what might first appear to be merely a status symbol, challenges Diomedes, "And pay thy life thou owest me for my horse" (V, 6, 7). Whether Shakespeare meant this to be a slip of his tongue in the confusion of the battle or whether he was aware of the very nonheroic implications of this challenge, Troilus' fury seems at this moment directed not so much against Diomedes who stole Cressida from him, but against Diomedes the thief of his horse. That Shakespeare was not altogether unaware of the comically revealing significance of this confusion is seen in the repeated ambiguous references in this play to another horse, the one that belongs to Ajax and whose superiority over his master is stressed

by the remarkably clearheaded Greeks. Thus Thersites on a number of occasions rails at Ajax whose ownership of a horse seems
to be his only mark of distinction: "but I think thy horse will
sooner con an oration than thou learn a prayer without a
book . . ." (II, 1, 18). And again, "Let me bear another [letter]
to his horse, for that's the more capable creature (III, 3, 312).
Ulysses' reference to the somewhat surprising affinity between
Ajax and his horse is subtler though no less explicit. Praising
"the unknown Ajax" to Achilles in order to arouse the latter's
envy, he suddenly exclaims, "Heaven what a man is there! / A
very horse that has he knows not what" (III, 3, 126). Now Ajax
who, throughout the play, is described as "self-willed, blockish,
dull, and brainless," one "who sears his wit in his belly," but
whose limbs are "sinewy, valiant, dreadful and lusty," is thus
almost identified with his horse. As an embodiment of healthy
and vigorous appetite, he, together with his horse, stands for the
uncontrolled potency of instinctual urges, a very paragon of animals in whom the division into "higher" and "lower" is symbolized by his improbable brutishness, on the one hand, and by his
"horse," on the other. Evidently, the animal side of his personality, his horse-like vitality, is far superior to what may be described as his consciousness. That Troilus should be so eager to
take vengeance for the theft of his horse—and there is no reason
at all to assume that his steed is in any way superior to the one
with which Ajax himself is being compared—throws a somewhat
less than heroic light on the Trojan prince, whose longing for
vengeance is now freed of all the inhibiting influences of civilized conduct. For though the steed in mythology (though not
often in Shakespeare) is usually invested with heroic significance,
psychologically it represents "the non-human psyche, the subhuman, animal side, and therefore the unconscious. . . . As a
beast of burden it is closely related to the mother-archetype;
the Valkyries bear the dead hero to Valhalla and the Trojan
horse encloses the Greeks. As an animal lower than man it represents the lower part of the body and the animal drives that take

their rise from there. The horse . . . carries one away like a surge of instinct. . . . It is evident, then, that 'horse' is the equivalent of 'mother' with a slight shift in meaning. The mother stands for life at its origin, and the horse for the merely animal life of the body." [38]

What Troilus has "lost" and wishes to recapture is, in the language of heroism, his manhood, and in the language of psychology, his "worst weakness." Depriving him of his horse, Diomedes adds symbolic emasculation to intense emotional anguish: by sending it to Cressida he robs him of a maternal image and shows him the extent of his psychic disability at the very moment when both the higher and the lower contents of his psyche defeat the purity of his intentions.

There is little hope that Troilus will survive the loss of Cressida and of his horse. Nor is it likely that his hatred for Diomedes will redeem him from his twofold "dishonor." For the last word belongs, not to the true sons of Troy, but to the bastards: Thersites who is illegitimate in birth, in instruction, in mind, and in valor, will outlive them all. And when he meets another bastard, an illegitimate son of Troy, on the battlefield, he reminds him that the quarrel between Paris and Menelaus, and between Troilus and Diomedes, is "most ominous to us." For if the true children of Troy must be swallowed by the Terrible Mother "who leads the people into whoredom with her devilish temptation," [39] the bastards, at least, have no honor to lose and no redemption to fight for. Thersites' last words, then, dismiss the claims of honor in the name of commonsense: "If the son of a whore fights for a whore, he tempts judgment" (V, 7, 21).

Inexorably placed between his anima and his shadow, Troilus, in his last heroic attempt at strengthening his disintegrating ego, experiences a final division when he chooses a senseless death in the defense of a nonexistent honor.

3

The Shadow

JUNG'S REPEATED ATTEMPTS at defining the "shadow," be it as the dark side of the personal unconscious or as collective archetype, invariably make use of metaphorical language. Thus he frequently speaks in images when he wishes to describe the conflict between the "visible" ego, a man's persona, and that "invisible" portion of the human personality which is denoted by the unconscious. To the student of literature who feels at home in the language of poetic imagery, Jung's exuberantly metaphorical terminology with its multiple layers of meaning holds few secrets. For though the shadow, as a psychic phenomenon, is described as a projection of the personal unconscious on suitable persons or as an apparition to such persons in dreams, it is through metaphor alone that Jung can indicate the beneficial or harmful effect that the encounter with the shadow may have on the functioning of a man's psychic equilibrium.

Thus the shadow is first described as a mere "deprivation of light," implying a darkening of consciousness as the result of the invasion of unconscious contents. Later on, in a paper entitled "The Personification of Opposites," Jung completes the metaphor with the help of a quotation from the alchemist Michael Maier: "The sun and its shadow bring the work to perfection. . . . For what, in the end, is the sun without a shadow? The same as a bell without a clapper." [1]

When Jung wishes to portray the passionate involvement and anguish resulting from an encounter with the shadow, his metaphors become increasingly mixed. For this meeting with the darkest recesses of one's unconscious calls for the participation of the *whole* man. No image is too farfetched or too alien to represent the dehumanizing process of becoming one with the invisible: "The shadow is a tight passage, a narrow door, whose painful construction no one is spared who goes down to the deep well. . . . For what comes after the door is, surprisingly enough, a boundless expanse full of unprecedented uncertainty, with apparently no inside and no outside, no above and no below, no here and no there, no mine and no thine, no good and no bad. It is the world of water, where all life floats in suspension." [2]

Jung finds it equally difficult to convey in the ordinary language of everyday life the beneficial effect of such an encounter with one's shadow. For though it is always possible to speak of the shadow in abstract terms as "a moral problem that challenges the whole ego personality," it is in the living experience as communicated to the reader that the shadow acquires a "personality," almost a "character," of its own. Thus during one of his travels in Africa, Jung, musing on "the Arab's dusky complexion," transforms him into an "ethnic" shadow associated and contrasted not merely with the European's persona, but with the totality of the Western personality. Jung thinks of himself, at this moment, as a characteristically self-assured white man who prides himself on his rationalistic outlook, "without realizing that his rationality is won at the expense of his vitality, and that the primitive part of his personality is consequently condemned to a more or less underground existence." [3]

Jung finds his metaphors in literature no less than in life. While his encounter with the dark-skinned Oriental reminded him of what is still lacking to achieve completeness as a European, his reading of Goethe's *Faust* supplied an even stronger impetus toward individuation. Repeatedly Faust's need of Mephisto is described in terms of his meeting with "the dark side of his being, his sinister shadow." Yet Mephisto represents "the true spirit of life as against the arid scholar who hovers on the brink of suicide." [4]

To sum up, Jung's definitions of the personal unconscious stress those "psychic contents that are incompatible with the conscious attitude. This comprises a whole group of contents, chiefly those which appear morally, aesthetically, or intellectually inadmissible and are repressed on account of their incompatibility." [5] This is the dark side of the soul without which, however, psychic reality would remain incomplete. Though the shadow is a living concomitant of the personality, it leads an autonomous existence and as such has to be acknowledged. As the shadow side of the psyche it frequently is identical with "that hidden, repressed, for the most part inferior and guilt-laden personality whose ultimate ramifications reach back into the realms of our animal ancestors." [6] On the other hand, this same shadow may display, when properly disciplined, qualities of creative insight and visionary impulse. Though symbolizing "inferior" instinct-driven carnality, civilized man's as yet untamed violent urges toward chaos, it may be subjected to conscious guidance and control. This, in effect is an essential component in the psychotherapist's attempt at curing the patient.

[I]

THE SHADOW, then, has first to be known in order to be controlled. "The meeting with oneself," says Jung, "is at first the meeting with one's own shadow." [7] Such an encounter between the ego and the shadow it throws, on the one hand, and the self, on the other, is the most significant point in Shakespeare's portrayal of the process of individuation. In his history plays and tragedies, it is a confrontation fraught with fear and wonder. For once the hero has acknowledged the existence of the shadow as a dynamic part of his psyche, he has to come to terms with it. To "live with one's shadow" requires more than a looking glass wherein to discover one's face. For what King Richard really sees in the mirror lies behind his physical countenance. What he looks at is the shadow projected by his disintegrating persona. Having, for so long, denied the existence of the personal unconscious, embodied in the figure of Bolingbroke, who, significantly, is the one who provides him with the mirror, Richard now rejects his "usurping" shadow and looks for the "substance" of his grief in his "heart."

To argue one's shadow out of existence or to rationalize it into harmlessness is a form of self-deception practiced by the inwardly divided, the least conscious among Shakespeare's characters. Frequently their blindness is their only protection against their "hidden, repressed, guilt-laden" unconscious. Bolingbroke's mirror is a revealing instance. And when Hamlet holds up a mirror to his mother—"Where you may see the inmost part of you" (III, 4, 20)—he uncovers that part of the personal unconscious which she has repressed till then, her "compulsive ardour," the source of her unacknowledged sense of guilt and shame. What she sees now seems, indeed, incompatible with her persona as mother and queen:

> O Hamlet! speak no more;
> Thou turn'st mine eyes into my very soul;
> And then I see such black and grained spots
> As will not leave their tinct. (III, *4, 88*)

How morally ambivalent the effect of such a confrontation with one's "shadow" can be, is indicated by the friendship between Brutus and Cassius. Brutus at the beginning of the play appears to a very considerable extent to have repressed the contents of his personal unconscious. Alienated from the Roman people by personal temperament, superior intelligence, and a political insight that he finds hard to share with anyone, even his best friend, he does not admit to himself the element of guilt which characterizes the shadow side of his personality. To make it conscious and transform it into significant action, requires a "mirror." Thus the shadow that Cassius reveals to his friend consists of all the repressed elements of guilt, at not having lived up to his own expectations as a bringer of freedom, and at having cut himself off from the living tradition of the Roman people. Cassius whose own motives are morally questionable or, at least, of a politically doubtful nature, *is* Brutus' "shadow." Having been repressed for so long a time, it is now projected in the form of a temptation, the "inner voice" of the seducer who offers a "bait of falsehood" in order to catch a "carp of truth":

> And it is very much lamented, Brutus,
> That you have no such mirrors as will turn
> Your hidden worthiness into your eye,
> That you might see your shadow. . . . (I, 2, 54)

Brutus, at first, denies, the existence of any such shadow. He refuses to listen to the inner voice. At the moment of crisis when a decision has to be made and the choice is between his shadow or his conscious self, Brutus holds fast to his persona as a stranger to life and to politics. He even blames Cassius for trying to seek in him "for that which is not in me." His friend, knowing that none is "so firm that cannot be seduced" considers Brutus' denial merely an excuse for his blindness:

> I, your glass,
> Will modestly discover to yourself
> That of yourself which you yet know not of. (I, 2, 68)

What Cassius makes Brutus see is his "inmost part." To confront it, Cassius knows, requires the kind of moral courage that Brutus, alone among the Romans, possesses. Up to the end of the play Cassius remains his friend's shadow side. And the personal unconscious into which Brutus gazes, now that he has learnt to "see," is transformed into the "phantasma" and "hideous dream" that fill his solitary meditations. And as the "truth"

of Brutus' shadow is insurrection and the murder of Caesar, his
hands, the "mortal instruments," will now have to translate this
projection into action. It is Brutus' shadow made conscious and
integrated in Brutus' mind that kills Caesar. The light he gives
to the Romans returns to him in the questionable shape of his
"evil spirit," a "monstrous apparition," walking abroad "with
Ate by his side come hot from hell," the most hideous of all
his dreams—this time no longer his shadow, but transformed into
a primordial image of the collective unconscious.

Macbeth's shadow side, as he reveals it, resembles that of
Brutus. It originates in "thoughts whose murder yet is but
fantastical" and ends in "the affliction of these terrible dreams /
That shake us nightly." The mirrors in which he discovers his
shadow are, first, the prophetic projections of his own unconscious in the shape of the three witches and, later, of his wife,
who teaches him "to catch the nearest way," and to listen to the
inner voice of the serpent hidden under the innocent flower.
The knowledge and the power he dreams of are contained in
his "ignorant present." To achieve "sovereign sway and master-
dom" requires the projection of his shadow into a future where
knowledge will be identical with his unconscious, and power, no
longer dependent on time, will be absolute. All this can be
accomplished with the instruments of his shadow, the witches
and his wife. Having satisfied his appetite for power, they substitute their own shadow existence for Macbeth's brief candle of
self-awareness. After the murder has been committed, Macbeth,
finally, resembles that man "who is possessed by his shadow"
and therefore "is always standing in his own light and falling
into his own traps . . . because he is living below his own
level." [8]

Macbeth's true level is indicated in Shakespeare's play. He
is "valour's minion," "Bellona's bridegroom," he is brave and
noble; the language the king uses to express his thanks is
symbolical of fruitfulness and natural growth—"I have begun
to plant thee, and will labour / To make thee full of growing"

(I, 4, 28). Ambition, if properly regulated and directed toward a creative end, may assist man in the acquisition of deeper political insight and individual self-knowledge. But instead of the fruitbearing tree that Duncan planted, it is a "horrible shadow," the "unreal mockery" that grows in Macbeth's psyche. The shadows expand and multiply as Macbeth's unconscious outgrows the limits of his individual psyche, until it covers the whole universe. Then all life turns into unreal mockery: floating daggers, marrowless bones, boiling cauldrons, apparitions of armed heads and bloody children, and more horrible still, a "glass" in which he sees more living Banquos than could ever be contained in his consciousness.

Macbeth never really doubts the existence of these shadow projections on either the psychological or the physical plane. And when he shakes with fear at what his shadow suggests, his "seated heart" knocking at his ribs "against the use of nature," it is less at the image of the murder than at the image of himself, cut off from common humanity and face to face with a form of the collective unconscious that can no longer be mastered, even if he had the power to do so with his mind and body. Macbeth's anguish, at this moment, resembles that of Brutus before the battle at Philippi: they both experience the ultimate solitude of those who find themselves contaminated by what is most nonhuman in the collective unconscious. The effect of such a trans-personal projection is "to isolate the subject from his environment, since instead of a real relation to it there is now only an illusory one. Projections change the world into the replica of one's own unknown face." [9]

What Brutus and Macbeth see when they confront their "ill spirits" can no longer be defined as phantasma or terrible dream. Nor has the mirror into which they look any of the attributes of what art or nature ever created. Caesar's spirit and Banquo's ghost are not determined by visual distortions due to faulty eyesight. Brutus and Macbeth see as far as their inner eye will carry them. Theirs is the "rare and shattering experience . . .

to gaze into the face of absolute evil." [10] This is what makes Macbeth implore the ghost to "take any shape but that," while Brutus realizes that it is Caesar's spirit, and not bad strategy, that "turns our swords / In our proper entrails." Their "state of man" is no longer theirs to control. It is given over to a primordial spirit of hell, an ultimate nonhuman form of destruction.

These are indeed "perturbed spirits," that come to visit mortals when their shadow sides claim integration within their consciousness. Brutus, Macbeth, and Hamlet confront the visiting spirit with their eyes open. They question not its existence but the purpose of its coming. The story of hell that the ghost of Hamlet's father cannot tell his son, is that of the other two spirits as well. For they dwell in a "prison-house" filled with shadows, a description of which

> Would harrow up thy soul, freeze thy young blood,
> Make thy two eyes, like stars, start from their spheres,
> Thy knotted and combined hair to stand on end
> Like quills upon the fretful porpentine. (I, 5, *15*)

What these spirits communicate is damnation for those that created them. None of these three protagonists ever integrates the shadow he projects. The spirits they see darken the day and make night hideous. They shake man's disposition "with thoughts beyond the reaches of our soul." They embody the perils of the psyche which, if it cannot become one with its shadow, will be swallowed by it. It is, perhaps, not altogether surprising that so primitive a fear of the shadow should find so powerful an echo in the soul of some of Shakespeare's most sophisticated characters. According to anthropological investigation, "often [the savage] regards his shadow or reflection as his soul, or at all events, as a vital part of himself, and as such it is necessarily a source of danger to him. For if it is trampled upon, struck, or stabbed, he will feel the injury as if it were done to his own person; and if it is detached from him entirely (as he believes that it might be) he will die." [11]

Frazer mentions this dependence on the spirit world as typical of the superstitious beliefs among savages. Jung's studies in the nature and structure of the psyche, without ever referring to Shakespeare's insistence on the supernatural as an essential component of the unconscious, reach conclusions which prove that "civilized" man might experience similar psychic phenomena without necessarily suffering from neurotic dissociation. While the primitive still takes ghosts and apparitions for granted, civilized man explains these visions as dreams, hallucinations or fantasies. While to the primitive mind the materialization of a departed soul may seem both natural and, in certain circumstances, even inevitable, the Western mind interprets the belief in it in terms of pathological and delusional ideas. By rationalizing such psychic phenomena (being quite unable to integrate them in any other way but through the intellect) modern man places, as it were, the spirit outside himself, and since to the normal eye such spirit-manifestations remain invisible, they are, to the apparently well-adjusted person, nonexistent. Yet what civilized man considers normal is an objective and scientific assessment of such phenomena. The shadow side of the psyche, however, is "visible" only to those who project it beyond the confines of their consciousness. Those who see the world through their ego only, therefore, remain "blind" to the exhortation of the spirit. Gertrude does not see her husband's ghost; Lady Macbeth is unaware of the presence of blood-boltered Banquo at the banquet; Cassius, throughout the play, is insensitive to the might of Caesar's spirit after his death. Jung's conclusion seems to agree with Frazer's when he says that "Spirits . . . viewed from the psychological angle, are unconscious autonomous complexes which appear as projections because they have no direct association with the ego." [12]

Being "autonomous" as indeed they are in Shakespeare's plays, they symbolize that part of the soul that has become detached and now threatens the personality with extinction. The spirit no longer relates to the one that created it. Experiencing its presence, apparently without the assistance of the "seeing" eye, is a harrowing, an annihilating event in the life of the soul. It is then, when one is least ready for it, that one meets the last shadow of all—before the decisive battle, at the moment of final usurpation, in the midst of a son's ecstatic admonition to his mother. It is always a moment of destiny, chosen by the shadow, to confront the soul with a truth it had previously denied. It is also at that moment that it becomes "detached" and invades the consciousness. Physical death causes the soul to split into the personal and the collective unconscious. And though Cassius tells his friend that Brutus "will start a spirit as soon as Caesar," it is Caesar's spirit, come hot from hell, that will do the killing. At the time of his death Brutus is fully aware of what it is that is killing him. He has seen his death with his own eyes. Cassius dies with his face covered. Even in his death, he remains Brutus' shadow.

[II]

"THE SHADOW," says Jung, "is a living part of the personality and therefore wants to live with it in some form." Its presence is a constant reminder of the duality threatening the soul with disintegration. Thus many of Shakespeare's heroes are accompanied by a shadow, their "offending Adam" who, unknown to them, undermines their conscious hold on life. Symbolically, this shadow is always their own creation, a faithful image of the wilderness inhabited by their "wolfish" desires. "Consideration" and "policy" may, and sometimes do, subdue the extravagant and erring riot of the unconscious. When Prince Hal exiles Falstaff, the "new" Adam defeats the "old." Other less self-controlled princes fail to vanquish the personal unconscious. The tragic polarity which Shakespeare reveals in the Brutus-Cassius relationship remains unsolved to the very end of the play. The same may be said about Macbeth's defeat by his unconscious. That in one case the shadow should appear in masculine shape, whereas in the other it is feminine, indicates its psychic ambivalence. Yet Cassius, as he himself says, possesses specific feminine characteristics (inherited from his mother, he suggests), while Lady Macbeth indulges in strongly masculine daydreams. A man's persona may indeed throw its shadow on whomever and in whatever way it pleases, regardless of biological differences or emotional allegiances. Thus one's shadow may be one's friend or one's enemy. And Jung's reference to "old Adam" as the shadow of modern man does not exclude Eve, without whom Adam could not have become what he, in civilized imagination, has always been: "The 'old Adam' corresponds to the primitive man, the 'shadow' of our present-day consciousness, and the primitive man has his roots in the animal man (the 'tailed Adam') who has long since vanished from our consciousness. Even the primitive man has become a stranger to us, so that we have to rediscover his psychology." [13]

This is what Troilus, very much against his will, discovers when he projects his shadow into "the sinister darkness of the animal world of instinct" embodied in the figure of Diomedes, the "tailed Adam" tempting his Eve. Yet Cressida stands as much for the contents of Troilus's unconscious as does Diomedes. Troilus finds himself placed between two kinds of projections both originating in his own unconscious. And when his anima and his shadow embrace before his disbelieving eyes, his civilized consciousness rejects this sight as a sliding back into animality which he has tried so hard to avoid. It is not "the penalty of Adam" that worries Troilus, but rather the one that the over-civilized ego has to pay when, instead of mastering his shadow, he becomes its victim.

The psychic conflict revealed in the relationship between the persona and its shadow, as symbolized in the case of Hal and Falstaff, Brutus and Cassius, Troilus and Diomedes, is even more fully developed in the friendship between Bertram and Parolles in *All's Well*. Here the association between the two young men is woven into the total texture of the play far beyond anything Shakespeare had previously attempted. Falstaff, Cassius, and Diomedes, whether as "tutor," friend, or enemy, fulfill their dramatic function as "characters" in their own right. They are endowed with natural gifts of speech and action, consciously cultivated and exhibited before others. To look upon them only as shadows of those with whom they so closely associate would be to misconstrue their significance as active participants in the story as Shakespeare told it.

Their existence as part of the hero's personal unconscious is revealed only when Hal, Brutus, and Troilus are subjected to analysis in depth. Then their stage presence, including even Falstaff's, acquires a psychological dimension that transcends the mask they wear, the robes they borrow, and the intonation of the voice they have learned so well to imitate. Though they *are* themselves on the stage, they also *represent* the unacknowledged portion of the hero's personality, what Jung calls "the repressed tendencies," the shadow which, though not necessarily evil and not even always morally questionable, is still "somewhat inferior, primitive, unadapted, and awkward." This same shadow, continues Jung, may contain qualities "which would in a way vitalize and embellish human existence," [14] if they were given a chance to do so.

What has troubled so many readers of *All's Well*, is that Bertram, from the very beginning of the play, is assumed to be torn between two conflicting and apparently irreconcilable tendencies. While repudiating Helena's selfless love, he encourages Parolles' prosaic opportunism which regards both love and war as "commodities" to be enjoyed without having to pay a price. Bertram and Parolles seem, in effect, made of the same common stuff. Never before or after did Shakespeare identify more completely the substance with the shadow.

The question whether there really was any need to introduce so undesirable a "character" as Parolles into a play in which Helena occupies so central a position, has never been adequately answered. Historically, Parolles seems to stand for what Shake-speare most abhorred, "the Renaissance gentleman on the French-Italian model, a spineless creature . . . a parrot, a parasite, a flatterer, an echo, a copy-cat, a so-say-I, a fool of time." [15] Placed within the context of dramatic tradition, he appears to symbolize the Evil Angel of medieval Morality Plays. According to this approach he would be one of the main keys to the meaning of the play. In the battle for Bertram's soul Parolles first wins an easy victory (by shipping him off to the war); later on, Helena, as Bertram's Good Angel, "saves" him by her self-sacrifice, from the degraded world of lust and lies into which he has fallen.[16] In this sense Parolles' temptation of Bertram may serve as a counter-point—indeed, a parody—of Helena's patience in her pursuit of love. Others again are of the opinion that Parolles is the real failure of the play,[17] a watered-down Falstaff whose "words" (as his name indicates) show only what he would like to be, rather than what he really is.[18] As a character he is less con-vincing than any other figure in the play. The editor of the Arden edition (1959) compares him to Lear's "superfluous man" whose clothes are worn merely to conceal the hollowness within, "a nut without a kernel, a word without meaning." Therefore, the editor reflects, "there is no psychological depth in his follies; the follies *are* the character." [19]

The very unpleasantness of Parolles' character lies at the root of the problem. If he can be analysed as psychologically independent of Bertram, then indeed one can attribute to him all those qualities that are associated with the type of the "seducer," the evil-intentioned friend. Then Bertram himself can be reduced to being "the simple dupe of Parolles' preten-sions." [20] If, however, we think of Bertram's singular story as an unwilling pilgrimage from ignorance to self-knowledge, then the part Parolles plays in it acquires a significance beyond that of a counter-hero, preventing the integration of society and, because of his libertine point of view, blocking the union of the

hero and the heroine. Involved as he is in Bertram's own individuation, he then fulfills the function of Bertram's shadow,
his inferior personality, in a more consistent way than any of
the previous figures discussed in this chapter.

For Parolles is clearly not a *character* in the conventional
naturalistic meaning of the term. He stands for Bertram's unconscious, his "old Adam" whose primitive tendencies deprive
him of the ability of either making a conscious and reasonable
choice or of relating himself to an anima figure the integration
of which is essential for the achievement of individual happiness.
Instead he joins Parolles on their way toward "the sinister
darkness of the animal world of instincts."

Bertram's return to consciousness can take place only after
the shadow itself has been overcome and integrated in society.
In psychotherapeutic treatment (and Bertram might have greatly
profited by it) "the individuation process is invariably started
off by the patient's becoming conscious of the shadow. . . ." In
Shakespeare's play no less, "this integration cannot take place
and be put to a useful purpose unless one can admit the tendencies bound up with the shadow and allow them a measure of
realization—tempered, of course, with the necessary criticism." [21]

What the text tells us about Parolles is explicit enough as far
as the criticism is concerned. No one in the play ever accepts
him at his face value, for he has no "face." Though they all seem
to refer to him as a "character," the Clown alone defines him
in terms of the "nothingness" that the unconscious symbolizes:
"To say nothing, to do nothing, to know nothing, and to have
nothing, is to be a great part of your title, which is within a
very little of nothing" (II, 4, 26). As Bertram's shadow he is essentially hollow and his hollowness is transparent—everyone can
see through him, especially Lafeu: "Yet the scarfs and bannerets
about thee did manifoldly dissuade me from believing thee a
vessel of too great a burthen. . . . So my window of lattice, fare
thee well; thy casement I need not open, for I look through thee"

(II, 3, 212). His relationship with Bertram is generally defined as the main cause of Bertram's degradation. The countess, Bertram's mother, calls him,

> A very tainted fellow, and full of wickedness;
> My son corrupts a well-derived nature
> With his inducement. (III, 2, 89)

When Bertram asks the First Lord whether he could be so greatly deceived in his friend, the Frenchman first calls Parolles "a bubble" and then "a most notable coward, an infinite and endless liar, an hourly promise-breaker, the owner of no one good quality worthy your lordship's entertainment" (III, 6, 9). Parolles describes himself as a go-between in assisting Bertram to seduce Diana at a time when "he was mad for her and talk'd of Satan and of Limbo and of furies and I know not what" (V, 3, 255). Parolles acted in this way without any scruple because he "knew the young count to be a dangerous and lascivious boy, who is a whale to virginity, and devours up all the fry he finds" (IV, 3, 211). Lafeu's description of Parolles as a devil's disciple and "a general offence" sums up Bertram's "shadow" as a demonic figure whose domination over his friend is as complete as it is pernicious.

When Helena speaks about Parolles she uses very different language. As she loves Bertram, she cannot deny his shadow. Knowing him for what he is, she calls him "a notorious liar . . . a fool . . . a coward. . . ." She also realizes that "these fix'd evils sit so fit in him" because, in her imagination, they are related to the man she loves. Therefore she can make fun of Parolles and his "superfluous folly" while at the same time admitting that she "loves" him for Bertram's sake. And yet it is he, Parolles, who writes a sonnet to Diana "in behalf of the count of Rousillon."

His blindfolding carries the analogy with the shadow to its logical conclusion. He now calls Bertram "a foolish idle boy, but for all that very ruttish," at last speaking the truth right into his face. Describing Bertram as he really is, without the mitigating circumstances of love or friendship, he in effect describes himself. When, at last, he is reduced to "a poor, decayed, ingenious, foolish, rascally knave," his nothingness begging for mercy, he is granted admission to society on condition that he ceases to be Bertram's shadow. He is, however, permitted to be "himself" which, considering his "nothingness," will be little enough: "Simply the thing I am / Shall make me live," he remarks. His conditional integration into the society of Rousillon, however, prepares the way for Bertram's own "reformation." The religious analogy which, in recent times, has so often provided a novel interpretation of this play, may supply a somewhat different emphasis in explaining the vanishing of Bertram's shadow: "The very aim of religious education," says Jung, "from the exhortation to put off the old Adam, right back to the rebirth rituals of primitive races, is to transform the human being into a new future man, and to allow the old to die away." [22]

[III]

SHAKESPEARE'S VILLAINS frequently are embodiments of the tragic hero's unconscious. As the shadow side of the psyche they justify their existence by constant rationalization. The strength of the shadow resides in its power of persuasion through reason. It initially seduces with arguments of practical proof. It supplies the scientific evidence whenever required. Its approach to evil is functional, opportunistic, and strictly impersonal. It is at home anywhere, in war, in politics, in love. It is the only mirror that shows the absolute truth about the one who looks within. It strips the hero of his clothes, and, having deprived him of his persona, leaves him exposed to ridicule or despair. Yet if there had been no Cassius, Brutus would have had to invent him; if Cressida had not been taken by Diomedes, Troilus would have had to dream this scene into existence; without Parolles Bertram might still have stumbled, but he needed the "blindness" of Parolles to show him the way into even greater indignity.

The shadow, then, is both tutor and devil. It instructs in order "to plague the inventor." The shadow has the power to release the hero from bondage; it may equally well enslave him. Its destructiveness does not reflect the hero's weak resistance to evil. On the contrary, the more than life-size hero will project a gigantic superhuman shadow, while a morally and intellectually frivolous figure will produce a correspondingly commonplace and indifferent shadow. Thus Parolles' "nothingness" is a true reflection of Bertram's moral and sexual nullity. The appalling strength of Iago's evil, on the other hand, is a faithful shadow thrown by Othello's over life-size integrity of soul.

Yet what Othello projects into his universe of love is more than a "personal" shadow: it is a primordial image of evil originating in the collective unconscious, a devil-figure whose existence is no longer definable in terms of this or that dramatic convention or of psychological analysis, however subtle. Iago as archetype derives his strength from Othello's own unconscious. Thus the irrationality of Othello's suspicions and jealousy renders Iago's evil incomprehensible to others. It is Othello's "inner voice" which, by definition, must remain inaudible to anyone else.[23] It acquires its potency from Othello's own predisposition to listen to it and be persuaded by it. Possibly it is the shadow of that portion of Othello's simple soul which had to remain hidden, a reflection of the repressed guilt of forbidden impulses, such as those of sexual jealousy.

This is what Iago stirs up when calumniating Desdemona. By bringing the forbidden impulses into the open, he reveals the true though unacknowledged nature of Othello's love for Desdemona. Iago's various rationalizations, all tending in the same direction, give the shadow an animal complexion. The supreme value of Othello's love for Desdemona acquires all the repulsive features of the sterile inferno of lust. What the shadow shows

Othello is the malevolence of the flesh, the ocular proof of the act of sport performed in public. Thus Iago will limit his shadow-image to the body and its sexual needs. His speech articulates this archetypal preoccupation:

"Your daughter and the Moor are now making the beast with two backs. . . ." (I, *1, 117*)
"It is merely a lust of the blood. . . ." (I, *3, 339*)
"When she is sated with his body. . . ." (I, *3, 356*)
"When the blood is made dull with the act of sport. . . ." (II, *1, 230*)
"That she repeals him for her body's lust. . . ." (II, *3, 366*)
"There's many a beast, then, in a populous city. . . ." (IV, *1, 64*)

As Iago reveals himself increasingly to be an autonomous content of Othello's personal unconscious, he eludes detection. There is nothing left to be detected since no one is aware of his manipulations. Othello himself, in the simplicity and nobility of his soul, never grasps Iago's real identity, though he alone could have comprehended the threat to his bliss which this projection of his unconscious symbolizes. It lies in the nature of such a projection that it can be grasped only through a fully mature and wide-awake consciousness. To "integrate" the evil once more, involves an effort of awareness of which Othello is not only incapable but which he is even unwilling to make. For Iago *is* the truth in its most archetypal form, revealing what Othello has always known but could never admit to himself:

> O curse of marriage
> That we can call these delicate creatures ours,
> And not their appetites. . . . (III, *3, 268*)
> Even then this forked plague is fated us,
> When we do quicken. . . . (III, *3, 276*)

The archetype to which Othello succumbs need not "hunt" for motives. It is an end in itself. It does not commit itself to any personalized psychological system. None of the motives that Iago propounds when he is alone, holds good in public. The naturalistic approach discovers an Iago that never was in nature. Neither envy, nor hatred, nor sexual jealousy, the three motives most frequently mentioned by him, carry conviction. His manipulations of all the characters in the play do not depend on such emotional involvement. Iago remains throughout morally, psychologically, and emotionally, uninvolved. His "reasons" for hating do not fit the circumstances of the case, or are expressed in so casual a manner that there appears to be no incentive, no provocation, not even genuine enmity justifying his hatred. To call him "a showman who produces [the play] and the chorus that interprets it" and whose only "essential relationship is with the audience" [24] begs the question, and reduces him to the role of a practical joker whose jokes are "aimed at particular individuals with the reformatory intent of de-intoxicating them from their illusions." [25]

"I am not what I am," describes him truly as Othello's shadow. He is, as it were, driven to act the way he does by his realization of being "nobody." Iago then embodies the absolute nothingness of all shadows. His evil is a form of self-hatred directed most against the one of whose positive strength he can merely be the negative shadow. His evil is always perpetrated "in public"; for when he is alone and compelled to face his own nothingness, he frantically looks for motives. Even when he believes he has found them, they do not make sense: for the sole motive that a shadow requires is the strength of the unconscious that created it. To negate its own nothingness, it must first deny the soul out of which it grew. Negation of love and denial of purity are the natural forms of hatred that Othello's shadow takes.

Auden's definition of Iago as a "practical joker" is analogous to that given by Heilman to Iago as Othello's "tutor." [26] By teaching him to see what is invisible because nonexistent, Iago plays the practical joker of the ocular proof most effectively. That the joke is founded on the belief that all scientific enquiry is intrinsically beneficial because it encourages the disinterested acquisition of knowledge, turns the joker into a parody of the psychiatrist who, by studying the various layers of the psyche wishes to find out what the patient—in this case Othello—is really like. When the joke has been played to its tragic conclusion, and Othello asks Iago "Why he hath thus ensnared my soul and body?" Iago's reply is unequivocal: "What you know, you know."

By whatever name one wishes to call this negative "knowledge" that Othello acquired from his "tutor," it is of a primordial and nonhuman nature, and therefore can no longer be subject to psychological investigation. Whether as an artist of evil or a joker, a student of human nature or a calumniator, Iago first darkens and then annihilates the universe of love that Othello built when he married Desdemona. He is the ultimate embodiment of Shakespeare's tragic vision of a singularly repulsive form of trans-personal evil. Though unfamiliar to the eyes and the minds of the civilized spectator who no longer believes in the shadow as an archetype of the unconscious, this "monstrous apparition" is no unsubstantial ghost, "come hot from hell," but "derives its existence from the hinterland of man's mind." Othello's encounter with Iago, then, "is a primordial experience which surpasses man's understanding, and to which he is therefore in danger of succumbing. The value and the force of the experience are given by its enormity. It arises from timeless depths; it is foreign and cold, many-sided, demonic and grotesque." [27]

It is to this archetype of the collective unconscious that Othello, the noblest of all the souls that Shakespeare created, surrenders.

[IV]

THE MOST LEGENDARY FORM that the shadow archetype assumes in myth and dream is that of the "hostile brother."

What was originally the cosmic opposition of light and darkness became, first, the conflict between the divine twin brothers and, later on, was reflected in countless folk-tales describing in story form the personalized conflict between the "good" and the "evil" brothers, exemplified best of all in the biblical story of Cain and Abel. But as mythical thinking ignores the conventional division into empirical and transcendental and between the temporary and eternal, the myth retells the same story in different settings an infinite number of times, only vaguely responsive to the historical changes brought about by the gradual awakening of human consciousness. In the course of time the myth of the hostile brother loses its religious connotation. From being an archetype of evil rooted in the imagination of archaic man, he is personalized into the various figures that, in ancient legends, symbolize the destroyer of whatever is kind, generous, and beautiful, the insidious bearer of violence lurking in darkness for his unsuspecting victim. He is the barbarous warrior whose physical courage allied to cunning easily vanquishes the subtle grace of a gentler and more civilized mind.

Thus Set, according to an Egyptian myth, cut his "good" brother Osiris into fourteen pieces; he had the head of a donkey and was a warrior and a hunter. In the language of mythology he *is* Edom and Cain, Cham and Ismael and Esau: whenever the myth reconstructs the primordial setting of a divine being metamorphosed into a mortal, the shadow is incorporated into the myth as an indivisible part of the dual and antithetical nature of man. Abel, Jacob and Joseph, in the timeless revisions of myth, shared the same shadow because they shared the same dual nature. Their mythical identity is collective. Whatever individual differences are revealed they belong to the setting which is part of the human mind rather than of human history. For myth, like the dream and like the work of art, merely creates different symbols for the same psychic antagonism.

The "dark" brother is generally, though not always, the

older of the two. When the elder brother is a fighter, a hunter, and a rival for parental blessing, the younger brother is put on the defensive. The psychological analogy can easily be drawn. As so often before, the myth provides the primordial situation and the only possible escape from a polarity that of necessity must destroy both the good and the evil if the antagonism is not resolved in time. Thus the "hostile brother" has to be faced, overcome, incorporated into one's own psyche. Only in such a way can the ego evolve from partial self-knowledge to complete assimilation of the unconscious. The psychological truth that underlies this myth symbolizes the process of individuation more absolutely than does any other that has been outlined previously in this study. For what has been called the "shadow" before, fulfills a necessary function in the process of self-discovery. By showing the need of assimilating the "hostile brother" and thereby reconciling oneself to the demands made by one's unconscious as an indispensable part of the self, the archetypal motif of the Twin Brother is rendered psychologically intelligible. For, having issued from the same womb, "he is not just the 'hostile brother,' but the companion and friend, and it is sometimes difficult to tell whether this twin is the shadow or the self. . . . The way to the self lies through him; behind the dark aspect he represents there stands the aspect of wholeness, and only by making friends with the shadow do we gain the friendship of the self." [28]

The hero's dual nature must needs lead to conflict. The result of such a conflict may be the assimilation of the shadow into the self, which may mean the death of the shadow or the death of the self. Whenever the younger brother represents the victory of light over darkness, he symbolizes the archetype of the "hero" whose consciousness, defending itself against the aggressive instincts that are always centered in the shadow, finally succeeds in integrating them. The dualism out of which his consciousness grows is thereby not abolished; nor does the conflict ever terminate in complete victory of the conscious over the unconscious. For "the self lies hidden in the shadow, he is the 'keeper of the gate,' the guardian of the threshold." [29]

Thus the shadow never dies. Whether it is light that wins over darkness, or darkness defeating light, the presence of the "hostile brother" will ever be felt. In drama criticism, insofar as it refers to the distinction between comedy and tragedy, the hero's successful assimilation of darkness, or his defeat at the hands of his shadow, must needs determine the spectator's response in terms of self-criticism, compassionate identification, or revulsion. And as every spectator comes to the theatre accompanied by his own shadow, of whose existence he may, in all likelihood, be quite unaware, the spectacle on the stage may serve as a guide toward completeness—even in cases where darkness defeats light, and the "hostile brother" achieves his illusory victory. For only when the "good" brother "dies," does the spectator become fully aware of the peril that threatens his own soul. This shock of recognition is part of what Aristotle called *catharsis*. The spectator who has, quite literally, lost his identity in witnessing the spectacle of Othello's agony and defeat, will know that Iago *is* Othello's "hostile brother," and that the drama that is being enacted on Shakespeare's stage is as immemorial as the myth from which it originates.

The archetype of the shadow, it has been noted before, acts by persuasion, seduction, rationalization. The image of the serpent, as a symbol of the unconscious, represents cunning, the art of articulation, the attempt at providing a scientifically objective solution to the complexities of a human situation. If the "hostile brother" in myth is a fighter and a hunter, he is represented as fighting for survival in an essentially antagonistic environment. He hunts down those whose consciousness has been weakened by too much introspection and a recognizably "civilized" disposition toward self-analysis. Basically, the conflict between the "shadow" and the self is synonymous with the fight carried on in the mind of man between what the senses perceive and elaborate into a system of material survival and what the psyche intuitively recognizes as more important, though much less tangible: the need to acquire self-knowledge before material survival is either desirable or possible. The cosmic opposition of light and darkness has, in truth, a very modern equivalent. Jung provides an effective formula: "Rationalistic materialism, an attitude that does not seem at all suspect, is really a psychological countermove to mysticism—*that* is the secret antagonist who has to be combatted. Materialism and mysticism are a psychological pair of opposites, just like atheism and theism. They are hostile brothers, two different methods of grappling with these powerful influences of the unconscious, the one by denying, the other by recognizing them." [30]

Shakespeare's archetypal use of the hostile brother theme can be fitted into this definition with striking consistency. Every one of the evil brothers in comedy or in tragedy "rationalizes," as it were, his unconscious out of existence. His intelligence, his power of persuasion, his unscrupulous use of intellectual argument in the service of evil, are his most outstanding psychological characteristics. If ever he defeats his brother, it is by a consistent denial of his unconscious, of those psychic contents that cannot be "rationally" explained. Therefore he prides himself in being what he is, "a plain-dealing villain" who cannot flatter nor serve anyone's pleasure but his own. Don John, Don Pedro's brother in *Much Ado,* supplies the *leitmotif*: "I cannot hide what I am . . . I had rather be a canker in a hedge than a rose in his grace, and it better fits my blood to be disdained of all than to fashion a carriage to rob love from any. . . . If I had a mouth, I would bite. If I had my liberty, I would do my liking. In the meantime, let me be that I am, and seek not to alter me" (I, 3, 14).[31] Don John's "pleasure" is rooted in his capacity to do evil. He never fully succeeds in expressing in rational language the unconscious whence the evil he wishes to commit originates. For to rationalize the irrational should be the singular privilege of the shadow: "Only to despite them, I will endeavour any thing," is all he can say to justify himself. Though this seems a weak enough argument upon which to base criminal action, the evil that Don John actually commits almost succeeds in destroying the happiness of two innocent lovers. For it is Don John who supplies the false evidence of Hero's unchastity. He does so, like Iago after him, with the aid of an ocular proof. Don John is the first of Shakespeare's fake-scientists whose functional interpretation of the love-impulse constitutes the original source of the evil that is going to be done. To reduce Hero to the status of a whore (as Iago will do later on with Desdemona) is the purpose of his scheme. When it fails, he does not put up a fight but attempts to escape. All that Shakespeare tells us of him at the end of the play is that he "is ta'en in flight / And brought with armed men back to Messina" (V, 4, 129). Some kind of "punishment" is in store for him. Shakespeare must have known that to "tame" and integrate him into a new society requires a stronger and more comprehensive soul than his mild and benevolent brother possesses. Thus the shadow merely melts into the sunlight of Messina and is never heard of again.

Oliver, in *As You Like It,* is a much more carefully delineated "hostile brother" than Don John. His evil nature seems not merely inborn and altogether unmotivated, but, at least in part, the result of envy. By rationalizing his envy, he transforms his brother Orlando into an unnatural monster of iniquity. Thus he tells Charles the wrestler that Orlando is "a secret and villainous contriver against me his natural brother . . . should I anatomize him to thee, as he is, I must blush, and weep, and thou must look pale and wonder" (I, 1, 152). But when he meditates on his brother's true self, he finds him "gentle, never school'd, and yet learned, full of noble device, of all sorts enchantingly beloved, and indeed so much in the heart of the world, and especially of my own people, who best know him, that I am altogether misprised." These two descriptions of Orlando complement each other as the shadow corresponds to the source of light whence it comes. To reconcile the two, Orlando must learn to "love" his evil brother, to absorb his darkness, and make it his own. At the beginning of the play Oliver is all hatred, "for my soul, yet I know not why, hates nothing more than he" (I, 1, 174). Orlando is a true Abel-figure. His servant, significantly called Adam, describes him in truly archetypal terms:

> Why are you virtuous? Why do people love you?
> And wherefore are you gentle, strong and valiant? . . . .
> Your virtues, gentle master,
> Are sanctified and holy traitors to you;
> Oh what a world is this, when what is comely,
> Envenoms him that bears it? (II, 3, 5)

In the Forest of Arden the cosmic opposition of light and darkness is resolved in terms of Oliver's "conversion" and Orlando's "kindness, nobler than revenge." When Oliver decides to remain in the Forest and live the life of a shepherd, the antagonism between his former "materialism" (symbolized by his envy, greed, and hatred) and Orlando's "mysticism" (symbolized by the sanctity of his virtues) is resolved into the enlarged personality of Orlando: in his new self the unconscious finds a place side by side with his consciousness, while the proportion of rational and irrational impulses is expressed in the equal scope given to both in the process of individuation. Oliver and Orlando have become one through exile, suffering, conversion, and love. For they marry the daughters of the two other brothers whose "hostility" and reconciliation serve as a background to the action in the Forest. For though it is the younger Duke that exiles the older, the final encounter takes place on the same level of mystical union:

> And to the skirts of this wild wood he came,
> Where, meeting with an old religious man,
> After some question with him, was converted
> Both from his enterprise, and from the world. (v, 4, 166)

These two pairs of hostile brothers in *As You Like It* may serve as an example of twin shadows in Shakespeare's work. Whether the younger threatens the older with extinction, or *vice versa,* the survival of either is rendered possible only by the voluntary acceptance of the shadow roots of the personality. It may almost appear as if in Shakespeare's use of the archetype Abel is no less guilty of repression than Cain. Orlando's "holy" virtues are like torches that do not "go forth from [him]," and illumine nothing until he meets Cain in the forest and forgives him his evil. By dispensing forgiveness, he, for the first time, applies the light of his virtues to the darkness of his brother's evil nature. By blessing his "twin," he establishes communion between his self and his shadow, and opens the gate to self-knowledge.[32]

In Shakespeare's comedies the shadow as hostile brother is either "punished," as Don John's disappearance at the end of *Much Ado* indicates, or "converted" from his assumed intellectual superiority to a position of humility and grace. In Shakespeare's tragic universe, the archetypal situation is revealed in all its primordial horror. For there the shadow does not wish to be forgiven. It rather wants to be acknowledged as the sole master of the hero's fate. Claudius, Hamlet's uncle, kills his brother; Edmund, Gloucester's bastard son, plots Edgar's death; and, finally, Antonio, Prospero's brother, usurps his kingdom and sends Prospero and his infant daughter into exile and certain death. What these three have in common is a lack of any deeper personal idiosyncrasy. They are compulsively obsessed by their ambition for power. Having brought upon themselves "the primal eldest curse" they attempt to extricate themselves by a variety of rationalizations. Unlike Macbeth, they are daytime figures. They walk through life their eyes open, the mark of Cain on their foreheads.

As hostile brothers the destructive element they represent lies in their power to seduce. Eloquence is their most striking attribute. Their intellectual superiority may be employed for

political, but equally for erotic, purposes. Hamlet's father speaks
of his brother's "traitorous gifts," his "wicked wit," which helped
him to seduce the "will" of his wife. Hamlet himself is struck
by his uncle's "smile" which he, quite rightly, relates to his
cunning and his wit. Claudius himself grows wonderfully eloquent when he delivers his speech on the death of fathers, and
blames his nephew for showing "unmanly grief." It is a speech
full of arguments founded on logic and the ocular proof that
nature gives of the ever-repeated death of fathers. It is the
scientist's most convincing evidence of nature's inexorable domination over the shaky metaphysical foundations on which man
builds his spiritual convictions. Hamlet's excessive grief, then, is

> a fault to nature,
> To reason most absurd, whose common theme
> Is death of fathers, and who still hath cried,
> From the first corse till he that died to-day,
> 'This must be so.' (I, 2, *102*)

The implied division between the two kinds of reason—man's
intellectual attempts at judging natural phenomena by the aid
of scientific evidence and, on the other hand, his metaphysical
belief in the reason underlying all divine dispensation—symbolizes the archetypal polarity between the two "brothers." If,
as Claudius argues, the "common theme" of reason is the death
of fathers because nature ordained it so, there must be, on the
other side of the scale, another kind of reason, determined by
man's reliance on God's laws rather than on the laws of nature.
Then "the death of fathers," viewed as it were from above, is
seen for what it is, namely a brother's murder. It bears a different and very nonscientific complexion; for in heaven, Claudius
himself says so, "There is no shuffling, there the action lies / In
his true nature" (III, 3, 60).

Claudius, the most archetypal Cain-figure that Shakespeare
created, is increasingly troubled by his conscience. Yet it is his
eloquence rather than his repentance that carries the day. He
knows that his words are "painted," even at the very moment

that his conscience begins to stir. And when he tries to pray he
fails to convince heaven no less than himself,

> My words fly up, my thoughts remain below;
> Words without thoughts never to heaven go. (III, 3, 97)

Edmund's eloquence and power of persuasion are equally
remarkable. He "seduces" everyone he comes in contact with.
The first who believes him is his brother Edgar, followed by his
father. Both Goneril and Regan are taken in by his persuasive
charm. Once more it is Nature dressed as Reason that supplies
the criterion for action. As a pure materialist, Edmund sees in
nature the functional principle of a life-urge that dispenses with
any moral distinctions. And as nature is the tutor to all living
things, to draw artificial distinctions between bastards and legitimate children as well as between right and wrong, is "to reason
most absurd." The intellectually most attractive of all Shakespeare's hostile brothers, he pokes fun at the quasi-metaphysical
arguments that his father uses to arrive at an understanding of
what "nature" does to man. Thus, when Gloucester wonders
why if "the wisdom of nature can reason it thus and thus, yet
nature finds itself scourged by the sequent effects," Edmund
supplies the ironically scientific answer: for by blaming nature
for all the evil we are doing, we evade our personal responsibility
which, Edmund rightly assumes, lies within us and not in some
"spherical predominance" or "planetary influence."

Yet Edmund's concept of Nature is as "absurd" as the Reason
that Claudius holds up to Hamlet. Lacking in depth of moral
awareness, it is merely a convenient standard by which to distinguish the foolishly humble from the worldly-wise. Reason
which Edmund identifies with Nature, is a "commodity" which,
if properly used, may enable one to advance from "wisdom" to
power. Any other kind of reason will merely reveal the nature of
"unaccommodated man" in all his naked helplessness: "Is there
any cause in nature that makes these hard hearts?" asks Lear
when his wits are already half gone. Yet this is the least absurd

of questions. It relates not merely to the "hard hearts" of Goneril and Regan, but to Edmund's identification of nature and reason, which alone justifies the evil he is committing. After all, Lear's loss of reason is his first step toward redemption. The killing of Edmund by his brother is not an act of revenge, but of survival. Only by completely destroying the shadow into which Edgar had fallen when it forced him to deny his own self, could he translate "the art of known and feeling sorrows" into that "ripeness" which is the essential meaning of individuation.

Antonio is the most consistent in the three sets of hostile brothers. Claudius, at one time at least, wrestles with his conscience. Edmund, at the point of dying, appears to repent—"some good I mean to do / Despite mine own nature." Prospero's brother is not only untroubled by any pangs of conscience, but rationalizes this lack of moral scruples "scientifically": there is no more conscience in "nature" than there is in "reason." Therefore, would it not be "to reason most absurd" to look for conscience where there can be none? Sebastian's bewildered question, "But for your conscience?" is deflated of all possible moral implications by Antonio's,

> Ay, Sir; where lies that? if 'twere a kibe,
> 'Twould put me to my slipper: but I feel not
> The deity in my bosom: twenty consciences
> That stand 'twixt me and Milan, candied be they
> And melt, ere they molest. (II, *1, 284*)

The Antonio that is revealed in this conversation corresponds to the picture painted of him by his brother Prospero in the story he tells Miranda at the beginning of the play. Twelve years have passed since his enforced exile; yet Antonio's firm belief in "reason" as sole criterion for action is as strong as it was then. And just as in the case of Claudius and Edmund, it is "nature" that supplies him with those principles of conduct that led to treachery, usurpation, and absolute power. Prospero, like Hamlet's father, Lear, and Gloucester before him, still sees in nature a divine and metaphysical principle at work. According to the antithetical spirit of light and darkness, the artificial identity of reason and nature, created by man for his own convenience, stands for the shadow, the unconscious gaining predominance over man's mind, the loss of the gift of moral discrimination. By casting the government of the country upon Antonio, "in my false brother / Awak'd an evil nature" (I, 2, 92). In almost the same terms Prospero accuses his brother at the end of the play of having "entertain'd ambition / Expell'd remorse and nature" (V, 1, 75).

Antonio's belief in Reason as synonymous with unscrupulous political commonsense relates him to the other two brothers, Claudius and Edmund, in a more significant way still. For their "reason" is directed against those very Abel-figures whose life is illumined by an irrational belief in the virtue of self-knowledge and personal maturity. Thus Hamlet's father is described as Hyperion, his countenance that "of Jove himself," "an eye like Mars," "a station like the herald Mercury / New lighted on a heaven-kissing hill." Edgar, in Edmund's own words is

> a brother noble
> Whose nature is so far from doing harms
> That he suspects none; on whose foolish honesty
> My practices rise easy. . . . (I, 2, *201*)

Lastly, Prospero, "rapt in his secret studies," grows a stranger to the people he is supposed to govern, neglects "worldly ends" and "all dedicated / To closeness and the bettering of [his] mind" substitutes the art of his magic for "reason." After mastering nature, he can also control human consciousness. When he finds Antonio's mind at his mercy, he "forgives" him—very much as Orlando forgave his evil brother Oliver in the Forest of Arden. Antonio, however, does not become converted to his brother's compassionate insight; nor does he ever show repentance. All that Prospero's controlling mind can do is to re-integrate his brother into a new society of which he is the creator.

Though Prospero's widened consciousness can forgive Antonio, it is incapable of compelling him to repent. This describes the limits of the process of individuation as envisaged by Jung. The first step is the recognition of the shadow as an integral part of one's total personality. What follows, however, can best be expressed in metaphorical language; for only after the conflict between opposites has strained the psyche to the breaking point, can the solution which is a joining together of persona and shadow be felt as a kind of grace, "an unfathomable mixture of conscious and unconscious factors, and therefore a symbol, a coin split into two halves which fit together precisely." [33]

The ego and the shadow do not become one except as an image in a dream. In life they remain divided, though complementing each other and supplying vital energy to all parts of the personality. The self remains an ideal still to be pursued. For the ultimate union of mutually destructive aspects in the psyche pertains to the alchemy of the soul. However precisely the two halves of the coin may fit, the "new" Prospero need not be imagined as Antonio's equal. Yet he is no longer the magician whose consciousness ruled the world, but a humbler and wiser man than he used to be before his hostile brother landed on his island to challenge him into forgiveness.

4

The Inner Voice

AMONG ALL THE PROFESSIONS, only in that of acting is the performer deprived of his shadow. Shakespeare's preoccupation with various forms of acting, whether on the stage or in life, indicates his concern with the man who has lost his shadow through complete identification with the ego. Angelo, in *Measure for Measure,* is such a performer in the full ambiguity of his function as a public figure. Though Shakespeare portrays him as a private individual when the play opens, his persona is already well established. The dilemma of having to choose between private and public consciousness is thrust upon Angelo by the Duke. As his Deputy he will have to speak and act "through his mask" on a variety of contradictory levels of reality. Thereby he will inevitably evoke conflicting responses from his various audiences. He must first convince the Duke, Isabella, Claudio, Lucio, and even Pompey of the "reality" of his persona which he himself believes to be identical with his true psychic nature. At the same time he will have to "act" for the benefit of the audience in the theatre, convincing them that the stage-illusion of the "angel with horns" is equally true to life. The public significance of his acting then is twofold: first, he plays on the stage before an audience who are mostly unsympathetic and always ready to pounce upon the outsider who claims moral superiority over them, and second, he confronts the audience in the theatre, hypothetically divided into two groups—the Elizabethan playgoers for whom Shakespeare wrote, and who must have found Angelo much less of a moral riddle than he may appear to us today—and the twentieth-century spectator whose motive for going to see the play might have something to do with the specifically contemporary difficulty of adjusting one's individual sensibility to the demands made upon it by one's public persona.

Angelo exhibits a split personality, represented by the incompatible claims made by his ego upon his unconscious. The former, symbolized by his persona, his public disguise, observes, calculates, passes judgment, whereas the latter reveals itself as a whirlpool of intense and overmastering emotions, only half understood, though therefore no less subject to scrutiny, analysis and introspection. When the two meet in a head-on clash, Angelo is like an actor who has forgotten his part in a sudden fit of amnesia, and is compelled, on the spur of the moment and never quite oblivious of the two audiences, the one on the stage and the other in the theatre, to improvise a new role for himself. From being a "public" figure endowed with the persona of the Duke's Deputy, he all of a sudden, exhibits all the symptoms of a "private" neurosis. What Shakespeare portrays in this play, then, is man's inability to live up to the mask he has assumed before the world. Yet the conflict takes its inevitable course. It is transferred from the public stage to the semi-darkness of the personal unconscious. It scarcely seems accidental that Jung should describe such a process in terms of dramatic art: "A chain of fantasy ideas develops and gradually takes on a dramatic character: the passive process becomes an action. At first it consists of projected figures, and these images are observed, like scenes in a theatre. In other words, you dream with open eyes. . . . The piece that is being played does not *want* merely to be watched impartially, it *wants* to compel his participation. If the observer understands that his own drama is being performed on this inner stage, he cannot remain indifferent to the plot and its denouement. He will notice, as the actors appear one by one and the plot thickens, that they all have some purposeful relationship to his conscious situation, that he is being addressed by his unconscious and that it causes these fantasy-images to appear before him." [1]

What Angelo seems to be doing is to be continuing to play "without a mask," forgetting that he is still "on the stage," facing not only Isabella but a divided world of imagination and reality. Deprived of his mask, Angelo appears to be truer to life—even though on the level of Caliban—than the Deputy of the Duke, whose persona has become his second nature, a "higher" and public consciousness. Jung, in a singularly revealing passage, attempts to clarify the distinction between public and private consciousness in terms of the psychology of an over-eager actor who, when the play is over, forgets to change over from the public persona to his private self: "Our intellectual consciousness is like an actor who has forgotten that he is playing a part. But when the play is over, he must be able to recollect his subjective reality, for he cannot continue to live as Julius Caesar or Othello, but only as his particular self, from which a temporary deception of consciousness had separated him. He must realize once again that he was merely a figure on a stage where a play of Shakespeare was being played." [2]

[I]

SHAKESPEARE'S TREATMENT of Angelo deserves closer scrutiny. For his deputyship was directed by a conscious choice —not his own but the Duke's. As his representative, Angelo has to cultivate a pose of authority, without being fully aware of all that such a pose implies in potential good or evil. Full consciousness of what he has taken upon himself comes to him only when the strength and validity of his authority is tested by someone whose assumed stature is as strong as his. For when chaste Isabella comes to plead for her brother (whom Angelo has condemned to death for having "fall'n by prompture of the blood") the innocence of her self-conscious virginity proves to be his undoing. The essential shallowness of his pose becomes disconcertingly evident to himself when she asks him to

> go to your bosom,
> Knock there, and ask your heart what it doth know
> That's like my brother's fault. (II, 2, *136*)

Although he is persuaded that his bosom will reveal no similar fault committed in the past, his pose begins to crumble, and his "conscious attitude" that has till now protected him against temptations of this kind collapses. What he succumbs to is not merely the possibility of an erotic adventure (such as Troilus succumbing to the "imaginary relish" enchanting his senses long before Cressida's arrival) but an "inner voice" that reveals to him the truth about his own distorted psyche: "She speaks and 'tis such sense / That my sense breeds with it" (II, 2, 142). Isabella, at this moment, does not stand for the principle of compassion, but for the inevitable choice that Angelo must now make between his pose as Deputy of the Duke and the true nature of his unconscious (of which he has just become dimly aware) and which is symbolized by the twofold meaning of the word "sense."

When Isabella speaks contemptuously of the pose of strength that enabled Angelo to condemn her brother, "Dress'd in a little brief authority" and behaving like "an angry ape," she expresses the kind of "sense" to which Angelo is most susceptible: for the limits of his power have never been determined by the Duke. His deputyship appears to be based on the Duke's assumption that Angelo's remarkable psychic stability, centered as it is in his ego, may fail him when he needs it most. The "breeding" of his sense, the unexpected arousal of his sensuality (which will lead to his outrageous sexual blackmail) is the first responsive stirring of his unconscious. Isabella's "temptation" then has a twofold function: to awaken Angelo's repressed libido and thereby to lead him into doing evil, and, ultimately, to reveal to him the meaning of the choice between sense as sanity and sense as the insane "breeding" of blood. Isabella, then, is in Jung's terminology, the "inner voice" to which Angelo succumbs.

Although each individual psyche creates its own inner voice, it generally appears as an archetype of temptation and appeals to the instinctive urge to transcend the limitations of a consciously regulated life. Therefore man's attitude to his inner voice is ambivalent: it frightens him out of his spurious self-confidence, while, at the same time, stimulating his desire to test the validity of his consciousness by new and nonconformist standards. What this inner voice whispers to him is usually

> something negative, if not actually evil. This must be so, first of all because we are usually not as unconscious of our virtues as of our vices, and then because we suffer less from the good than from the bad in us. The inner voice . . . makes us conscious of the evil from which the whole community is suffering. . . . But it presents the evil in an individual form, so that one might at first suppose it to be only an individual characteristic. The inner voice brings the evil before us in a very tempting and convincing way in order to make us succumb. If we do not partially succumb nothing of this apparent evil enters into us, and no regeneration of healing can take place. If we succumb completely, then the contents, expressed by the inner voice, act as so many devils, and a catastrophe ensues.[3]

That Angelo should succumb to the inner voice symbolized by Isabella's chastity is perfectly in keeping with his extraordinary self-restraint in his relation with women till the moment he meets her. For Isabella, unknown to herself, reveals to him his "breeding" sense as if it were reflected in a mirror. Although Angelo, on one occasion, tells her that her sense "pursues" not his, their senses do meet, though neither of them at first is fully

aware of the implication of this meeting. Both indeed are blind
to the natural strength of their repressed sensuality. Isabella
appears to Angelo sexually more persuasive in her chaste pose of
eloquent compassion than we see that Cressida is to Troilus.
Thus Isabella's brother describes her as a true "inner voice"
whose temptation is yet without guile and devoid of all evil:

> For in her youth
> There is a prone and speechless dialect
> Such as move men; beside, she hath prosperous art
> When she will play with reason and discourse,
> And well she can persuade. (I, 2, *193*)

That she, again without ever being aware of it, "plays" with
sense, trying to persuade Angelo in terms of her own chaste
sensuality, is strongly hinted at when she exclaims that, before
yielding up her body to Angelo,

> Th' impression of keen whips I'd wear as rubies,
> And strip myself to death as to a bed
> That longing have been sick for . . . . (II, *4, 102*)

Both Angelo and Isabella hide their incomplete, crippled
personalities behind a pose of chastity and self-control. Neither
of them hesitates to condemn Claudio to death, Angelo as the
Duke's Deputy and Isabella as a servant of God: they do so in
the name of the twofold "sense" that may either control or loosen
the principle regulating relationships between men and women.
Claudio's death, if and when it should come, will be the result
of a semantic ambiguity. He will be a victim of too much "sense."
Thus Angelo's repressed sensuality grows in proportion to his
realization of Isabella's chastity. "Can it be," he asks, "That
modesty may more betray our sense / Than woman's lightness?"
(II, 2, 168). Possibly, had Isabella been a Cressida coming to
plead for her doomed brother, she would have proved less persuasive. His "sense" would have remained unmoved by hers, and
her immodesty (encouraged by her bawdy-talking uncle) would
have strengthened his self-restraint.

Angelo's uncompromisingly puritanical attitude toward sex

is entirely ego-centered. In a society freely given to uninhibited gratification of the senses he is an outsider, if not actually a misfit. Temptation never seems to have come his way, and if it ever did, resistance to it seemed easier than surrender. Every time that temptation was successfully opposed, the fearful possibilities of having to share tenderness and affection with another human being was repudiated in the name of virtue. Except for a short-lived engagement to Mariana, several years previously, which he broke off because of the loss of most of her dowry at sea, there appears to have been no woman in his life. Before his fateful encounter with Isabella, he finds his state of celibacy perfectly natural and the behavior of others absurd: "Even till now/ When men were fond, I smil'd and wonder'd how" (II, 2, 186).

When the Duke appoints Angelo his deputy, he does so in order to test his sincerity. This experiment in establishing the limits of ego-consciousness—controlled by the Duke at every stage in its progress—is, incidentally, based on premises not altogether applicable to Angelo. For when the latter becomes aware of "the strong and swelling evil / Of my conception" (II, 4, 6) and immediately communicates the sense of this conception to Isabella, he remains true to his own crippled ego. The question of insincerity or what Isabella calls "seeming" scarcely arises: for when Angelo yields to the temptation of the senses, he is being consistent in a way that neither the Duke who controls the experiment nor Lucio who so violently disapproves of it could fully grasp.[4]

Angelo's self-restraint, then, is neither pretense nor the result of scheming dishonesty. What other people think of him corresponds to his own image of his moral stature. The Duke speaks of him as "A man of stricture and firm abstinence" (I, 3, 12), and calls him "precise" (the same word as is used for him later on ironically by Claudio). Again, according to the Duke, Angelo

> Scarce confesses
> That his blood flows, or that his appetite
> Is more to bread than stone. (I, 3, 51)

That this was the generally accepted opinion about the Duke's Deputy, shared by those who held and exercised power in Vienna, is indicated by the regret expressed by Escalus to Angelo after the latter's admission of having yielded to temptation:

> I am sorry one so learned and so wise
> As you, Lord Angelo, have still appeared,
> Should slip so grossly, both in the heat of blood
> And lack of temper'd judgment afterwards. (v, *1, 472*)

Angelo, in his astounding simple-mindedness, would have been the first to agree with him: for did he not, in an earlier conversation with that same "ancient lord," reject his plea for mercy on the ground that " 'Tis one thing to be tempted, Escalus, / Another thing to fall" (II, 1, 17).

Lucio who among all the figures in the play has no illusions as regards the equivocal nature of "sense," has already described Claudio's offence in terms of "breeding," when he tells Isabella about the

> blossoming time
> That from the seedness the bare fallow brings
> To teeming foison. (I, *4, 41*)

When he discovers that Angelo, as the Duke's Deputy, has passed judgment on Claudio for a "vice" that never seems to have troubled Angelo unduly, he describes him to Isabella as a man unmoved by "sense" and therefore incapable of responding to his unconscious except in intellectual terms—

> A man whose blood
> Is very snow-broth; one who never feels
> The wanton stings and motion of the sense;
> But doth rebate and blunt the natural edge
> With profits of the mind, study, and fast. (I, *4, 57*)

Once more Angelo would have approved of this description of false integrity and self-deceiving virtue. Lucio is more explicitly contemptuous when—after the spectator has already been taken into confidence and has witnessed Angelo's fall—he tells the Duke, disguised as a friar, what the common people really think of Angelo's unbelievable continence. His birth, surely, could not have been the result of "breeding," nor did a woman ever conceive him. According to popular belief, Angelo was not

> made by man and woman, after this downright way of creation. . . . Some report, a sea-maid spawned him. Some, that he was begotten between two stockfishes. . . . And he is a motion unregenerative. . . . This ungenitured agent will unpeople the province with continency. (III, 2, *114*)

The Duke's experiment fails because Angelo is not a "seemer" nor "outward-sainted": his unawakened senses remain unmoved until Isabella arouses them to life. Yet whatever self-knowledge he can achieve is through his senses. Thus when Angelo decides to "write good angel on the devil's horn" (II, 4, 16) he, evidently for the first time in his life, listens to his inner voice and, wholeheartedly, surrenders to the temptation of the senses:

> I have begun
> And now I give my sensual race the rein:
> Fit thy consent to my sharp appetite;
> Lay by all nicety and prolixious blushes
> That banish what they sue for. (II, *4, 160*)

Though the image of the "devil's horn" applies to Angelo rather than to Isabella, the archetypal tempter comes to man in feminine shape to lure him away from "study and fast" and persuade him, with her still, small voice, to commit evil. Isabella whose "sincerity" is equally beyond doubt is yet Angelo's "devil" whose voice reaches him at the very moment he is most in need of it. For her power of persuasion "faces [him] with ultimate moral decisions without which [he] can never achieve full consciousness." [5] That the "inner voice" should come to him in erotic disguise proves its archetypal nature. For what appears to Angelo (and to us) an individual and consciously desired relationship is, in truth, a repetition of a primordial human situation where the projection of a man's anima on to a beloved woman reflects an essentially "primitive mythological mentality that consists of archetypes, and whose totality constitutes a collective unconscious. Accordingly, such a relationship is at bottom collective and not individual." [6]

The archetype of chastity alone, sanctioned by religion and dressed in the "little brief authority" of her sisterhood can lure Angelo into temptation. He is the first to realize the archetypal situation:

> O cunning enemy, that, to catch a saint,
> With saints dost bait thy hook! (II, 2, *180*)

Whatever might be the outcome of the gamble he undertakes, he will from now on have to live with his inner voice. To come to terms with it is a "test" far beyond the scope of the experiment that the Duke organized when he selected Angelo to be his deputy.

[II]

SHAKESPEARE'S PREOCCUPATION with the conscious ego in search of the self that would give wholeness to the human personality constitutes the main characteristic of those plays— tragedies or comedies—that deal with man's disposition to question the validity of his moral judgment. Man's consciousness, being so frequently founded on faulty sense-perception, is seldom sufficiently well-equipped to withstand the impact of a collective archetype: if he attempts to integrate it, either it may be absorbed by his unconscious, causing loss of identity and regression —as when we see Troilus vainly endeavoring to "take vengeance" at the end of the play—or, through a gradual and painful process of individuation, consciousness may be restored, but within the larger framework of the rediscovered self. The newly experienced "reality" would, then, consist, in equal measure, of elements deriving from the conscious and the unconscious, and sense-perception would no longer be the main cause for man's delusions (as, for example, in the case of Othello's "ocular proof"). His reborn identity will confront the world new-made, as it were, through an insight that has taught him to see the contradictory nature of reality with his inner eye and to listen with his inner ear to the disharmony of "inner voices," each one attempting to persuade him with a different kind of untruth.

To experience the chaos of such an inner landscape with its conflicting sights and sounds, and to reach, beyond conflict and contradiction, a level of awareness not accessible to mere sense perception, is, then, the first step toward the knowledge of Self. And if what he "sees" and "hears" within proves to be a denial and a rejection of all that he held dear in the past, producing, in effect, the kind of upheaval without which no individuation is possible, surrender to evil becomes a blessing in disguise. So greatly does man desire to know his true Self that he would rather create his own temptation than do without it. Thus Shakespeare's young problem heroes, the ones to whom the modern spectator feels most nearly akin, when put to the test lose whatever little identity they possess in moments of ecstatic self-abandonment. They thereby acquire a false sense of identity meant to deceive both themselves and others. It is in the name of this false Self that they act out their various lusts and behind which they hide their unacknowledged fears.

Thus Claudio, in *Much Ado,* a few moments before making public what he thinks to be Hero's shameful loss of virginity, exclaims in the certainty of his conviction, "O what men dare do! What men may do! What men daily do, not knowing what they do!" (IV, 1, 19), though it is he who is most ignorant of what he is doing at this moment, both to himself and to the girl he presumes to love. In *All's Well* Bertram's loss of identity is described in similar terms. Once more, misled by faulty sense perception and ignorant of what he is doing, he yet accomplishes an act that (had Helena not substituted herself for Diana) would

have strengthened his ego and ruined the girl to whose "temptation" he succumbs. The First Lord sums up the situation in
words reminiscent of those used by Claudio: "As we are ourselves, what things we are!" (IV, 3, 24). In both cases it is man's
"sense" that betrays him, whether it be his understanding, his
inborn sensuality, or his unreliable sense perception. The cure,
we remember, is a "study of imagination" which reveals a reborn
Hero to a greatly chastened Claudio. In the words of the same
First Lord the true Bertram exists in terms of the inner voice
that led him to temptation. What this remarkably shrewd lord
assumes is, indeed, that without the surrender to evil no self-
knowledge could ever arise:

> The web of our life is of a mingled yarn, good and ill together;
> our virtues would be proud if our faults whipp'd them not and
> our crimes would despair if they were not cherish'd by our vir-
> tues. (IV, 3, 83)

Angelo's case is even more illuminating since he experiences
the archetypal situation in full consciousness of the moral dilemma he has created for himself. Thus, the Duke, quite rightly,
generalizes the angel-devil synonymity, where being and seeming
are no longer valid contradictions. Nor can the purity or im-
purity of motive serve as explanation for what men may do or
for what they are:

> O, what may man within him hide,
> Though angel on the outward side. (III, 2, 293)

Yet, the conclusion of the play is once more based upon the
recognition that the "true" Self can only arise out of the darkness
of stumbling "sense," that indeed the temptation of sense—in
whatever meaning one may now interpret this word—is indispensable to direct the growth of human consciousness toward an
acceptance of the whole of man's psychic reality. The First Lord's
generalization about man, in *All's Well,* is more particularly
applicable to Angelo when the one woman who has least reason to

show forgiveness, Mariana, substituting for Isabella, spends
the night with Angelo without his knowing of the substitution:

> They say best men are moulded out of faults,
> And for the most, become much more the better
> For being a little bad. (v, *1, 440*)

"Sense" in Bertram and Angelo starts "breeding" when they
encounter Diana and Isabella. The Don Juan and the Puritan,
compulsively affirming or denying their "senses," yet equally de-
fenceless before the archetype which is their own anima-projection, realize the peril of visual attraction and look for darkness
in which to translate the "imaginary relish" of their senses into
reality. Having been betrayed by their eyes, they now impose
that blindness upon themselves which alone could save them
from seeing too well. In the stillness of all-dissolving darkness
their wedding ritual is transformed into a rape. They re-enact
the archetypal encounter between the sexes where the consciousness of the male succumbs to the anonymity of the inner voice
which is that of woman. This surrender of the ego to the archetype prevents recognition: their blindness is both symbolical and
real. The woman they rape is, indeed, any woman. Shakespeare
represents such an encounter on these two similar occasions.
What attracted him here could not have been the mere comic
implication: for neither Helena nor Mariana could afford laughing at the viciousness exhibited by those who, after all, were assumed to be their husbands. Nor does the absurd humor of the
statement that "no man in an Elizabethan play can tell one
woman from another in the dark" [7] do justice to Shakespeare's
insight into human nature. What this scene in the dark does to
the spectator is to reveal to him tragedy in the disguise of comedy.
For having put Angelo within the tragic context of two equally
preposterous alternatives of action—regardless as to whether he
be "true" or "false" to himself, he will in any case be compelled
to cause suffering—Shakespeare now administers a comic *coup de
grace* and blinds Angelo for the rest of the night.

The story of Eros and Psyche as retold by Apuleius may provide the explanation in depth of the lovers' blindness. In *Much Ado,* for instance, the encounter between Hero and the stranger takes place in Claudio's imagination, so that the "new" Hero—after Claudio has regained his "sight"—differs from the former only in the perspective applied to her by her overcredulous lover. The play does not tell us whether Claudio's "sense" is ever made to "breed." Angelo's rape of Mariana whom he believes to be Isabella is as real as is his faulty eyesight. For the night when he is smitten with comic blindness is the night of his own soul. What saves him from completely succumbing to the darkness is Mariana's readiness to serve as a substitute, thereby fulfilling her own feminine destiny. By imposing on herself a voluntary anonymity, she, as it were, approves of her partner's blindness in order the better to guide his senses. She also seems aware of the transpersonal nature of their encounter; otherwise it would be difficult to imagine her tolerating the indignity of submitting to Angelo's appetite—knowing as she inevitably does that the love emotion will be absent from the act. For what, from the masculine point of view, may be nothing but "aggression, victory, rape, and the satisfaction of desire . . . is for the feminine destiny, transformation, and the profoundest mystery of life." [8] The words spoken by Psyche to Eros when he first came to her bed without being seen by her, could well have been those that Helena or Mariana whispered into her husband's ear: "I seek no more to see your face; not even the dark of night can be a hindrance to my joy, for I hold you in my arms, life of my life." [9] That in spite of the deceptive nature of the encounter (for the god never shows his face to Psyche) she addresses him as the "light" of her life reveals the inner illumination that makes her submit to this one-sided encounter. True love, however, is possible only when the darkness that encloses her anonymity is broken and she overcomes her fear of seeing and of being seen. As a victim of his uncontrolled senses she has until then been acquainted with the animal nature of the god whom she worships. Now that she holds up the lantern and a drop of oil falls on her husband's skin and wakes him from unconscious sleep, "she experiences a fateful transformation, in which she discovers that the separation between beast and husband is not valid . . . she recognizes Eros as a God, who is the upper and lower in one, and who connects the two." [10] This is the beginning of her true love for him. It is also the starting point of his renewed consciousness, which in the case of the legend leads to even more suffering and sacrifice, while in Shakespeare's problem plays this scene is, for obvious reasons, kept in darkness, though it constitutes a kind of short cut to the final confrontation between husband and wife, no longer in the anonymity of their unconscious but as the ultimate goal of their individuation. What appears to be a literary convention and a psychological absurdity is seen to be part of a process of self-discovery, one that guides man from the ignorance caused by faulty sense perception to the humility of self-knowledge, no longer in darkness but in the light of common day.

Both Bertram and Angelo are made to stumble into truth through the unseeing compulsion of their blood. Helena's and Mariana's senses, however, do not deceive them when they "see" their husbands joining them in the dark. Helena, more articulate and more consciously involved in this appalling encounter, provides the feminine point of view:

> But, O strange men!
> That can such sweet use make of what they hate,
> When saucy trusting of the cozen'd thoughts
> Defiles the pitchy night; so lust doth play
> With what it loathes for that which is away. (IV, *4, 21*)

While Helena acts alone, Mariana is guided by the Duke "who would have dark deeds darkly answered" (III, *2*, 190). The "pitchy night" toward which Angelo is so compulsively drawn is the disguise that is required to make him know himself. Thus the Duke sets the scene and pulls the strings "that the place may have all shadow and silence in it." If therefore "the encounter acknowledge itself hereafter, it may compel him to her recompense" (III, 1, 262). The "false" darkness in which the encounter takes place may, the Duke believes, cure Angelo of his own falsehood:

> So disguise shall by th'disguise
> Pay with falsehood false exacting
> And perform an old contracting. (III, 2, 302)

Though the Duke assures Mariana that "To bring you thus together 'tis no sin" (IV, 1, 74), and uses a harvest image to justify the deception—"Our corn to reap, for yet our tithe's to sow" (IV, 1, 77)—Mariana could scarcely have been under any illusion as to the form this encounter in the dark would take. Yet the defilement thus committed ceases to be "disguise" and "falsehood": Mariana, in her role as Angelo's Psyche, confronts him with his own projected anima, and can now, in public, reveal the extent of his masculine blindness without which, however, he could never have "known" her as she wanted to be known by him.

> I have known my husband; yet my husband
> Knows not that ever he knew me
>   . . . and that is Angelo,
> Who thinks he knows that he ne'er knew my body,
> But knows, he thinks, that he knows Isabel's.
> . . . But Tuesday night, last gone, in's garden house
> He knew me as a wife. (v, 1, 182)

Mariana's triumph of "knowledge" is paralleled by Isabella's triumph of mercy. For in this same scene when Mariana pleads for her new husband as being a good man "moulded out of faults," Isabella who does not yet know that her brother is alive, is yet ready to forgive Angelo; for, she seems to imply, it is not he but his senses that have betrayed him:

> I partly think
> A due sincerity govern'd his deeds
> Till he did look on me. (v, 1, 446)

That Angelo should ask for death indicates the measure of his new self-knowledge: for what his enlarged consciousness reveals to him is the amount of suffering that he has caused when he surrendered to the "breeding" of his sense:

> I am sorry that such sorrow I procure.
> And so deep sticks it in my penitent heart
> That I crave death more willingly than mercy. (v, *1, 475*)

The process of individuation that Angelo must undergo before he can marry Mariana involves the rejection of his former defective vision. His restored eyesight can but repudiate the darkness in which he met Mariana thinking her to be Isabella. For as "by reason of its solar nature, the eye is a symbol of consciousness," [11] the daylight in which he now "sees" her (and is thus seen by her) provides Angelo with the focus that turns the act of seeing into a conscious choice. When the Duke, then, asks him to "love her," it is as husband rather than as surreptitious lover in the dark that he returns to her. The knowledge he gained transforms him from being the untamed blind Eros of the myth imposing his dark authority on unsuspecting victims, into a human being, at last ready to assume his new identity in the daylight world of the senses.

Blind Cupid is far from being, at all times, the harmless and playful young god of popular legend, shooting his arrows in a somewhat haphazard manner, blindly as it were, and in whatever direction he pleases. In Shakespeare's plays, his blindness is frequently associated with the violence and emotional instability caused by lust. Thus, in the comedies, his blindness is associated with the phallic symbol found hanging in front of brothels to attract customers. It is in this quite unambiguous and anti-romantic sense that Berowne, in *Love's Labour Lost,* speaks of Cupid as

> This whimpled, whining, purblind, wayward boy,
> This signor junior, giant-dwarf, Dan Cupid . . .
> Dread prince of plackets, king of codpieces. . . . (III, *1, 189*)

Such an ironic analogy between blind Cupid and a house of ill-fame is constantly drawn in *Much Ado* where he is called "a good hare-finder" (I, 1, 192) and "the little hangman" (III, 2, 10), while Benedick swears he will never marry unless his friend Don Pedro "pick out mine eyes with a ballad-maker's pen, and hang me up at the door of a brothel-house for the sign of blind Cupid" (I, 1, 261).

Cupid's blindness, within the context of comedy, seems to threaten no one unless it be Benedick's conceited bachelorhood or Beatrice's assertive virginity. But when Lear meets Gloucester on the heath and addresses him as "blind Cupid" (IV, 6, 138), the very incongruity of it strikes an ominous note. As an invitation to visit a brothel and applied to Gloucester in his blindness, it appears to be the result of Lear's disordered imagination which, a few lines previously, had made him exclaim, "Let copulation thrive . . . / To't, Luxury, pell-mell." Yet at the same time one remembers Gloucester's own jocular description of Edmund's "conception" in the degrading surroundings of a brothel—"there was good sport at his making" (I, 1, 23). Edmund's mother conceived out of wedlock, and therefore "this knave came something saucily to the world before he was sent for."

The erotic implications of Gloucester's blindness are scarcely more than hinted at. Yet, at the end of the play, Edgar reminds his bastard brother of their father's uncontrolled lust which he describes as being the cause of his present blindness:

> The gods are just, and of our pleasant vices
> Make instruments to plague us:
> The dark and vicious place where thee he got
> Cost him his eyes.[12] (v, 3, 172)

Angelo, whose initial blindness resembles that of Gloucester, cannot distinguish Mariana from Isabella in the dark. He also prefers what in Edmund's language is "the lusty stealth of nature" to a "dull, stale, tired" wedding bed. Yet, he is, miraculously, cured when his senses are restored to him and he, once again, learns to see and to discriminate, even in the dark. For the inner voice, which was that of Isabella, has spoken the truth. It has made Angelo "conscious of the evil from which the whole community is suffering." The city of Vienna, after all, continues to be haunted by its "blind Cupids." And Mistress Overdone will continue plying her trade, for as Pompey, her servant and pimp, informs her, "You that have worn your eyes almost out in the service, you will be considered" (I, 2, 119).

[III]

ONE OF THE MOST PUZZLING THINGS about this play is the casual manner in which the laws prohibiting sexual inter-course between unmarried partners are once more forgotten after the Duke's return to Vienna. Yet, they are the means by which Angelo has been tested. And when he falls he succumbs to what is inherently absurd in them. The laws are, on various occasions in the play, called *strict, biting, hideous, severe,* and *angry.* No one seems to have thought of reviving them until the Duke, at a time when the inhabitants of the city no longer even remember their existence, chooses Angelo to enforce them once again. This choice imposes obligations on Angelo transcending his in-dividual virtues, however great they may be. For after the Duke has

> Lent him our terror, drest him with our love,
> And given his deputation all the organs
> Of our own power, (I, *1, 19*)

he raises him above the collective standards of morality that had prevailed in Vienna for so many years, and makes Angelo's con-sciousness the sole arbiter of right or wrong. The Duke informs Angelo of the scope of his power in very ambiguous terms, leav-ing it to his Deputy's "soul" to define his authority as may seem fit:

> Your scope is as mine own,
> So to enforce or qualify the laws
> As to your soul seems good. (I, *I*, *64*)

The choice falls on Angelo because he appears to be a paragon of virtue, a man whose aloofness, indeed nonattachment to things and people, qualify him for the exalted position of judge. No one else but he could resurrect "the drowsy and neglected act" both by example and strict application of the laws. Yet Angelo's virtue must have seemed to the Duke a morally questionable, if not socially undesirable personal trait. The test he imposes on Angelo necessarily takes for granted some sort of ethical common denominator, an acceptable collective standard of conduct, against which Angelo's virtue may then be measured.

It is, therefore, possible, indeed necessary, to start with the assumption that Angelo himself was largely unaware of the extraordinary purity of his life before he was appointed the Duke's Deputy. This unexpected elevation to the highest position in society where he has to dispense justice by applying the standards of his apparent moral perfection to others, provides him with the means to change the face of society by civilizing men's manners and helping them to progress towards greater self-control in their relationship with others. The only use that Angelo makes of his new authority is to punish with death those that "do coin heaven's image / In stamps that are forbid" (II, 4, 42). What is forbid is not the act which in Angelo's (and Isabella's) vocabulary is consistently called a "vice," but the breeding of bastards. One is inclined to agree with Lucio when he tells the Duke, "What a ruthless thing is this in him, for the rebellion of a codpiece to take away the life of a man" (III, 2, 100). The psychological dilemma which the Duke forces upon Angelo (who by the very nature of his deputyship is quite unable to avoid such a dilemma) may be defined in terms of an all-powerful identification with an object that has taken complete possession of his ego. His consciousness then acts as if from within a prison cell which it had built for its own protection and which now prevents the necessary escape from a form of compulsive psychic energy that leads to its own ruin: in such a case as Angelo's, "the ego is drawn into this focus of energy so powerfully that it identifies with it and thinks it desires and needs nothing further. In this way a craze develops, a monomania or possession, an acute one-sidedness which most seriously imperils the psychic equilibrium." [13]

Shakespeare portrays the various stages in this progressive identification between the ego and the object of its consciousness which, in Angelo's case, is "the law." Claudio who is its first victim speaks of the authority invested in the law as a "demigod" dispensing justice haphazardly: "on whom it will, it will; / On whom it will not, so . . ." (I, 2, 131). Isabella, defending Claudio's "vice" against Angelo's "virtue" sees nothing but pride and vanity in the one who upholds the law in total ignorance "of what he is most assur'd / His glassy essence" (II, 2, 119), which may mean the divine spark of compassion hidden within him or the human soul as a "glassy" image of God. Yet, it is Angelo's "ignorance," his consistent identification with the "law," his acceptance of authority, at first in all the candor of virtuousness and later with the cunning of his aroused "vice," that Shakespeare portrays with singular insistence. Whatever psychic energy there is in the play pertains to Angelo. Isabella and her brother Claudio plead, suffer, and endure what is imposed on them from outside. Angelo alone—though himself under constant observation—is compulsively engaged in action. "It is the law, not I, condemn your brother" (II, 2, 80) expresses Angelo's attempt at rationalizing the loss of his own identity in favor of "the law." By applying the law to Claudio and his "vice," he in all sincerity believes that the evil of the past will be redeemed, and more controlled behavior-patterns in future be made possible. As "the voice of the recorded law" (II, 4, 62) he indeed justifies the Duke's "election" by dismissing his own identity as irrelevant. Angelo thus identifies his compulsive private ethics which do not admit of the existence of "the vice" on the plane of consciousness (the only one of which Angelo is aware) with the law:

>   Now 'tis awake
> Takes note of what is done, and like a prophet
> Looks in a glass that shows what future evils,
> Either new, or by remissness new conceiv'd
> And so in progress to be hatch'd and born,
> Are now to have no successive degrees
> But ere they live, to end. (II, 2, 93)

The best proof of Angelo's basic innocence, his unawareness of the potentialities of his own undiscovered Self, until he meets Isabella, consists in his readiness to apply the same "hideous" law to himself as he has already applied to Claudio. When he condemns Claudio to death in the name of a law, the mystique of which he interprets with his conscious mind, while the deeper layers of his unconscious remain unaffected by it, he passes judgment on himself. Now that Angelo the man and Angelo the Deputy have become one, and his interpretation of the law *is* the law, what he condemns is his own private ethics insofar as he thinks them to be synonymous with public morality. This is the price he has to pay for assuming a position of strength in society without having the necessary inner resources to relate his ego-consciousness to the very real demands of his unconscious. Depth psychology, especially in its emphasis on the conflict that arises when anima and animus elements are unequally distributed and the psychic unity of the individual is threatened, would interpret Angelo's divided rule, as a private model of virtue and as a public symbol of "vice," in terms of an anima-oriented weakness that proves to be a most formidable disability in a position of power: "The socially 'strong man' is in his private life often a mere child where his own states of feeling are concerned; his public discipline (which he demands quite particularly of others) goes miserably to pieces in private . . . his 'spotless' public morality looks strange behind the mask. . . . Outwardly an effective and powerful role is played, while inwardly an effeminate weakness develops in face of every influence coming from the unconscious.

. . . The persona, the ideal picture of a man as he should be, is inwardly compensated by feminine weakness, and as the individual outwardly plays the strong man, so he becomes inwardly a woman, i.e. the anima." Therefore, Jung continues, a man like Angelo, initially handicapped by the rationalization of his "virtues" must, before it is too late, "become conscious of his invisible system of relations to the unconscious, and especially of the anima, so as to be able to distinguish himself from her." [14] Angelo's consciousness can achieve the equilibrium it lost only when Mariana is substituted for Isabella in the dark. When he finds out that his anima has "deceived" him, that indeed it has the power to make him "do" what he never intended doing, he realizes the weakness inherent in all his previous rationalizations.

The Duke never declares the experiment to have failed, nor is the law ever abrogated and the dubious collective standard of conduct, which has ruled Vienna for so long a time, upheld. Instead of admitting defeat, the Duke distributes punishment and reward, not in accordance with the long-neglected laws of the city, but in view of man's "glassy essence" which is both bright and brittle, an image of grace as well as of damnation. Thus he first asks Mariana to marry Angelo "before the law," then immediately imposes a verdict of death on her new husband; and lastly, when Claudio is found to be still alive, orders Angelo to "love" his new wife. Does the Duke, then, approve of Angelo's vice as essentially of a collective and archetypal nature, and therefore not punishable at all? And if this is so, does not then Angelo's coming to terms with his anima symbolize his own acceptance of transpersonal reality which makes the law, the purpose of which it is to regulate and discipline the "breeding" of the senses, look as hideous as indeed it is?

On a more primitive level of awareness than the Duke's, Pompey, the pimp, provides the most convincing evidence why no one ever mentions the law again after the Duke's experiment has so evidently failed to prove what it set out to prove:

'Twas never a merry world since, of two usuries, the merrier was put down, and the worser allowed by order of law; a furred gown to keep him warm; and furred with fox, on lambskins too, to signify that craft, being richer than innocency, stands for the facing. (III, 2, 6)

What Pompey complains of is not only that lechery, the "merrier" of the two usuries, has been "put down," but that the judge himself, though guilty of the same vice, goes scotfree because his mask, his "facing," protects him from the law. When Shakespeare puts words of similar import into Lear's mouth, the "madness" of his speech goes a long way to emphasize the commonsense of Pompey's observation:

> The usurer hangs the cozener.
> Thorough tatter'd clothes small vices to appear;
> Robes and furr'd gowns hide all. (IV, 6, 168)

It is only by imposing a standard of conduct according to which the judge and the criminal are subject to the same law that sanity on the individual and social levels can be re-established. The Duke says as much to the Provost: "Claudio, whom here you have warrant to execute, is no greater forfeit to the law than Angelo who hath sentenced him" (IV, 2, 165). When Angelo falls, the law falls with him. What he experiences is a fulfillment "in the dark." By denying the law which has made him lose his identity, he takes the first step toward his own individuation. He learns to walk in darkness. By embracing Mariana instead of Isabella, he comes to terms with a law—no longer "hideous" and "angry"—that is the law of life itself. By acting in conformity with a collective code of conduct, he no more cuts himself off in lofty isolation from other human beings, but returns to the folds of a society which imposes individuation upon him for the very reason that he "failed" in the test to which he has been subjected. If indeed "individuation does not shut one out from the world, but gathers the world to oneself" [15] while at the same time "the individuated ego senses itself as the object of an unknown and superordinate subject," [16] Angelo's election as Deputy to the Duke, his proclamation and enacting of the law, his stumbling and his fall in the dark, leading, finally, to the discovery of the relatedness between his ego and the world around him, are all stages in the process of his individuation.

Shakespeare ends the play with the assumption that such a process will create a psychic equilibrium which alone can guarantee an active and conscious participation in the life of society. A new center of balance has been achieved. To depart from it would mean aberration, illness, and suffering. Its meaning is no longer identified with the mask of the judge that, in his own eyes and in the eyes of others, supplied him not only with a deceptive strength, but also with the ability to distinguish between what he *is* and what the unconscious thrusts upon him. Whatever "authority" he possesses, will now come from within his own integrated psyche. Whether one looks upon him, in his role of the Duke's Deputy, as an angel with horns or as an angry ape, now that his identity has been recreated, the only authority he will ever submit to will derive from his awareness of man's glassy essence in which he finds reflected the true scope of his own soul. Standing before Mariana and the Duke and experiencing his own resurrection at the very moment of dying, he now bows before that "unknown and superordinate" power that has enabled him to gather the world to himself.

PART TWO

Anima

5

Logos: Fathers & Daughters

THE DIFFICULTY of putting Jung's theory of archetypes into empirical terms becomes manifest when the unconscious contents of the psyche have to be, as it were, translated for the Shakespearean stage as visible components of character and dramatic action. Among them the anima and animus archetypes, which Jung also calls Eros and Logos, when defined empirically as part of the process of individuation, are the most elusive of all. As they reside within the psyche they cannot be "personalized" though they adopt a variety of shapes according to individual differences. They have neither "character" nor "personality." Any attempt at consciously representing them through art or literary symbols would produce equivocal results, for the invisible psychic contents necessarily elude all conscious portrayal.

They manifest themselves in religious customs and social rituals of primitive tribes, in myths, in dreams, and in what Jung calls "visionary" art. In the individual they originate in the tension resulting from an over-developed ego in conflict with the suppressed unconscious. As they are invisible they are invariably projected onto others. Thus the first bearer of the anima image is the mother, while the father comes to symbolize the animus archetype. As man grows into adulthood, the separation from father and mother constitutes a significant and, at times, critical point in the development of his consciousness.

Even though it is impossible to speak of anima and animus as having "personalities," they are related to primordial man's experience of woman and woman's experience of man. Each one of these archetypes fulfills a compensatory function, the anima counterbalancing masculine consciousness, while the animus, itself of masculine character, stands for an infinite variety of opinions, judgments, rationalizations that a woman projects upon a man. Thus the two are constantly interrelated, acting upon one another with equal vehemence. In the same way as "a man brings forth his work as a complete creation out of his inner feminine nature, so the inner masculine side of a woman brings forth creative seeds which have the power to fertilize the feminine side of man." [1] A relative state of stability between these opposites can only be achieved when and if a process of individuation resolves the psychic contradiction.

The anima archetype appears in very similar form in Shakespeare's comedies and tragedies. Since it is a stable content of the unconscious, it is impossible to speak of a "progress" in Shakespeare's own attitude toward it. His dramatic art underwent all those changes that are commonly associated with an artist's growth from immaturity to maturity and, in particular, from his acceptance of the conventional to increasingly perceptive insights into human nature. Such changes as these, however important in the study of Shakespeare's artistic range, do not affect his predisposition to represent what is universal and archetypal rather than particular and individual. Insofar as the anima archetype is concerned, it is present, for instance, whenever a young woman's growth from maid to wife and, ultimately, to motherhood is represented. Whether in comedy or in tragedy, the anima is projected onto a masculine consciousness, first the father's, then the lover's.

There is no "development" of archetypes in Shakespeare's dramatic vision. As they are psychic contents, they elude historical analysis. They have no duration in time. Since they lie below the level of consciousness, they form no part of any philosophical system. Being images and symbols of ever-recurring human constellations, they can only be understood in terms of those universal assumptions that have, from time immemorial, guided human destiny.

[I]

IN THE CASE of the unmarried daughters in Shakespeare's plays the conflict situation is one where the animus in a young woman's soul, her capacity for logical thinking, her purposiveness, her power of conscious persuasion, is shown to be in need of a man's Eros, his capacity for deep and sustained feeling and his ready submission to instinctual spontaneity. The roles that men and women are commonly and mistakenly assumed to play in life are reversed in Shakespeare's mature comedies, where the young women are characterized by a strong "paternal" Logos, while those who are the objects of their love exercise a singular, though powerful, attraction by their unconscious Eros. Jung's formula is applicable in these plays to the young woman, as well as the young man, although in the early Shakespeare the former are given prominence while the latter are seldom more than supporting parts: "Just as the mother seems to be the first carrier of the projection-making factor (i.e. the anima) for the son, so is the father (i.e. the animus) for the daughter. . . . The animus corresponds to the paternal Logos just as the anima corresponds to the maternal Eros . . . just as the anima becomes, through integration, the Eros of consciousness, so the animus becomes a Logos: and in the same way that the anima gives relationship and relatedness to a man's consciousness, the animus gives woman's consciousness a capacity for reflection, deliberation, and self-knowledge." [2]

In following the dictates of the unconscious, Shakespeare's

young heroines make ample use of the Logos, for the guidance
they receive from within their own essentially feminine beings
is "paternal." This is certainly true, in a transpersonal and archetypal sense, in the case of the death-bed inspirations of Portia's
and Helena's fathers. There is something "secret" and "holy"
about a prescription that raises the virtue of humility to the
highest point of human perfection. If the Logos understands
only in part, the unconscious responds wholly and immediately.
Yet to fulfill their fathers' inspirations, Logos and Eros have to
achieve true union. By making their love speak in impassioned
language they project the anima from father-image to lover, thus
integrating the paternal Logos inherited from their fathers at the
moment of death, with the maternal Eros as represented by their
lovers.

Only in terms of such an archetypal situation does a woman's
individuation become possible. Elements of the conscious and
the unconscious, of masculinity and femininity are likely to fuse
in this process. Jung provides a relevant commentary to many
of Shakespeare's most bewildering accounts of such a love-relationship: "The love of woman claims the whole man, not mere
masculinity as such, but also just that in him which implies the
negation of it. The love of woman is not sentiment—that is only
man's way—but a life-will that at times is terrifyingly unsenti-
mental and can even force her to self-sacrifice. A man who is
loved in this way cannot escape his inferior side, for he can only
answer this reality with his own." [3]

There is much psychological subtlety in the fact that these
young heroines, in Shakespeare's early plays as well as in his
tragedies and romances, should be shown as deprived of a
mother's sympathetic support. Portia, Rosalind, Viola, Hero, and
Helena grow up in the shadow of their fathers: as symbols of
femininity they yet are motherless. But when they love, they reveal themselves in the twofold archetypal guise of woman, as
Maid and as Mother. The virginity of each, guarded by a powerful father-image is offered up as a sacrifice to their lovers for the

sake of future motherhood. The sacrifice—whether accomplished symbolically in the course of the festive conclusion, the wedding-feast that ends each of these plays, or as a naturalistic "bed-trick" performed behind the stage—is undergone as an intrinsic part of a woman's growth from Maid to Mother. Such a growth to be healthy must discard a father's animus, symbolizing her past existence as a Maid, and attract her lover's anima which stands for her future existence as a Mother.

From the point of view of dramatic structure every one of these plays must necessarily, and in keeping with the archetypal situation, start with that point in a young woman's development from Maid to Mother where some form of maladjustment in her relation to father or lover has to be overcome. The first few scenes in these plays, therefore, will have to be devoted to an analysis of the particular difficulties that stand in the way of the healthy development of a girl's instinctual life. Helena's and Portia's successful transference of the Eros element from a father-figure to the image of the beloved (whether real or imaginary) is facilitated by the fact that both fathers are dead. The "prescriptions" of both men at the moment of death are evidently rooted in the desire to see their wisdom resurrected in their own daughters: Portia's future motherhood is already implied in Bassanio's conscious choice of the leaden casket, while Helena's conscious sacrifice of her virginity is implied in the wisdom of rejuvenation with the help of which she cures the ailing king. In both cases the father has to "give up" his soul, to renounce his anima, to enable the maid to become a mother.

Shakespeare's young heroines, in his "romantic" comedies, do not hesitate: they seem to choose their future husbands without giving the matter a second thought. Having chosen by instinct rather than by logic, they—not altogether surprisingly—are confronted by men who are apparently deficient in both Eros and Logos, and each of whom either exhibits a primitive kind of virility or indulges in truly feminine equivocation. Such men are quite unfit to respond wholly or even in part to the young women. They have to be taught the meaning of love, as seen through a woman's eyes, that is in terms of sacrifice. What then happens—and this is a recurrent theme in Shakespeare's mature comedies—is that only when a man's anima is found to correspond to his image of woman, her soul, may a love-relationship ending in marriage be achieved. Whether such a marriage will necessarily be happy is a question that Shakespeare consistently refuses to consider. And since the anima element in woman as well as in man belongs to the "dark" world of the unconscious, there is no reason to assume that the apparent incompatibility of Portia and Bassanio, Helena and Bertram, Viola and Orsino, Hero and Claudio, is bound to result in perpetual emotional maladjustment. All that can be said—and Shakespeare has said it in such eloquent language that psychology can add very little to his poetry—is that "in his love choice, a man is strongly tempted to win the woman who best corresponds to his own unconscious femininity, a woman, in short, who can unhesitatingly receive the projection of his soul," [4] because, continues Jung, "woman stands just where man's shadow falls, so that he is only too liable to confuse her with his own shadow." [5] And, one is tempted to add, a man's shadow will fall where it is most likely to be confounded with her unconscious because "woman loves the weaknesses of the strong more than his strength, and the stupidity of the clever more than his cleverness." [6]

The obstacles put in the way of such a love relationship are —like images in a dream—symbolically significant, though Shakespeare also makes full dramatic use of them as part of the fairyland reality he creates in these comedies. Thus Viola, in *Twelfth Night,* is shipwrecked on the coast of Illyria, a dream-country of no fixed geographical boundaries, where together with the captain of the ship and some sailors, she starts her new life. Born out of the sea, the primal element that so often gives birth to the hero of the myth, she (like a near relative of hers very much later, Miranda, in *The Tempest*) is faced by an as yet undiscovered adult world of which she knows only one thing, told to her by her father: the name and family status of Illyria's ruling prince. This information appears to have been imparted quite some time ago, for at the end of the play we are told by the heroine herself that her father had died "when Viola from her birth / Had numbered thirteen years" (V, 1, 254). Sebastian, her brother, confirms this, for the day of his father's death is

> lively in my soul:
> He finished, indeed, his mortal act
> That day that made my sister thirteen years. (v, *1, 256*)

Beyond the day of his death and the fact that he had a mole upon his brow, we are told nothing at all about Viola's father —except that, for no obvious reason, he had mentioned Illyria to his daughter before he died and had, in no uncertain terms, described the present ruler of Illyria as a bachelor, omitting any further reference to his character, upbringing, or outlook on life: "Orsino! I have heard my father name him: / He was a bachelor then" (I, 2, 27). Whether this remarkable father spent his time discussing available bachelors in faraway countries with his pre-adolescent daughter remains undivulged. Yet Viola's immediate choice of this bachelor as her future husband has been made possible by a father's half-forgotten hint, only remembered at the moment of shipwreck. Now that the father is no longer there to provide the accustomed support, the paternal image arises out of her unconscious to remind her of Orsino's bachelorhood. It is indeed at this moment that the shipwreck is forgotten, and Viola, following the dictates of her own Logos makes her compulsive choice. She discovers that the Duke loves another woman, Olivia, who refuses to respond to his clumsy and obstinate advances. At that time Olivia herself is in mourning for a dead father (and therefore unwilling to transfer her emotional allegiance from an overidealized father-image to the very real, if somewhat self-centered, image of the man who claims to love

her). Viola, taking recourse to storytelling, attempts though at
first unsuccessfully, to put into words a conflict-situation that she
can no longer control.

For her "shadow" has fallen on one whose weak anima does
not and cannot as yet correspond to the strength that urges her
forward. Here is something that her father had neglected to tell
her and of which she could but be ignorant: Orsino's quite un-
repressed femininity responds to her masculine attire, her disguise as animus, in a different way from that she intended. He
only sees in her the Logos that he lacks and that he wishes to
make use of in order to persuade Olivia of the existence of his
love for her. Actually, only Viola can be aware of the perils of
a homo-erotic relationship between her and Orsino, and the
growth of a similar lesbian involvement with Olivia.[7] Her soul
is, in effect, torn between two equally undesirable situations.
To introduce Logos into the dark groping of her two "shadows,"
Orsino's equivocal anima and Olivia's no less ambiguous animus,
she relates to the Duke a story that is supposed to have happened
in some distant and undefined past. Dressed as a man, she naturally has to tell her story in the third person. In keeping with
the archetypal nature of her story, she starts with her father:

> *Viola:* My father had a daughter lov'd a man,
>   As it might be perhaps, were I a woman,
>   I would your lordship.
> *Duke:*   And what's her history?
> *Viola:* A blank, my lord. She never told her love,
>   But let concealment, like a worm i' the bud,
>   Feed on her damask cheek: she pin'd in thought;
>   And with a green and yellow melancholy
>   She sat like Patience on a monument
>   Smiling at grief. (II, *4, 109*)

It is Viola's own story. By telling it in the third person, she
objectifies her own condition, looks at it from a perspective of
aloofness, and thus prevents spiritual discord leading to neurosis
from taking hold of her soul and destroying it. Evidently, the

main difference between Viola and her "father's daughter" (all other elements being equal) is that she can communicate her anima to the man she loves and in this manner prepare the ground for what she alone knows has to happen—the Duke's apparently voluntary choice of Viola as "your master's mistress." It must have been one more case of "holy inspiration" that made her father tell her, when she was still a child, the story of Illyria and its handsome, albeit dejected and moping, bachelor-prince.

Rosalind's father, the banished Duke, never mentions Orlando to her. Yet we come to know, in the course of the play, that he and Orlando's father had been friends a long time ago, probably even before Rosalind and Orlando were born. Sir Rowland having died in the meantime, it is Rosalind's father alone who, in the Forest of Arden, watches over his daughter's cheerful pursuit of Orlando's love. "I am the Duke / That loved your father—" (II, 7, 198) serves as a happy prologue to Orlando's final recognition that "the fair, the chaste, and inexpressive she" is indeed Rosalind, the Duke's daughter, and not some ancient mythological being such as Diana, the goddess of hunting and of night.

Her father, who is absent from court when Rosalind first sees Orlando at a wrestling match, seems to be one, if not the main, cause of her sudden and intense infatuation with that "excellent young man." For when her uncle expresses disapproval of the fact that Orlando is the son of the late Sir Rowland, she exclaims with quite unexpected vehemence:

> My father lov'd Sir Rowland as his soul,
> And all the world was of my father's mind:
> Had I before known this young man his son,
> I should have given him tears unto entreaties,
> Ere he should thus have ventur'd. (I, 2, 252)

Dead and exiled fathers, then, have to be resurrected first, the once powerful animus of each brought back to life, before Rosalind's and Orlando's love can come to full fruition. Yet to be able to attract Orlando she must, at the outset, (even before setting eyes on him) "forget" her father.[8] "Teach me to forget a banished father," she asks Celia who can only promise her that she would help her "to make sport withal" which includes loving men, though not yet "in good earnest." When, however, Rosalind finds loving a "sport" full of pitfalls (some of them, indeed, caused by the interference of fathers where there should have been nothing but lovers), the transition from paternal attachment to the passion aroused by Orlando's remarkable wrestling match becomes a compulsion which it would be quite vain to resist. When therefore Celia asks Rosalind whether her dejection —after having seen Orlando defeating Charles the wrestler— still is for her father, she wistfully replies, "No, some of it is for my child's father . . ." (I, 3, 11).

Their meeting in the Forest of Arden takes place, almost literally, under the eyes of the exiled Duke. He speaks with both of them, though separately, discovers whose son Orlando is, and wonders at the striking resemblance between Rosalind dressed as Ganymede, and his own daughter. Rosalind who has not quite succeeded to forget her father, tries hard to dismiss his image from her mind—"But what talk we of fathers, when there is such a man as Orlando?" (III, 4, 39). A final emotional balance is established only when father, daughter, and lover recognize one another. The relationship that has grown between them in the course of the play is the result of a father's freely-given admission that his anima is not his to keep but to be passed on to the man his daughter has chosen. Rosalind's "shadow" falls where Orlando stands, his Eros at last ready to respond to her Logos. Having disciplined her emotions she can now divide her love for both father and husband on equal terms: "I'll have no father, if you be not he: / I'll have no husband, if you be not he" (V, 4, 129).

Among all the fathers we shall encounter in Shakespeare's plays, Rosalind's is one of the most archetypal. Like Prospero, his banishment is in part voluntary, serving the purpose of attaining self-knowledge through close communion with nature. Such a self-imposed exile has freed him from "painted pomp" and the "envious Court": the hardships he has to undergo when leaving civilization behind him "are counsellors / That feelingly persuade me what I am" (II, 1, 11). He is, again like Prospero, though to a lesser degree, an image of human perfection. Looking down upon the world of men with more than ordinary understanding and compassion, he sees beyond the present moment of individual perplexity, and thus is enabled to help others to find themselves and to survive in the very teeth of adversity. Here, in effect, we have one of Shakespeare's first intimations of the ideal of nonattachment:

> Thou seest, we are not all alone unhappy:
> This wide and universal theatre
> Presents more woeful pageants than the scene
> Wherein we play in. (II, 7, 136)

The forest in which the two lovers meet is an archetypal landscape where the trees themselves seem to speak a language understandable to primordial man only. For the love poems that Orlando hangs on them are not only bad verse, but also the result of an ill-digested civilization. When Celia discovers Orlando in the forest, she finds him lying "under a tree like a dropp'd acorn," very much like Adam waiting for Eve in anticipation of the fruitfulness that is to come. It is an image of paradise regained where neither serpents nor wild beasts can tempt men away from their newly discovered innocence. Life in the forest is free of "the penalty of Adam." For, except for Jacques, there is no sense of guilt or shame inhibiting the thoughts and actions of men. If Rosalind's father knows it and therefore considers his exile not as an imposition that he has to suffer but as a gateway to wisdom and charity, Orlando, as yet almost untainted by the corrupting powers of civilization (as his poetry shows) and therefore more simple-minded than the Duke, grows in the forest from adolescence to maturity. For when he discovers his wicked brother

Oliver asleep under a tree and feels naturally tempted to let him be devoured by a ferocious lioness, he saves him out of "kindness" which (in the words of Oliver) is "nobler ever than revenge," and out of a natural feeling of compassion which is (once more it is Oliver who provides the formula) "stronger than his just occasion" (IV, 3, 131). Rosalind then marries not merely that "excellent young Orlando" of the wrestling match, innocently and unknowingly lying under a tree, but a new Orlando who has acknowledged the existence of his shadow symbolized by his "wicked" brother as an ineluctable part of his own self.

In such a way, in terms of an intuitive rather than logical consistency, Rosalind's future husband and her father achieve a level of completeness which symbolically joins the two halves of her unconscious, her animus and her anima, into one. There is, and need be, no conflict in Rosalind's soul when she marries Orlando: it is a marriage made in the innocence of the forest where her husband and father, divided only by the passing of time, meet in Rosalind's unconscious, transforming her from virgin to wife, and, in the ripeness of time, from maid to mother.[9]

[II]

ROSALIND IS UNINHIBITEDLY and vividly articulate. So is her father. Their ability to see things as they are is suitably matched by their gift of expressing what they see in words. Communication between human beings in the Forest of Arden is not yet a form of make-believe but of self-revelation. There is indeed little enough that father and daughter have to hide. Even Rosalind's disguise as a boy is merely a form of self-revelation.

All this is bound to change in a society where human relationships are determined by highly sophisticated social conventions and where the archetypal landscape of the Forest is replaced by the king's palace, life at court and in the city. In Messina in

Much Ado the "penalty of Adam" is taken for granted. Beatrice and Benedick have to disentangle themselves first from the formal artificialities of upper-class wit and erudition (Benedick also tries his hand at poetry and fails more wretchedly even than Orlando who at least is not erudite enough to know how bad his poetry is) before they can articulate their love. On the other hand, Claudio, who starts the play by eloquently declaring that he— before going to the war—had looked upon Hero "with a soldier's eye," now finds his war-thoughts have been replaced by "soft and delicate desires," and has to be penalized in order to prove himself worthy of her innocence.

This is indeed a story of lost faith and loyalty misguided. Hero herself hardly gets a chance to articulate her feelings. Placed as she is between an over-credulous lover (made jealous by a false ocular proof of her infidelity the night before her pro- posed wedding) and an over-affectionate and domineering father (a worthy predecessor of Capulet, Polonius, and Brabantio), she discreetly disappears into the underworld of an imaginary death to wait there for the commotion, the much ado about her vir- ginity, to subside.

In a make-believe society neither Logos nor Eros proves to be of any help if those nearest to one are themselves victims of make-believe situations. This is why Hero has so little to say in her own defense. She would have to use a make-believe language to communicate with her father and lover. Instead she withdraws into a silence which critics—judging her by naturalistic and pseudo-psychological criteria—have found incomprehensible. Lewis Carroll, in his well-known letter to Ellen Terry, asks, "Why in the world did not Hero . . . prove an 'alibi' in answer to the charge?" [10] Another reader of *Much Ado* considers "the disgrace of Hero an utterly incredible business." [11] We are even told that Shakespeare himself "could make little of her" and that he must have "asked himself what sort of woman must Hero be to take her dismissal so meekly, to swoon and 'die' . . . with no protest or reproof." [12] And what is one to think of the statement that "nubility is her sole characteristic and her only asset. Her duty is to look charming, conduct herself decorously and be a virgin." [13] From here it is only a short step to Granville-Barker's conclusion that "the end of the Claudio-Hero theme is cynically silly" [14] and to Richard David's casual reference to Hero as "a very dumb blonde—surely a beginner's part." [15]

Her uncle wishing undoubtedly to test her loyalty to her father and referring to the possibility of her future marriage, says, "Well niece, I trust you will be ruled by your father" (II, 1, 54). She does not reply, feeling, in all likelihood, that a daughter's obedience to her father is not a matter to be argued; on the other hand, she naturally refuses to commit herself. Beatrice who is present replies for her: "Yes faith, it is my cousin's duty to make curtsy and say, father, as it please you. But yet for all that cousin, let him be a handsome fellow, or else make another curtsy, and say, father, as it please me."

The dilemma that Hero has to face and that Friar Francis alone helps her to solve, is not of her own making. Does she "love" Claudio? She never says so. Her father's accusations seem to hurt her more than do Claudio's. This is revealed in her only attempt at self-defense addressed to Leonato. He has just now spoken of paternal love, significantly in terms of the purity of innocence that "belongs" to him: for her virginity is the most convincing symbol of patriarchal authority:

> But mine, and mine I loved, and mine I praised,
> And mine that I was proud on; mine so much
> That I myself was to myself not mine,
> Valuing of her. Why she, o she is fallen,
> Into a pit of ink, that the wide sea
> Hath drops too few to wash her clean again,
> And salt too little, which may season give
> To her foul tainted flesh. (IV, *1, 138*)

Hero, accepting Leonato's assumption that her innocence is his rather than hers to give away, replies—

> O my father,
> Prove you that any man with me conversed
> At hour unmeet, or that I yesternight
> Maintained the change of words with any creature,
> Refuse me, hate me, torture me to death. (IV, *1, 182*)

In *All's Well* assumed death is also Helena's solution to win Bertram's love. Her descent into the underworld of suffering includes an acceptance of devious ways of conduct that lead from deliberate deception to willing loss of virginity. Hero's anguish at being rejected by Claudio is as real as Helena's when Bertram mockingly refuses to consummate a marriage that he had never desired. Helena's "loss" is Hero's "gain": for the virginity that the former sacrifices to "prove" her love for Bertram, the latter keeps intact as evidence of *her* love for Claudio. Both are animated by similar emotions. In patriarchal societies such as those Shakespeare re-created in Renaissance France and in Renaissance Sicily it is the woman that is considered guilty before she can prove her innocence. Helena's guilt could easily be disproved: she merely consummates a marriage that has been legalized by the king. As for the assumption of Hero's guilt, it is equally absurd, for it is merely the result of Claudio's own lack of self-confidence regarding his virility, projected onto an imaginary rival whom he has "seen" on a dark and rainy night making love to Hero. The "rival" pertains to that kind of dream young men are likely to have who never yet truly loved and whose sexual experiences in the past have been founded on lust and not on tenderness and affection. Basically Bertram and Claudio are made of the same cheap metal: they are both sexual adventurers and therefore incapable of Eros and only superficially responsive to Logos.

This Hero then whose native element seems to be silence, "dies," as it were, into an even greater silence. Her resurrection, however, when it comes, is no rebirth. For she is the same after her "death" as she was before. She appears as a new Hero, while actually it is Claudio who has been reborn. His make-believe love has undergone a process of purification. Like Bertram he has done *nothing* to bring this about. Each of these young men is indeed prisoner of his anima, blindly following where his unconscious leads him. Neither of them comprehends the full value of the "sacrifice" to which the two young women submit. Only at the very last moment, and just before they are going to marry substitutes for those who have "died" for their sake, does the Eros in each respond to a Logos he can no longer deny. At last these shallow young men realize that to reach their aim, Hero and Helena have had to experience the ordeal of seeking their lovers through darkness, disguise, humiliation and pretended death until they find them.

When Shakespeare created Hero, not as a character but as a symbol of a woman's growth, he added to Viola's and Rosalind's pursuit of love through symbolic shipwreck and exile, the new dimension of death. Freed of her paternal animus, Hero can now easily be identified with archaic man's imaginary harvestmaid and corn-mother of which the most familiar mythical representatives are Demeter and Persephone in ancient Greek mythology: "The descent of Persephone into the lower world would thus be a mythical expression for the sowing of the seed: her reappearance in spring would signify the sprouting of the young corn. In this way the Persephone of one year becomes the Demeter of the next, and this may very well have been the original force of the myth." [16]

The rape of Persephone which in *Much Ado* is committed as it were by proxy as part of the make-believe world in which Hero lives, leads to her "descent." Viola's Illyria and Rosalind's Forest of Arden are still, if not geographically, at least psychologically conceivable. Hero's "death" within the framework of the artificial civilization of Messina has to be part of a wider illusion that embraces all human life. Therefore Hero's "maiden truth" has to be tested by human—that is, moral—not divine, standards. This can only be done by making the illusion of her death look like reality itself. Friar Francis then asks all those

present at the wedding in church to "do all rites / That apper-
tain unto a burial" (IV, 1, 209). It is he who explicitly refers to
Hero's ordeal as the precondition for her return from the dark:
"But on this travail look for greater birth" (IV, 1, 215). Claudio
takes up the theme of renewal when he reads out the scroll that
he is going to hang up on Hero's monument: "So the life that
died with shame / Lives in death with glorious fame" (V, 3, 7).
Lastly, the song that is being sung over her grave formally prays
to the "goddess of the night" to pardon "Those that slew thy
virgin knight." The ritual thus performed by Claudio as a form
of redemption from guilt once more refers to the miracle of rebirth when "Graves yawn, and yield your death, / Till death be
uttered" (V, 3, 19).

The prayer to the "goddess of the night" is spoken in a context of myth rather than naturalistic dramatic illusion. No analogy with real, familiar life is attempted. To a reader responsive
to the fundamental human ingredients of this scene rather than
to psychological subtleties—so conspicuously absent here—Hero
herself has become a "goddess of the night," a primal being
symbolizing woman's fate in an as yet undisclosed mythical form.
In this sense she may indeed be taken to be, whether we call her
Persephone, Artemis, or Psyche, "the symbol and expression of
all genesis and origination." [17] The Greeks called her by the
name of *Kore* which is simply the goddess "Maiden."

An application "in depth" of the Persephone myth might
well have been part of Shakespeare's vision when he dramatized
Hero's misfortunes in this play. Although, at first sight, it is
merely a story of mistaken identities and of near tragedy, leading
from wedding feast to funeral, he must have seen in it possibilities of tragic human experience that had been lying dormant
in it for ages. From the story as he knew it in conventional literary adaptations to the primeval myth, as it must have been re-
created in Shakespeare's own imagination, it was but a short step:
"Persephone was completely passive. She was picking flowers
when she was raped by the Lord of the Dead. . . . She was wor-

shipped in the most serious manner as the Queen of the Dead, and the rape of the bride was an allegory of death. Lost maidenhood and the crossing of the borders of Hades are allegorical equivalents." [18] Identification with such an equivocal primal figure means "to be pursued, to be robbed, raped, to fail to understand, to rage and grieve, but then to get everything back and be born again." [19] The association between wedding feast and funeral is of the very essence of the myth. It tells us of "the strange equation of marriage and death, the bridal chamber and the grave. Marriage in this connection has the character of murder. But not only does it call forth the lamentations of the celebrants, it also calls forth obscene speech and laughing at obscene actions. . . . We can speak of a connection between death and fertility." [20]

Hero's marriage is in the nature of a murder. The ceremony itself is interrupted by Claudio's gross references to her "savage sensuality" and the "obscene actions" that she committed in his sight. Her father adds his own comment on her "foul tainted flesh." That all this comes immediately after Borachio's whispered obscenities about "Pharaoh's soldiers in the reechy painting" and his remarks about Hercules' codpiece puts a symbolic emphasis on the sexual nature of the evil of which Claudio is guilty. A passive spectator of the "rape" that never was, he has now to redeem himself from an untruth that besmirches both him and Hero's over-credulous father. It is this "inner act" that alone justifies his ultimate reunion with Hero. In the mysteries of Eleusis, we are told, "the passivity of Persephone, of the bride, the maiden doomed to die, is re-experienced by means of an inner act—if only an act of surrender. Our sources speak of an 'imitation of Dionysian happenings.' As a sacrificial victim and one who is doomed, Dionysus is the male counterpart of Persephone." [21]

Persephone has been called the quintessence of all femininity, combining in one person all the virtues of endurance and patient suffering. Yet, she is a goddess and her fate divinely or-

dained: even her rebirth could only occur because of the intervention of the gods. For only gods were present at her rape and
heard her cry for help. But they "saw" nothing: the actual rape
took place "in darkness" after the earth had opened and a chasm
appeared in the Nysaean Fields from which Hades, the Lord of
the Underworld, sprang and carried the struggling maiden off.
These primal beings of the myth exist in a preconscious state
and therefore are not humanly aware of the consequences of
their action. They fulfill their godlike urges, they experience
pain and pleasure, in the mindless and uninhibited violence of
uncircumscribed time. Their local habitation and even their
names change with the ages. The conventional use that writers
make of such a myth supplies a bewildering variety of places
and names: in the most recent collection of source material for
Much Ado, and the Hero-Claudio theme in particular, eighteen
possible sources and analogues are mentioned,[22] written in Ital-
ian, French, Latin, German and English, between 1538 and 1601
alone. Yet the true analogy can be found in nonhistorical primordial time rather than the sixteenth century. For if Persephone is Hero's divine counterpart, the figure of Psyche in Apuleius'
retelling of the legend of Amor and Psyche in his *Golden Ass*
is her human equivalent.

The fact that the story "is still widely current as a primitive
folk tale in countries as far apart as Scotland and Hindustan," [23]
adds to the relevance of the analogy. All the elements that characterize the Persephone myth are there: a wedding turned into a
funeral, a rape committed in the dark, the disappearance of
Psyche, her deathlike sleep and her acquaintance with the underworld, her final return to life and light, and her rediscovery of
love. The one ingredient that is so conspicuously lacking in the
Persephone myth and that makes the Amor-Psyche legend a human allegory of love is the insistence on sight as a symbol of
human consciousness. Psyche, being human and a woman, wants
to "see" the face of the one who visits her at night. She expects
to find a monster "fierce and wild and of the dragon breed," one

that "makes his harvesting" with fire and sword, and infuses terror even into the "darksome river of the dead." [24] Instead, Psyche who was "a simple and gentle soul," [25] discovered "the kindest and sweetest of all wild beasts, Amor himself, fairest of gods and fair even in sleep." [26] She saw Eros by the light of a lantern.

Psyche who has not been unaware of the animal attraction of her nightly "rape" in the dark, now recognizes a more powerful attraction still, that of conscious love. The lantern which she holds in her hand throws a human rather than a divine light upon Eros and his love for her; it raises her from the ignorance of a mere physical identity with Eros to the all-illuminating consciousness of love. It is this new and as yet untested awareness of self that has to suffer loss and alienation, a descent into the underworld, the agonies of her three impossible labors patiently endured and successfully accomplished.

As part of a "psychology of encounter," [27] Psyche's ordeal is an allegory of the anguish that a woman's Logos may experience in its search for the true meaning of Eros. It also shows the way from the preconscious abandonment of physical encounter to the "travail of the personality leading through suffering to transformation and illumination." [28] When Claudio discovers "another" Hero it is a spiritually transformed Kore-Psyche, the "maiden truth" he has been unable to see before. His encounter with the new Hero returning from death corresponds to Eros finding Psyche asleep in the story as Apuleius tells it, after she has—like her primordial cousin Pandora—opened the casket given to her by Persephone as a gift to Venus. He *does* find her because all along it is Psyche, his own anima, that has guided him toward the liberation of the individual from the primordial mythical world, indeed toward the freeing of his own imprisoned soul. Her torments were his own in the same measure as her transformation will now be his as well. It is only now that the figures on the stage, as if awakening from a dream, become aware of the reality of human existence behind the veil of a make-believe civilization. They take off their masks and are themselves again.

Clinical observation of pathological behavior patterns in a situation resembling that which Shakespeare dramatized in *Much Ado* and *All's Well* may explain a good deal, though not all. According to this approach, Claudio and Bertram came to "know" their sexual partners in the dark, the former through the intermediary of an imaginary rival, the latter by mistaking one woman, his real wife, who he thinks does not arouse his libido, for another who is supposed to have yielded to his "sick desires." The knowledge they have thus gained is only partial, yet quite sufficient to arouse their passion. Only once in the play does Claudio show intense personal involvement: when he accuses Hero of having surrendered to sexual lust, while Bertram returns to Helena, whose inhibiting virginity has been disposed of by a trick, and who is now already (and as a result of his own sexual lust) a mother.

Freud provides a revealing though incomplete commentary to the love situation as developed by Shakespeare in these two plays. Dismissing as only partially correct what "poets and imaginative writers" have to say about the "conditions of love under which men and women make their choice of an object, and the way in which they reconcile the demands expressed in their phantasy with the exigencies of real life," he refers the reader to the impressions he collected during the psycho-analytic treatment of neurotics, and concludes that similar erotic behavior patterns are observable among "ordinary healthy persons," such as Claudio and Bertram may be supposed to be: ". . . a virtuous and reputable woman never possesses the charm required to exalt her to be an object of love; this attraction is exercised only by one who is more or less sexually discredited, whose fidelity and loyalty admit of some doubt. This last element may vary within the limits of significant series, from the faint breath of scandal attaching to a married woman who is not averse to flirtation up to the openly polygamous way of life of a prostitute, or of a *grande*

amoureuse—but the man who belongs to the type in question
will never dispense with something of the kind. . . . Not until
they have some occasion for jealousy does their passion reach its
height and the woman acquire her full value to them, and they
never fail to seize upon some incident by which this intensity of
feeling may thus be called out." [29]

This description may in a superficial way explain Claudio's
and Bertram's final and startling choice of love-objects. Yet
Freud's remark that writers are limited in expressing reality because "they have to evoke intellectual and aesthetic pleasure"
and therefore "can display no great interest . . . in the origin
and growth of those conditions of mind which they portray in
being" is true only when psycho-pathological criteria are applied.
If, on the other hand, the love metaphor that is being enacted on
Shakespeare's stage is taken to mean the groping of a man's soul
for his anima, the least stable element in his unconscious, and a
woman's quest for fulfillment through Logos rather than Eros,
then the individuals concerned in these love relationships can
no longer be judged as fulfilling their personal fate only, but as
sharing in a collective unconscious of the existence of which
Shakespeare must have been entirely unaware. Jung's description
of the tension resulting from the clash of contrary impulses that
is an intrinsic part of the anima-animus encounter fits Claudio's
and Bertram's otherwise incomprehensible conduct: "Affects
lower the level of the relationship and bring it closer to the common instinctual basis, which no longer has anything individual
about it. Very often the relationship runs its course heedless of
its human performers, who afterwards do not know what happened to them." [30] What then clinical observation reveals, are
those same transpersonal elements, in more extreme form than
can be seen in the behavior of perfectly "sane" persons. Yet
neither Claudio nor Hero ever fully realize what is happening
to them. Experiencing life through their unconscious their conduct can only be explained archetypically. Studies of character

and plot are no longer of much help, for the two lovers resemble the gods of the ancient world and together "they form a divine pair, one of whom, in accordance with his logos nature, is characterized by *pneuma* and *nous,* rather like Hermes with his ever-shifting hues, while the other, in accordance with her Eros nature, wears the features of Aphrodite, Helen (Selene), Persephone, and Hecate." [31]

As part of their individuation Claudio and Bertram accept and integrate the anima they have so contemptuously rejected before. In both cases a Wise Old Man is present to approve and give his blessing: Friar Francis in *Much Ado* and the rejuvenated King in *All's Well.* This, once more, corresponds to Jung's own conclusion: "The recognition of anima or animus gives rise, in a man, to a triad, one third of which is transcendent: the masculine subject, the opposing feminine subject, and the transcendent anima. . . . The missing fourth element that would make the triad a quarternity is, in a man, the archetype of the Wise Old Man. . . . These four constitute a half-immanent and half-transcendent quarternity, an archetype which I have called the marriage quarternio." [32]

[III]

THE HAMLET-OPHELIA RELATIONSHIP does not lend itself so readily to symbolical interpretation. For once, we know too little about it to indulge in generalizations. Ophelia herself admits to her father "I do not know, my lord, what I should think" when he questions her about the true nature of Hamlet's supposed love for her. Beyond this, Ophelia vaguely mentions Hamlet's "tenders of affection" and the "holy vows of heaven" with which he has given "countenance" to his declaration of love for her.

Only once—over Ophelia's grave—does Hamlet commit himself in public and in the presence of his mother and his uncle, when in an access of quite understandable fury at Laertes' "phrase of sorrow" he exclaims,

> I loved Ophelia: forty thousand brothers
> Could not, with all their quantity of love,
> Make up my sum. (v, *1*, *291*)

For the rest of the play, neither Ophelia nor Hamlet ever speak seriously about their love. They are never alone, but always under the watchful eye of Polonius, Hamlet's mother and his uncle. And as they know that they are being observed, they do not and cannot behave naturally. The only occasion when they have met face to face without anyone else being present is described by Ophelia to her father: it is Hamlet's farewell to her. No word is spoken by either of the two. Again Ophelia is uncertain as to the meaning of Hamlet's extraordinary behavior, for all she can say in reply to Polonius' question whether Hamlet is "mad for thy love" is: "My lord, I do not know, / But, truly, I do fear it" (II, 1, 85). Ophelia's attitude to Hamlet is characterized by lack of self-confidence. She does not seem to trust him; nor does she trust herself.

As for Hamlet, he confides in no one, not even Horatio, the only one to whom he might have spoken the truth of the matter, if indeed there was anything to be said about it at all. All that one gathers is that Ophelia's inner life (whatever there is of it) is dominated by a powerful paternal image which renders beyond her strength any transference of emotional allegiance from father to lover. Her weak and undeveloped ego utterly fails to stand up against the moral casuistry, the political know-how, the formal dogmatism of a father who symbolizes an essentially masculine Logos (however perverted it may appear to be), and therefore stands for a patriarchal way of life as represented by the court of Elsinore, ruled over by unscrupulous and cunning men who, like him, are ready to sacrifice their own souls for the achievement of some political or personal ambition. Ophelia feels attracted to

Hamlet, who must have seemed to her different from all the other men she has met at the court, endowed with a more complex sensitivity, given to brooding, yet capable of quick spontaneous action. Before his father's death, she has found in him

> The courtier's, soldier's, scholar's eye, tongue, sword;
> The expectancy and rose of the fair state,
> The glass of fashion and the mould of form,
> The observed of all observers. (iii, *1, 160*)

Placed between the two masculine extremes of extrovert father and introvert lover, Ophelia's unconscious, torn in opposite directions and quite incapable of any form of integration, "remained suspended, oscillating between her father and a man who was not altogether suitable. The progress of her life was thus held up, and that inner disunity so characteristic of a neurosis promptly made its appearance. The so-called normal person would probably be able to break the emotional bond in one or the other direction by a powerful act of will, or else—and this is perhaps the more usual thing—he would come through the difficulty unconsciously, on the smooth path of instinct." [33] The passage does not come from a critical study of *Hamlet,* but describes the case of one of Jung's women patients who had come to him because of "a mild hysterical neurosis" the cause of which he diagnosed as residing in a "father-complex." On the other hand, Hamlet's intense attachment to his mother (which forms no part of Jung's diagnosis) leading to his revulsion at her speedy re-marriage with a man who seems to him "unsuitable," appears to have prevented him from ever looking upon Ophelia as an object of love, though at one time, he himself implies, and Ophelia does not contradict it, she might have been an object of lust.

As neither instinct nor will are strong enough, Ophelia chooses the way of least resistance, that of obedience to her father. His "prescriptions" to her consist mostly of prohibitions regarding Hamlet and her meetings with him. The first long interview between father and daughter ends with Ophelia's words, "I shall obey, my lord" (I, 3, 136). To Polonius' question, "Have you given him any hard words of late?" she replies,

> No, my good lord; but as you did command,
> I did repel his letters, and denied
> His access to me. (II, *1, 107*)

Polonius is fully aware of his daughter's quite unusual loyalty. Since "obedience" is a social virtue much practiced at Elsinore, though for ulterior motives, Polonius, speaking with the king and the queen, stresses Ophelia's readiness to supply him with information regarding Hamlet's intentions toward her. The letter he reads out to them, supposedly written by Hamlet to Ophelia, and his own comments upon it, constitute an unintentional diagnosis of a young woman's split personality, alienated from her own ego, a victim of her father's compulsive preoccupation with patriarchal codes of conduct. According to this diagnosis Ophelia stands where her father's shadow falls. He, in effect, describes a daughter's inability to free her anima from her father's Logos, a situation that Shakespeare frequently hinted at, before and after he wrote *Hamlet,* in a variety of father-daughter relationships:

> I have a daughter, have whilst she is mine,
> Who in her duty and obedience, mark,
> Hath given me this. . . . (II, 2, *106*)

> This, in obedience, hath my daughter shown me:
> And more above, hath his solicitings,
> As they fell out by time, by means and place,
> All given to mine ear. . . . (II, 2, *125*)

> And then I prescripts gave her,
> That she should lock herself from his resort,
> Admit no messengers, receive no tokens,
> Which done, she took the fruits of my advice. . . . (II, 2, *142*)

The scene ends with Polonius' infamous suggestion to "loose my daughter to him" in order to discover whether it is "hot love on the wing" that troubles Hamlet or "something in his soul . . . O'er which his melancholy sits on brood" and which might prove to be "some danger" to the person of the king. Ophelia continues to the end to be a willing tool in her father's hand. Being deprived of Eros by Hamlet's unconscious attachment to his mother, while her father's Logos inhibits whatever attempts she might have made to "be herself," all that she can do is to disguise her own emotional ambiguity "with devotion's visage / And pious action" from the one man who was most in need of a guidance she could not give.

Father and lover alike contribute to Ophelia's ultimate loss of identity. In her madness the disintegration of her personality takes its inevitable course: faced by divided loyalties that are irreconcilable, her unconscious is split into apparently meaningless fragments. The songs she sings emanate from some hidden layers of her unconscious that had to be repressed by her conscious mind in the past. We are told that in her madness "she speaks much of her father" (IV, 5, 4), and actually some of her songs evidently refer to the death and burial of Polonius. Some other songs, however, are frankly bawdy, telling the story of a young and chaste maid who lost her virginity one early morning on St. Valentine's Day because she wanted to, and because "Young men will do't, if they come to't / By Cock, they are to blame" (IV, 5, 61). This particular young man's only motive for having "done it," is revealing: he would indeed have married her, and of his own free will too, he implies, "And thou hadst not come to my bed."

What are we to make of the obviously compulsive nature of Ophelia's songs? They express sexual fantasies which in part may be wish-fulfillments but may also be reminiscences of happenings in her own life that she had until then successfully repressed. Her own loss of virginity might have been "imaginary"—as in the case of chaste Hero—or "real"—as in the case of Helena. In the previous plays the loss of virginity, whether real or imaginary, led to a return to sanity which had only temporarily been threatened. Ophelia's chastity—as far as her conscious life is concerned —has never been put to doubt; yet she dies like one who has known not merely the significance of the sexual act; but beyond the limited knowledge of personal fulfillment, her unconscious appears to participate in an experience of far vaster dimensions than her simple songs might indicate. As part of a fertility ritual emanating from her unconscious—liberated only in her madness from the paternal image—she enacts in her death the archetypal drowning of a vegetation spirit.[34] She finds her death among flowers floating on the surface of the water, some of which evoke sexual associations. They were known as "long purples . . . that liberal shepherds give a grosser name / But our cold maids do dead men's fingers call them" (IV, 7, 170). We are, rather irrelevantly, informed in a footnote to this passage in the Variorum edition first published in 1877, that the "long purples" were known by "various names too gross for repetition. . . ." but that "one of the grosser names Gertrude had a particular reason to avoid—the rampant widow." [35]

Ophelia's return to the element of water of which she was "a creature native and indued" symbolizes her disintegrating consciousness. When she is pulled to her "muddy death," her ego is finally destroyed and she returns to her original state as an anima figure. Though it appears to be a regression into insanity and suicide, her association in death with water, flowers, and spring points toward rebirth. We have met this renewal pattern before, though under different guises. It is inherent in Shakespeare's symbolic portrayal of a woman's growth from Maid to Mother. It must have lain dormant in Shakespeare's creative imagination when, at a later stage, he let Cordelia fulfill her fate as her father's anima, and created Miranda rising out of the water into which Ophelia had sunk, embodying a chastity consciously preserved and knowingly shared with her lover.

[IV]

CORDELIA HAS AROUSED little or no curiosity among amateur psychologists. In her case, questions that were asked concerning Hero's incomprehensible conduct, Helena's obstinate pursuit of Bertram, or Ophelia's escape into madness, are seen to be no longer relevant. Cordelia exists on a different plane of reality, if indeed it *is* reality that provides the criteria by which Cordelia and her relationship to her father should be understood.

The nineteenth century tended to see in Cordelia a morally ambiguous figure. Coleridge first spoke of "some little faulty admixture of pride and sullenness in Cordelia's 'Nothing'" in reply to her father's question: "Which of you shall we say doth love us most?" (I, 1, 53). The next step in assessing Cordelia's behavior in the first scene of the play was to see in her own suffering and death a kind of divine punishment inflicted upon her for not having lived up to her father's expectation of her. Moral judgment then becomes the touchstone by which Cordelia's death is to be understood. She failed her father and therefore had to die: "Cordelia pays the penalty of the fault she committed when, instead of affectionately humouring the weakness of her aged father, she met him with unfilial forwardness, and answered his, no doubt, foolish questions with unbecoming harshness, and asperity." [36]

If however one disregards her supposed initial "tragic" fault, she may be considered to be a victim of circumstances over which she had no control—her father's peculiar request to articulate her love for him, her sisters' hypocrisy and cruelty, a machiavellian society that, from the very outset, defeated the minority of honest people represented by herself, Kent, and Edgar. Then her death may be seen as the senseless culmination of her suffering, brought about not by herself but by powers of evil which she was too tender and gentle to resist. One may accordingly look upon her in the end "simply, as we regard Ophelia or Desdemona, as an innocent victim swept away in the convulsion caused by the error or guilt of others." [37]

Such a naturalistic interpretation of Cordelia starts with the assumption that she is a "character" having to fulfill a given dramatic function in the time, space, and action of the play. Nothing could be further from the truth as Shakespeare appears to have conceived it: Cordelia is seen on the stage in only four scenes and speaks less than a hundred lines. To the literary critic accustomed to apply standards of reality to the figures Shakespeare created, she constitutes an even greater dilemma than Hero, Helena, or Ophelia. *They* at least participated in the main action of the play: Cordelia appears to be peripheral, hardly more than a disembodied spirit, and, on superficial reading, enduring her suffering and ultimate death in utmost passivity.

Though Cordelia is physically absent from the stage most of the time, her presence is felt throughout the play as a focus of metaphorical significance. Having been rejected by one man, her father, and chosen by another, her future husband, the King of France, for exactly the same reason, namely her inability to express her love in words, she—as Freud has pointed out—resembles the symbol of the leaden casket rejected by the Prince of Morocco and the Prince of Arragon, but chosen by Bassanio, in *The Merchant of Venice*. Her silence which brings her father's curse upon her has a leaden quality, and, whether it is the result of pride or humility, it turns her into a symbol of all that is inarticulate—nature, the earth, and even the supernatural. By not speaking out, she remains defenseless; unable to communicate her love through language, and having nothing else to communicate *but* her love, she is made to disappear, not in order to pursue an unwilling lover, but to convert an unbelieving father to her love. Her husband makes his choice as a matter of moral conviction. We are not told whether he "loves" her. Cordelia, now that she has been cast out of her father's heart, appears to the one who chooses her "most rich, being poor, / Most

choice, forsaken; and most lov'd, despised" (I, 1, 253). This second
Bassanio is never seen on the stage again. Yet he does all in his
power to alleviate Cordelia's suffering for her father: out of pity
for her "mourning and importun'd tears," he sends his army
along with her to England to restore her father's kingship. It is,
she says, "But love, dear love, and our ag'd father's right" (IV,
4, 28), that made him do it. He is not present at the reunion
between father and daughter, having in the meantime returned
to France where his presence "was most requir'd and necessary."

Shakespeare, throughout the play, looks upon Cordelia as a
daughter rather than a wife. Her marriage, at the beginning of
King Lear, does not fundamentally change her metaphorical significance. Yet she does not transfer her emotional allegiance from
father-figure to husband as Shakespeare's young women do so
easily in his comedies, and as Desdemona unhesitatingly accomplishes when she elopes with Othello (though her marriage,
ultimately, kills her father when "pure grief / Shore his old
thread in twain" [V, 2, 203]). Their reunion is not solely the
result of Lear's unconscious search for his lost daughter, but is
also Cordelia's conscious attempt to assist her father in his dark
groping toward her love.

Freud, in an early essay, entitled "The Theme of the Three
Caskets," relates Lear's rejection of and ultimate return to Cordelia almost at the very moment of his death, to the symbolism
of dreams as expressed in folk legends and myths. He starts with
a number of assumptions which must be understood in order to
enable the reader to accept his conclusions:

a) "Cordelia masks her true self, becomes as unassuming as
   lead, she remains dumb, she 'loves and is silent'."

b) Concealment, disappearance, dumbness . . . are in dreams
   "an unmistakable symbol of death."

c) Lear's choice of the fairest and best among his three daugh-
   ters "was prepared by an ancient ambivalence. . . . The
   Goddess of Love herself, who now took the place of the
   Goddess of Death, had once been identical with her."

d) "Cordelia *is* Death." [38]

Freud starts his illuminating though controversial essay by referring the reader to three myths in all of which occurs the same initial situation as in *King Lear,* the choice to be made among three sisters, of whom the youngest is declared to be the fairest or the most virtuous. Paris chooses Aphrodite, Cinderella is preferred by the prince to two elder sisters, and Psyche in the tale of Apuleius is the youngest and fairest of three sisters. Freud mentions a number of dreams and fairy tales, the symbolism of which connects "plainness" or "paleness" with death, and caskets "like boxes large or small, baskets, and so on" with women or, as Freud puts it, "symbols of the essential thing in women." A man's choice of a woman—insofar as myths and dreams are concerned—is transformed "by virtue of a displacement that is not infrequent" into a choice, inescapable in the case of Lear, of death. For Lear, being an old man, has nothing to expect from women but to be received again into the womb of Mother Earth. In this sense the "youngest daughter" is one of the Fates, the Parcae or the Norns, the third of whom is called Atropos, the inexorable. They were originally known as the Graces and the Horae, the Hours, dispensing rain and dew, divine representatives of the Seasons, and goddesses of vegetation. Presiding over the laws of nature they symbolized the unalterable succession of birth, growth and death, not only in nature but in man's life as well. The names of these three Spinners, Freud tells us, hint at the equivocal relationship between man and his fate: "Lachesis, the name of the second, seems to mean 'the accidental within the decrees of destiny' . . . while Atropos means 'the inevitable'—Death—and then for Clotho there remains 'the fateful tendencies each one of us brings into the world.' "

Thus, according to Freud, the ancient identity between the goddess who gives life and fertility and the goddess who brings death and destruction is to be found in the figure of Cordelia. And he points out that there really is no "free choice" at all "if every kind of evil is not to come about, as in *Lear*": for, he con-

tinues, "eternal wisdom, in the garb of the primitive myth, bids
the old man renounce love, choose death and make friends with
the necessity of dying."

The Jungian as distinguished from the Freudian approach
reaches different conclusions. Cordelia is seen as a power of redemption, a "healer" whose curative gifts are rooted in the earth.
Like nature herself she unifies all contradictory elements into
one. In her grief she is "Sunshine and rain at once, her smiles
and tears / Were like a better way" (IV, 3, 20). Her tears are compared to "holy water," not merely fertilizing the earth, but also
intended as a medicine to cure her father. She implores the earth
to help her in doing this:

> All bless'd secrets,
> All you unpublished virtues of the earth,
> Spring with my tears! be aidant and remediate
> In the good man's distress. (IV, *4, 17*)

To alleviate her father's suffering she has to apply her remedies
to mankind as a whole. It is as if Shakespeare had created her as
a symbol for universal redemption and as if he wanted to portray
Cordelia's final encounter with her father as symbolizing the
primordial encounter of father and daughter in terms of God,
the creator, and the soul that is his own handiwork, and without
which no life at all would be possible. For this is implied in the
most inclusive definition given of Cordelia:

> Thou hast one daughter,
> Who redeems nature from the general curse
> Which twain have brought her to. (IV, *6, 210*)

Freud emphasizes the symbolical significance of Cordelia to
such an extent that Lear appears somewhat diminished, a very
old, dying man whose "choice" (and previous rejection) of his
third daughter (as the goddess of Death) is imposed upon him by
the ineluctability of death itself. All that Freud proves (and this
hardly required the assistance of myths and dreams) is that Lear,
in his reunion with Cordelia, "makes friends with the necessity

of dying," and thus the "leaden casket" he recognized too late is turned into a coffin.[39]

But surely Lear is a more complex figure than this; his is a complexity which—in spite of the fact that we see Cordelia so rarely on the stage—is reflected in her reaction to her father and in the judgment others pass on him. These judgments stand for contrary states of being: for Lear is subjected to inner changes as part of the process of his own individuation. These apparently contradictory aspects of his personality are given prominence by the various speakers. Thus we have no reason to doubt the correctness of Goneril's and Regan's cold-blooded assessment of their father, immediately after his rejection of Cordelia: "he hath ever but slenderly known himself . . ." (I, 1, 297). Although they associate this uncontrolled choleric behavior with "the infirmity of his old age," they also remember "the imperfections of long-engraffed condition"—evidently implying that his blood and judgment had never been "well commingled." Kent's almost simultaneous acceptance of Lear as "master" because his countenance radiates "authority," seems to contradict Goneril's and Regan's previous estimate of their father. Yet their exaggerated Logos and Kent's emotionally determined submission to the old man's disintegrating spirit complement each other. The Fool's caustic remarks to Lear reveal an equal distribution of Logos and Eros elements: he speaks to his master with the affection of one who has seen through all pretences and who, therefore, is left without any charitable illusions as regards Lear's fatherhood and kingship. When he tells Lear that he is "an O without a figure" and some lines later answers Lear's question "who is it that can tell me what I am?" with a wistful "Lear's shadow," he thereby illustrates the essential "nothingness" of Lear's condition which his two daughters had been the first to recognize through their intellects, while he, the Fool, impelled to follow his master almost against his better convictions, becomes aware of it through shared suffering.

When Cordelia asks the gods (in the presence of a doctor) to cure "th'untuned and jarring senses / Of this child-changed father" (IV, 7, 16), thinking of him as a child, a "poor *perdu*," and in need of a mother's nursing care, she adds a new dimension to the picture of her father's purgatory that started with Lear's rejection of the one he loved most "and thought to set my rest / On her kind nursery" (I, 1, 125). Lear as the archetype of fatherhood combines the opposing elements that constitute the dual nature of the paternal image: he is both tyrannical and seeking protection, he possesses "authority" and is a child lost in the storm, he "divides" his kingdom only to be divided against his own self. He is indeed a symbol for the "splitting of the father figure when considered in the light of the ambivalent attitude of child towards parent." [40] This split is given symbolic expression through the cruelty of Lear's two daughters, on the one hand, and Cordelia's tenderness, on the other. What we see on the stage is one and the same Lear moving from his "darker purpose" through old age "foolishness" to redemption.

Goneril and Regan see their father in terms of the inner division that the father-figure symbolizes for them. It is a reflection of their own unconscious image of paternal and irresponsible tyranny and its opposite, the protection-seeking "foolish fond old man" in need of feminine support, be it that of daughter, wife, or mother. Yet the image that is thus reflected is also that of Lear's own unconscious come to the surface and made "visible" after a long period of time during which this unconscious remained successfully repressed. His "tragedy" then (of which Freud has nothing to say) lies in his initial inability to face his own individuation, his refusal to accept self-knowledge when Goneril and Regan supply him with all the tools necessary to achieve it. They literally force individuation upon him: but he turns toward Cordelia whose love—expressed through silence—is foolishly misconstrued as indifference or even worse. The "ailing king," at the beginning of *King Lear,* stands for the mana personality that has been invaded by the forces of his own unconscious, no longer an archetype of self but an incomplete ego swallowed up in his own "darker purpose." The intended division of his kingdom in terms of "divided" and calculated love, results in his mistaken preference for the Logos of his two elder daughters and the rejection of Eros, his own anima, as symbolized by Cordelia.

Even this misguided choice between animus and anima need not have led to tragedy had Lear been able to control the consequences of such a choice. This would have been possible so long as the tendencies of the conscious and the unconscious did not diverge too greatly. Cordelia's refusal to cooperate with her father's "darker purpose" resulted in Lear's affect-reaction which, at first sight, is so incomprehensible to the normally constituted mind. It is then that "these functions [of anima and animus], harmless till then, confront the conscious mind in personified form, and behave rather like systems split off from the personality, or like part souls . . . [therefore] both these archetypes possess a fatality that can on occasion produce tragic results. They are quite literally the father and mother of all the disastrous entanglements of fate, and have long been recognized as such by the whole world." [41]

The final resolution of tragedy takes place on the human, not the political, plane. When the play ends, we come to see Lear through the tears of his youngest daughter, just as we see her through his tear-dimmed eyes as a "soul in bliss." The knowledge he acquires is that of patience in the face of reality. But this reality encompasses all the best and the worst that can be known of nature and of man. Having rediscovered his "soul," he experiences death itself as a form of renewal. Thus Cordelia seems to watch over "Lear's purgatorial progress to self-knowledge," [42] and as the play moves towards its harrowing conclusion she becomes in ever-increasing measure a symbol of perfection and "an absolute of human experience." [43]

When Lear imagines their life in prison as a return to paradise, a permanent retreat from the reality of human society, he visualizes it in terms of innocence regained. In this primordial world they will at last find solitude. There they will sing "like birds i'th'cage" and "tell old tales, and laugh / At gilded butter-flies. . . ." (V, 3, 12). They will leave behind them the "packs and sects of great ones / That ebb and flow by the moon." Instead of court news, the rise and fall of trivial reputations, they will take upon them "the mystery of things." Looking down upon the petty world of men from their walled prison, they will be like "God's spies"—though still of this world, but no longer participating in the senseless game of gaining and losing power.

[V]

THE PICTURE Lear projects is fully realized at the beginning of *The Tempest* when Prospero and Miranda, a resurrected father and his daughter, are found to be living on their island, a "wall'd prison" that had kept them isolated from the sort of reality experienced in Shakespeare's previous plays by less uncommon fathers and their daughters. Prospero's self-knowledge is complete: it is a civilizing power that transforms Nature into Art and makes that Art look as if it were Nature. If Miranda is "ignorant" of what she is, Prospero will teach her to "know herself." The story he tells her deals indeed with "court news"—"who's in, who's out," the handy-dandy of political existence in Renaissance Italy. It is the story of his own failure as a king. He might equally have failed as a father, had not she supported him; it is like an echo from *King Lear,* when we hear Prospero say

> O, a cherubin
> Thou wast that did preserve me. Thou didst smile,
> Infused with a fortitude from heaven. (I, 2, *152*)

Yet, true self-knowledge can come to Miranda only after the arrival of Ferdinand on the island. It is her naive reaction to the young man's disturbing intrusion into the innocence of her life, and her father's constant admonition to discipline their emotions that open the way toward a mature understanding of her own self. Her love for Ferdinand is in no way different from that known at first sight by Rosalind for Orlando and by Viola for Orsino. It grows in stature from her first candid admission— "I might call him / A thing divine; for nothing natural / I ever saw so noble" (I, 2, 414)—to the tears she sheds because of her unworthiness "that dare not offer / What I desire to give; and much less to take / What I shall die to want" (III, 1, 77).

In previous plays the giving and the taking of innocence resulting in loss of virginity, was an act shrouded in mystery and performed either by proxy as part of a premarital wish-fulfillment (as in *Much Ado*), or through disguise and deception in order to compel a husband to consummate a marriage (as in *All's Well*), or in terms of uncontrolled and socially undesirable impulses (as hinted at in Ophelia's song). In each of these cases the sexual act itself, whether imagined or real, was related to psychic phenomena residing in the unconscious and therefore largely uncontrolled. Insofar as it is an instinctual act carried out from necessity, and frequently without conscious motivation, it constitutes an archetype of the collective unconscious, symbolically represented by the darkness surrounding it. Even the "knowledge" gained by it appears to be "dark," "threatening," "forbidden." For what the act reveals is knowledge of the unconscious as it invades the affective life of those that share in it. The disciplining power of consciousness has no place in it unless the sexual act itself becomes part of a civilizing process which corresponds to a kind of collective individuation. This is what Prospero attempts when he imposes chastity on Ferdinand as a necessary element in his premarital love for Miranda. A comparison between Polonius' advice to his daughter within the corrupt society of Elsinore and Prospero's teaching might indicate how greatly Shakespeare's insight into unregenerate human nature has matured between these two plays. For Polonius

speaks to Ophelia in the language of the court, assuming that a
prince's vows could not be anything but

> . . . mere implorators of unholy suits,
> Breathing life sanctified and pious bonds,
> The better to beguile. (I, 3, 129)

Polonius' frame of reference is *social,* in a peculiarly diminishing
sort of way. Love is then no longer determined by individual
purity of intention or by sexual innocence which (considering
that Polonius must have witnessed and approved Gertrude's
"compulsive ardour" which led to her present marriage) he
would scarcely look for in the morally rank society of which he
is the chief magistrate.

Prospero is fully aware of the threat posed by the arrival of
Ferdinand on his island. For the court at Naples in which
Ferdinand was brought up, and where he must have been
aware of the machiavellian conduct of Antonio, Prospero's
brother, was no better than the court at Elsinore. To bring all
this home to Miranda, Prospero first calls him a spy, then a
traitor, and lastly an impostor whose conscience he describes
in terms of the civilization from which he came—for it "is
possess'd with guilt" like Caliban's.

It is a fairy-tale trial of love that Prospero stages for the
benefit of his daughter. Ferdinand is by no means innocent,
for he has known and "liked" other women, though "never
any / With so full soul," and one may imagine that he—though
no Claudio and no Bertram—was not ignorant of the delights of
love. Miranda has never seen any man except her father and
Caliban, the one representing the apex of human consciousness,
the other a fearful symbol of uncontrolled instinctual drives.
Only Prospero knows that there is a Caliban hidden in every
Ferdinand: this explains the "trial" and the final command,
addressed to the young man in almost religious solemnity, to
respect Miranda's virginity until her marriage day. We have
gone a long way from Polonius' courtly chatter:

> But
>
> If thou break her virgin-knot before
> All sanctimonious ceremonies may
> With full and holy rite be minister'd,
> No sweet aspersion shall the heavens let fall
> To make this contract grow; but barren hate,
> Sour-ey'd disdain and discord shall bestrew
> The union of your bed with weeds so loathly
> That you shall hate it both: therefore take heed,
> As Hymen's lamps shall light you. (IV, *1, 14*)

Ferdinand's reply uses imagery taken from the language of primordial myth. Though this may appear unnecessarily conventional in the mouth of a young man very much in love, it fits in with Prospero's own seriousness. His "honour," would "take away"

> The edge of that day's celebration
> When I shall think, or Phoebus steeds are foundered
> Or Night kept chain'd below. (IV, *1, 29*)

Should lust overwhelm him, he implies, it would be as if the horses of the sun had stumbled in darkness and the moon had been prevented from rising, he himself having become a prisoner of his own unconscious.

This is the ultimate innocence of self-knowledge transmitted by Prospero to bridegroom and bride. It is also the least sophisticated form of perfection we have encountered so far. Deprived of all the trappings of an artificial civilization they are "blessed" in a way that no previous pair of lovers ever was. They can leave Prospero's island, that demi-paradise of human consciousness, to set sail for Naples carrying with them an ideal image of paternal perfection which, one is permitted to hope, will help them to face whatever Prospero's "Art" had left imperfect in man's nature.

6

Eros: Sons & Mothers

T HE ABSENCE of any significant mother-figure in Shakespeare's portrayal of a young woman's growth from adolescence to maturity is of considerable psychological interest. Rosalind, Viola, Portia, Hero, Helena, and Cordelia are motherless—their own psychic femininity encompasses all the stages of a woman's development from girlhood to motherhood. The four scenes in which Cordelia appears on the stage in *King Lear* symbolize the range of her growth, for while it is as father and child that Lear and Cordelia speak in the first scene of the play, she addresses him as if she were a mother in search of her lost child when she meets him again after the storm. Lear then is her "poor *perdu*" in need of maternal comfort and tender care.

Shakespeare's young women carry the germ of motherhood within them long before they are married. Had mothers accompanied them in any of these plays, these maternal images might have proved formidable obstacles to the young women's individuation. What mother would have put up with Rosalind's inexplicable infatuation with Orlando, Viola's unreasonable attachment to Orsino, or Portia's fervent declaration of selfless love addressed to Bassanio? The young women's fathers, on the other hand, fulfilled a very real psychological need, that of being

the recipient of their daughters' anima-projection long before
the lover and prospective husband appeared on the stage.

Though generally in Shakespeare's plays sons, for equally obvious psychological reasons, are fatherless, their mothers, in a
few exceptional instances, are very much in evidence. Hamlet
and Coriolanus fail to reach the stage in their development
where individuation might still have been possible, because their
egos are defeated, or as Jung would have said, "swallowed," by
mother-figures, each invariably a projection of the son's unconscious. These are exceptional sons because, as a rule, Shakespeare's young protagonists enter the play at a time when such
projections can be or have already been successfully transferred
from mother to beloved. Orlando, Orsino, Bassanio (though not
Claudio, in *Much Ado,* or Bertram, in *All's Well*) are free of
any unconscious maternal attachment. Hamlet and Coriolanus
are bound to singularly destructive anima-figures whose strength
easily overpowers the sons' as yet insecure egos. Thus, while
Hamlet deplores his mother's "frailty" by which he means her
uncontrolled "appetite," her "wicked speed" and "dexterity,"
he is equally appalled by her strength, her hypocrisy, her un-
questioning acceptance of evil, her readiness to find excuses for
herself, and the sexual bondage in which she holds her present
husband.

A mother's "frailty" may indeed be her most powerful weapon
in the war between the sexes. The more cynical the son's attitude to women in general, the more readily will he attribute
to his mother those vices that he expects to find in any other
woman. Bertram, in *All's Well,* as every Don Juan, "unconsciously seeks his mother in every woman he meets." [1] Thus,
when he lusts after Diana, he tries to persuade her that all she
has to do is to conform to her mother's conduct when she
[Diana] was conceived. Her reply,

> My mother did but duty; such, my lord,
> As you owe to your wife, (IV, 2, *12*)

fails to impress him. Though he looks for a mother-image in her, he is not ready to play the husband/father.

Troilus, neither a cynic nor a Don Juan, is similarly disposed to generalize on mothers in terms of woman's "frailty." What may well appear to be Cressida's destructive strength as an anima-figure provokes Troilus' amazement, "Let it not be believed of womanhood / Think we had mothers—" (V, 2, 126). Though Troilus never before has shown any particular insight into a mother's psyche, he now projects his own image of purity and loyalty onto an ideal mother-figure to which, as a matter of psychic identity, Cressida should conform. Ulysses, standing by his side and looking at Cressida's willing response to Diomedes' amorous advances, supplies the worldly-wise, the disilliusioned point of view, "What hath she done, Prince, that can soil our mothers?". What Ulysses sees when he gazes into Diomedes' tent, differs considerably from Troilus' emotionally distorted vision. Ulysses accepts Cressida's responsiveness to Diomedes' love-making as a matter of sexual expediency. He has never expected Cressida to behave differently. Neither his nor anyone else's mother is involved in what is to Troilus an experience, not merely of love betrayed, but of future motherhood dishonored.

Even married men may, in moments of emotional crisis, generalize upon their wives' real or imagined disloyalty in terms of a mother's "frailty." When Leontes, in *Winter's Tale,* neurotically aware of his supposed rival's greater sexual attraction, succumbs to an unresolved conflict of which he had previously been unaware, he addresses his little boy in the disillusioned language of Ulysses. Hermione, just as Cressida, is no better than any "daughter of the game":

> . . . Thy mother plays, and I
> Play too. . . .
> It is a bawdy planet, that will strike
> When 'tis predominant. (I, 2, 187)

Posthumous, in *Cymbeline,* similarly generalizes upon the frailty
of motherhood when he is led to believe that his wife Imogen
has committed adultery.

> We are all bastards,
> And that most venerable man, which I
> Did call my father, was I know not where
> When I was stamped. Some coiner with his tools
> Made me a counterfeit: yet my mother seem'd
> The Dian of the time. (II, 5, 2)

A mother's frailty, then, is the projection of a son's psychic
disability that prevents integration of the self. It is but a short
step from his assumption of being a bastard because of his
mother's unchastity to his fear of emasculation because of a
mother's indomitable anima. For to be "swallowed" by one's
own mother is identical with the loss of one's manhood.
Coriolanus, at the moment of yielding to his mother's plea, uses
explicitly sexual imagery to emphasize the defeat of his ego:

> Well, I must do't:
> Away, my disposition, and possess me
> Some harlot's spirit! My throat of war be turn'd,
> Which quiréd with my drum, into a pipe
> Small as a eunuch's, or the virgin's voice
> That babies lull asleep! (III, 2, *110*)

In each of these instances the mother is felt to be an obstacle
to the full development of the ego. The sense of psychic impotence, of opportunities for a fuller life left unused, of never
truly achieving selfhood, grows in proportion as the strength of
the anima-projection is made conscious. It lies in the nature of
these relationships between son and mother that full consciousness is excluded. At best, the son may "psychologize" *about* the
relationship without being able to establish a psychic equilibrium between the opposing forces of his conscious ego and his
anima-dominated unconscious.

Cassius, in *Julius Caesar,* is a perfect example of the instability resulting from an unequal distribution of these psychic aspects of his personality. His only emotional attachment, as revealed in Act IV, is to Brutus, himself married to a woman of a strongly animus-oriented nature. Neither Cassius in his relation to Brutus, nor Brutus himself in his relation to his wife, shows emotional maturity. Portia complains of her husband's casual treatment of her which makes her "Brutus' harlot, not his wife." She hints at her "once commended beauty," but emphasizes the paternal image under which she grew up—"A woman well reputed, Cato's daughter," and enquires from her husband whether he could ever doubt her superiority over other women "being so father'd and so husbanded?" (II, 1, 297).

The meanings of "frailty" and "strength" are reversed throughout *Julius Caesar.* Portia is shown in her talk with Brutus to possess a masculine power of endurance. Later on, she commits suicide by swallowing fire, itself a masculine symbol when contrasted to the "maternal" water in which Ophelia drowns, making even her death conform to her Logos-dominated nature. On the other hand, Cassius who speaks so eloquently of his feelings of friendship for Brutus, and who "cannot drink too much of Brutus' love" (IV, 3, 161), is unmarried and evidently subject to quite feminine fits of temper. Brutus formulates this anima aspect of Cassius' personality when he says,

> O Cassius, you are yoked with a lamb
> That carries anger as the flint bears fire,
> Who, much enforced, shows a hasty spark,
> And straight is cold again. (III, *4, 109*)

This is a different fire from the one that Portia swallowed. It burns by fits and starts, it illumines nothing, it gives no warmth, it is symbolic of what other Shakespearean characters have defined as a woman's "frailty." Cassius himself is fully aware of such feminine characteristics in men. For, at the beginning of

the play, he relates the degeneracy of present day Romans to
the predominance of a maternal spirit that has vanquished their
former manly heroism.

> Our fathers' minds are dead,
> And we are govern'd with our mothers' spirits;
> Our yoke and sufferance show us womanish. (I, 3, 82)

Later on, in his quarrel with Brutus, he blames himself for
having been defeated by his own inner femininity:

> Have you not love enough to bear with me,
> When that rash humour which my mother gave me
> Makes me forgetful? (IV, 3, 118)

This passage is significant not because it stresses a disposition
of fecklessness inherited from his mother, but because of his
conscious identification with the anima archetype, here symbolized by a maternal image. In one of the very few passages in
Jung's work where Shakespeare is mentioned, he refers to Cassius' "womanish yearning for love and his despairing self-abandonment under the proud masculine will of Brutus. . . ."
thereby emphasizing (what the more conventional kind of Shakespeare criticism may find hard to accept) Cassius' "infantile disposition, which is as always characterized by a predominance of
the parental image, in this case that of the mother. . . ." Jung's
illuminating summing-up of Cassius' essential immaturity may
be applicable to a few other Shakespearean heroes who failed in
their attempts at meaningful relationships with members of the
opposite sex, or succeeded only after passing through the vicissitudes of an unresolved conflict between the direction that their
libido takes and their anima-dominated personality: "So far
as his emotional life is concerned, he has not yet caught up with
himself, as is often the case with people who are apparently so
masterful towards life and their fellows, but who have remained
infantile in regard to the demands of feelings." [2]

[II]

IN MOST PRECEDING INSTANCES the mother-image represents a psychic archetype that stands in the way of man's individuation. Regardless of whether the mother is actually present on the stage, as in *Hamlet* or in *Coriolanus,* or is merely part of a psychic constellation, as in Cassius' case, or, finally, is both a stage-figure and an image, as is the Countess of Roussilon in *All's Well,* she stands at the core of an apparently insoluble conflict situation. Any attempt at untying the knot involves a fusing of the son's ego-consciousness with the unconscious contents of his psyche symbolized by his mother. This attempt is likely to fail when the son's anima-projection has already led to either "boundless fascination, over-evaluation, and infatuation" or to "misogyny in all its graduation and variants." None of these psychic manifestations "can be explained by the real nature of the 'object' in question, but only by a transference of the mother-complex." [3]

While mothers are comparatively rare as stage figures in Shakespeare's dramatic universe, the maternal image as archetype, however, constitutes Shakespeare's "gateway into the unconscious." [4] This "gateway" is frequently described in terms of a metaphor relating the mother to the earth, her "womb" being both the origin of all life and the burial-place after death, the figurative darkness which man leaves behind when he is born and to which he returns when he dies. Most of his life is spent in yearning for a return to his mother earth and for a renewal of life-creating forces from contact with it. Thus the earth that sustains man in his life and gives him shelter in his death, is Shakespeare's favorite maternal metaphor for a collective unconscious hidden in "the womb of time" and therefore not perceivable by man except in rare moments of conscious rationalization.

That Shakespeare always thought of the earth as a mother-archetype is indicated in many passages that emphasize the earth's moral indifference toward what is being born and what dies. When Miranda tells her father that "good wombs have borne bad sons," she formulates the intrinsically ambivalent conclusion of Shakespeare's lifetime preoccupation with the mystery of birth—as a moral rather than a biological phenomenon. Miranda, without realizing it, also hints at the antithetical nature of all life when considered as a manifestation of the unconscious. Friar Laurence, in *Romeo and Juliet,* approaches the same subject with less naivete than Miranda, but his epigrams on mother earth do not add anything new to Miranda's (and Shakespeare's) final verdict:

> The earth that's nature's mother is her tomb,
> What is her burying grave that is her womb,
> And from her womb children of divers kind
> We sucking on her natural bosom find. (II, *3, 9*)

Almost every one of the main characters in *Richard II* addresses the earth as a mother or a nurse. At one time Bolingbroke speaks of "The fresh green lap of fair King Richard's land" (III, 3, 47), while his father, John of Gaunt, previously described England as "this teeming womb of royal kind" (II, 1, 50). Richard himself greets his "gentle earth . . . as a long-parted mother with her child / Plays fondly with her tears and smiles in meeting" (III, 2, 6). Yet, he prays to the earth to deprive his enemies of her "sweets,"

> But let thy spiders that suck up thy venom
> And heavy-gaited toads lie in their way . . .
> Yield stinging nettles to mine enemies,
> And when they from thy bosom pluck a flower,
> Guard it, I pray thee, with a lurking adder. . . . (III, 2, *14*)[5]

It is a prayer to the elements of destruction enclosed within the archetype, to give birth to more instruments of darkness than man can possibly cope with. When the evils that the "womb" has brought forth outnumber the blessings, then to die will be

to consummate a marriage with the earth: for the mother that
has given birth is, once more, ready to swallow her own children.
It is this ambivalence of the creative act in nature that Bolingbroke, now Henry IV, refers to when he announces the beginning
of his reign and therewith the hoped-for end of civil war: "No
more the thirsty entrance of this soil / Shall daub her lips with
her own children's blood" (1 HIV, I, 1, 5). Many years later, when
Shakespeare writes *Macbeth,* this archetypal aspect of mother
earth reappears. For if one looks upon Macbeth himself as a
"son" of the earth, a child of the "womb" (to which he returns
when, for the second time, he meets the three witches "at the pit
of Acheron"), one who is obsessed by his own unconscious and
the various "images of death" he himself creates, one may realize
the implications of Ross's remark about Scotland under Macbeth's tyrannical rule: "It cannot / Be call'd our mother, but
our grave" (IV, 3, 165). This is the most explicit statement, in
Macbeth, of an ambivalence that characterizes all that is "feminine" in this play, Lady Macbeth's animus-oriented destiny, the
bearded and death-dealing witches, and Hecate, the goddess of
the underworld. The "grave" that yawns for Macbeth as for all
Scotland represents the completely negative side of the mother
archetype, connoting "anything secret, hidden, dark; the abyss,
the world of the dead, anything that devours, seduces, and
poisons, that is terrifying and inescapable like fate." [6]

The twofold symbol of the womb as a place of renewal and
as a final shelter for the dead provides Shakespeare with an
endless variety of poetic ambiguities whenever he describes the
still point where birth and death meet, the moment of conception itself, the return of the son to his mother. When Orlando
challenges Charles the wrestler, he and Rosalind are clearly
aware of the deadly risk he is taking. But at the back of their
minds the reward of renewed life, should he win, is temptingly
present. Both these possibilities are hinted at in Charles's super-
cilious question: "Come, where is this young gallant, that is so
desirous to lie with his mother earth?" (I, 2, 216). Having de-

feated the wrestler, Orlando, who is as "motherless" as most of
Shakespeare's young lovers, will lie down "with his mother
earth," like an acorn dropped from a tree, waiting for Rosalind
to teach him how to "die" and be reborn again. The acorn stands
in the same relation to the tree as the son to his mother. To
"lie with his mother earth" then is to repeat, as it were, the
mystery of one's own conception—by lying with one's beloved,
the all-swallowing unconscious of the one having been replaced
by the all-conceiving unconscious of the other. In *Measure for
Measure,* a play full of sexual symbolism containing both the
creative and the destructive elements that may be revealed in
man's submission to the archetype, the identity between the act
of conception and the unconscious and therefore "blind" abundance of the earth is brought out again and again:

> Your brother and his lover have embrac'd:
> As those that feed grow full, as blossoming time
> That from the seedness the bare fallow brings
> To teeming foison, even so her plenteous womb
> Expresseth his full tilth and husbandry. (I, *4, 40*)

When Agrippa in *Antony and Cleopatra,* describes the love-
making of Caesar and Cleopatra, he uses the same earth metaphor with even greater precision:

> Royal wench!
> She made great Caesar lay his sword to bed:
> He ploughed her and she cropp'd. (II, *2, 234*)

Conception, then, may be either a blessing or a curse: it may
result in fruitfulness and renewal or give birth to the monsters
of the deep which—as Shakespeare says elsewhere—if they remain undisturbed, are merely "Cave-keeping evils that obscurely
sleep" (*Lucrece,* 1250), but which, once aroused, turn into instruments of darkness spreading poison and death all over the
earth. In Iago's generally precise terminology, the sexual act is
merely "an act of sport," but perceived through Othello's disturbed imagination it is "an act of shame." Edgar, in *King Lear,*

no doubt thinking of his father and the way his bastard brother was conceived, ominously hints at "the act of darkness" which his father had committed serving "the lust of [his] mistress' heart" (III, 4, 86), while Lear, in his madness, no longer in control of his imagination, compulsively recreates the archetype in terms of the ambivalence of the gravelike womb, "synonymous with the unconscious and the non-ego, hence with darkness, nothingness, the void, the bottomless pit." [7] For though the Gods "inherit" what is above the girdle,

> Beneath is all the fiends: there's hell, there's darkness,
> There is the sulphurous pit—burning, scalding,
> Stench, consumption. . . . (IV, 6, 130)

The darkness that envelops the two lovers is symbolical of the womb into which they withdraw and where conception takes place. The literal and the metaphorical levels of meaning meet when those that seek the darkness of the forest anticipate a return to a kind of prenatal bliss that daylight reality withholds from them. Yet, once more, it is the twofold symbolism of the womb that regulates life in the forest. On the one hand, it is a return to primeval simplicity and innocence where time is measured not by the "clock," but the "seasons' difference," and prayers are offered under the open sky, "for here we have no temple but the wood" (*AYLI,* III, 3, 52). On the other hand, it is a nightmare world of evil presaging that of later plays:

> . . . about his neck
> A green and gilded snake had wreath'd itself,
> Who with her head, nimble in threats approach'd
> The opening of his mouth. . . . (*AYLI,* IV, 3, 109)

Though Valentine, in *The Two Gentlemen,* experiences the pastoral blessings of "this shadowy desert, unfrequented woods" as a welcome shelter from "flourishing peoples towns," yet it is in this same forest that Proteus attempts to rape Silvia " 'gainst the nature of love" (V, 4, 58). It is also Timon's belief that the Forest will save him from the "detestable town" that makes him escape "to the woods . . . . where he shall find / The unkindest beast more kinder than mankind" (IV, 1, 36). But the selfsame wood that provides shelter, dispenses death by bringing forth things poisonous and evil. This "common mother," says Timon,

> Whose womb unmeasurable and infinite breast
> Teems and feeds all,

defends herself against man's arrogance and ingratitude by engendering

> . . . the black toad and adder blue
> The gilded newt and eyeless venom'd worm,
> With all th' abhorr'd births below crisp heaven
> Whereon Hyperion's quickening fire doth shine. (IV, 3, *178*)

The confrontation between the forces of conscious good and unconscious evil, between man and his shadow, between his judgment and his blood, takes place in the darkness of the "wood," as near the "womb" of mother earth as human imagination can reach. Whether forest or hollow tree, a cave on a mountain or on an island, or a cavern below ground, it is there alone that the mysteries of love and hate may be enacted. Maternal darkness, then, is a refuge for souls in bliss or a prison for the damned. Reunion with one's mother is an awesome experience for both alike: it may enable them to reach self-knowledge, but it may equally well deprive them of their identity and lead them into madness.

[III]

THE PATH THAT LEADS across the forest to the temple takes man out of the dark labyrinth of his unconscious toward the light of consciousness, from the confusion of uncontrolled affects to the daylight solemnity of the marriage ritual. For it is only with one's eyes open, when one is fully awake, that one is permitted to enter the temple. On the other hand, to trust in the darkness of the wood is to regress into sleep. What happens to the two pairs of lovers in *Midsummer Night's Dream* when they leave Athens to spend the night in a wood on the outskirts of the city is "comic" only insofar as we can reduce the forest to mere stage-scenery or concentrate entirely on the antics of the "hard-handed men" of Athens and the "tragical mirth" they rehearse under the shadow of trees. For the rest, Shakespeare motivates the lovers' retreat into the wood by the threats of a raving father who—like Brabantio very much later before the Senate of Venice—complains to the Duke that Lysander has "bewitch'd the bosom of my child," and that "With cunning hast thou filch'd my daughter's heart; / Turn'd her obedience, which is due to me . . ." (I, 1, 36). Theseus takes up the wronged father's argument, claiming that to the obedient daughter a father "should be as a god." When both Hermia and Lysander refuse to play the game according to the rules laid down by an irate paternal tyrant, Theseus threatens her with death or "to a vow of single life." It is noteworthy that throughout this absurd encounter between a tyrannical father and his daughter, no mother is ever mentioned. Both Lysander and Demetrius seem to be orphans, while Hermia and Helena are equally motherless. The only feminine figure mentioned by Lysander is a childless widow-aunt who looks upon him "as her only son." At her house he suggests to Hermia, they will get married since "to that place the sharp Athenian law / Cannot pursue us" (I, 1, 163). To reach her house they have to pass a wood "a league without the town." In that forest the two lovers, followed by Helena who loves Demetrius who, in turn, dotes on Hermia, will meet.

A father's angry curse, then, drives them into regressive darkness. Their meetingplace is the still and whirling point of the unconscious, the maternal womb where they are translated into sleep, and dreams create images of life and death, reflecting the confusion of a disordered libido. All the psychic energy that animated these lovers outside the forest is either paralyzed or turned into confusion, that is, into a self-denying direction. What they simultaneously experience in the darkness of the wood is a form of introversion, a regression of the libido, into a "mother's" womb. In the acting out of this metaphor, Puck is merely an instrument of the unconscious. Sexless, like Ariel in *The Tempest*, he is a tree-spirit, at home in the wood, "following darkness like a dream," one of maternal Hecate's most faithful disciples.

In that sense, Puck is himself an archetype closely resembling the "Trickster-figure" which Jung discovered in American Indian mythology. According to myth, he is "God, man, and animal at once. He is both subhuman and superhuman, a bestial and divine being whose chief and most charming characteristic is his unconsciousness. He is so unconscious of himself that his body is not a unity, and his two hands fight each other. . . . Even his sex is optional despite its phallic qualities. . . . Although he is not really evil, he does the most atrocious things from sheer unconsciousness and unrelatedness. . . . [He is] superior to man because of his superhuman qualities . . . and inferior to him because of his unreason and unconsciousness." [8]

The relation between Puck, the four bewildered lovers, Titania, and Bottom transformed into an ass, can be understood best of all in terms of the wood symbolism that constitutes the metaphorical background to their confusion. For "the forest, dark and impenetrable to the eye, like deep water and the sea, is the container of the unknown and the mysterious. It is an appropriate synonym for the unconscious. Trees, like fishes in water, represent the living contents of the unconscious. . . . The mighty old oak represents a central figure among the contents of the unconscious, possessing personality in the most marked degree. It is the prototype of the Self, a symbol of the source and goal of the individuation process. The oak stands for the still unconscious core of the personality, the plant symbolism indicating a state of deep unconsciousness. From this it may be concluded that the hero of the fairytale is profoundly unconscious of himself. He is one of the 'sleepers,' the 'blind' or 'blind-folded'. . . . They are the unawakened who are still unconscious of themselves who have not yet integrated their future more extensive personality, their 'wholeness'. . . ." [9]

Jung, in this passage, did not attempt to establish an analogy with Shakespeare's play. Yet it is peculiarly applicable both to the human protagonists and the forest setting. For when the lovers enter the wood they become, as it were, prisoners of a collective dream, a manifestation of their own unconscious. This particular kind of dream is the more readily available as their libido has been driven back upon itself and now looks for shelter "among the trees." At one time, in the distant past, Frazer tells us, trees had been considered tribal mothers, and many myths speak of human beings born of trees. Female deities were worshipped in tree-form and amidst sacred groves. Trees are as common in dreams as they are in myths: if in the latter their maternal significance is repeatedly stressed, in the former their ambivalent sexual character is always strikingly obvious. For tree-symbolism in dreams often refers to compensatory wish-fulfillments that have to remain repressed in waking life. Such a dream compensation may have feminine, but at times also has explicitly masculine characteristics. Then the dream-tree displays bisexual features as does the symbolic tree of knowledge in paradise. Jung remembers having come across a picture of Adam in a manuscript in Florence "showing the membrum virile as a tree." [10] The archetypal tree, then, as it makes its appearance in myths and dreams, does not mean "itself," it neither *is* the mother nor does it *represent* the male sexual organ, but should be taken as a symbol of the libido whose object at one time was the mother.

In the *Dream*, the collective myth and the personalized dream are so closely interwoven that a literal reading of the play may leave us puzzled. If all that Shakespeare wants to prove is Puck's superiority over men, which makes him exclaim, "Lord, what fools these mortals be!" there would be no need for the symbolic elaboration that goes to the making of the play. Yet when the "negative" masculine and feminine elements, the "cave-keeping evils" that reside in the unconscious, are let loose, and the anima-animus encounter produces self-defeating "animosity," the fight can no longer be carried on within the bounds of civilized conduct, but, as it were, blindly, in darkness, and in pitiful ignorance of its consequences.

Thus Demetrius following Hermia, who has eloped with Lysander, into the forest, yet himself pursued by Helena, calls himself "wood within this wood" (II, 1, 192) because darkness prevents him from finding Hermia, while Helena, a few lines later, dismisses that same darkness as nonexistent, because her unconscious lights her way and shows her Demetrius as it were in a dream: "It is not night when I do see your face, / Therefore I think I am not in the night" (II, 1, 221).

After the juice of the flower has blinded Lysander to the meaning of reality, emotional allegiance is shifted in an instant and the logic of the unconscious takes over. Deceived by the sudden upsurge of his blood (for he never "loved" Hermia as he now loves Helena), he justifies this emotional *volte face* by appealing to his judgment. "Reason becomes the marshall to my will," he exclaims (II, 2, 120)—which recalls Hamlet's outburst against his mother, whose conduct proves, he thinks, that her perverted judgment has defended the unreasonable cravings of her "blood," and that therefore her "reason panders will"— in both cases the Elizabethan sense of the word *will* being synonymous with sexual appetite.

Lysander's "reason" having been undermined by the darkness of the forest, he is no longer amenable to daylight-logic. He calls Hermia, whom he was supposed to marry after passing through the wood, his "surfeit" and his "heresy," leaving her asleep under a tree in order to follow Helena. Hermia, in the meantime, equally "wood within the wood" as Lysander has been before, experiences a dream within a dream. Her unconscious reproduces the archetypal situation, most suitable to her present con-

dition, in which the feminine symbol of the tree and the masculine symbol of the snake appear equally threatening and are
carried over into waking life. For when she opens her eyes to
find herself alone and in darkness, she realizes that neither her
feminine "frailty" nor Lysander's masculine "strength" will give
any support. The Adam that should have been lying by her
side has followed an irrational impulse of the blood into the
depths of the forest. It is not difficult to interpret her dream,
revealing as it does a form of psychic activity functioning on a
deeper level than is common in waking consciousness. Hermia
implores the absent Lysander—

> Do thy best
> To pluck this crawling serpent from my breast!
> Ay me, for pity! What a dream was here!
> Lysander, look how I do quake with fear!
> Methought a serpent eat my heart away,
> And you sat smiling at his cruel prey. (II, 2, *145*)

Whether we call this dream a premonition of what is to follow,
Lysander's "smiling" indifference to Hermia's suffering, or the
expression of a collective unconscious in which the snake-motif
figures as repressed sexuality, either as "a fiercely sensual, feminine daemon, as the Devil himself with Dionysian goat's legs
and obscene gestures, or as a terrifying serpent that squeezes its
victims to death," [11] its ambivalent sexual character is evident:
for the unconscious manifests itself in dreams regardless of the
daylight division of masculine and feminine, while it may, if
the dream-picture conforms to a longed-for but unattainable
reality, compensate for the weakness of either the one or the
other by exaggerating the femininity or the masculinity of any
given object of desire.

It is in terms of such a compensation that Titania embraces
an ass in the forest. The mischief that Puck does when he "trans-
lates" Bottom into an Ass is performed at Oberon's command.
Titania's "hateful fantasies" are the result of Oberon's violent
jealousy and her unwillingness to compromise. "Bottom's dream"

is Titania's undoing, for while he knows that he has "wit enough
to get out of this wood" if he wants to badly enough, Titania
is only too ready to give reasons for the blind craving of her
blood. She does not implore but compels the Ass to keep her
company and lie with her in the Forest. For "Out of this wood
do not desire to go: / Thou shalt remain here, whether thou
wilt or no" (III, 1, 159). What deeper layers of Titania's unconscious are involved when she lovingly embraces the ass are
indicated by the frankly erotic imagery used by her in describing
their love-making.

> So doth the woodbine the sweet honeysuckle
> Gently entwist; the female ivy so
> Enrings the barky fingers of the elm.
> O how I love thee! how I dote on thee. (IV, *1, 48*) [12]

That Titania in her "dream" should see an ass issuing from
behind a tree is less surprising than may appear at first sight.
Both ass and tree have at all times been fertility symbols, the
femininity of the latter and the masculinity of the former con-
tributing in equal measure to the healing power residing in
their magic conjunction. The symbolic sexual act performed between tree and ass constitutes a kind of primitive equation
guaranteeing renewal on earth: "The ass and the tree are evidently related [Jung refers here to chemical practice], because
they both represent the power of life, procreation, and healing.
. . . The ass is a daemon Triunus, a chthonic trinity, which
is portrayed in Latin alchemy as a three-headed monster and
identified with Mercurius, salt, and sulphur. . . . The monster
and the tree both stand for . . . the elixir, the alexipharmic,
and the panacea. The tree's peculiar power to change into any
animal shape is attributed to Mercurius." [13] Mercurius is the
mythological embodiment of the Trickster-figure. In Shakespeare's play this is Puck.

The adventure in the wood is an inseparable part of the encounter between the anima and the animus elements in those

that made darkness their home for one night: for this encounter takes place within their own unconscious. Their "dreams" indeed have "no bottom," but they are seldom "comic," being "fierce vexations" that reveal "senseless things" and cause "distracted fear." As long as they are in the wood all their civilized past is forgotten, "All schooldays' friendship, childhood, innocence" (III, 2, 202), and whatever future they anticipated is swallowed up by a meaningless present. The lovers call each other names derived from the "cave-keeping" monsters that dwell in the unconscious. Thus Lysander to Hermia:

> Hang off, thou cat, thou burr! vile thing, let loose,
> Or I will shake thee from me like a serpent. . . .
> . . . You tawny Tartar . . . you dwarf,
> You minimus, of hindering knot-grass made;
> You bead, you acorn. . . . (III, 2, 260)

When they leave the wood at sunrise, they do so to the accompaniment of "musical confusion," a harmonious echo to the nightmare confusion they experienced during the dark. They wake up to a new, transformed present in which they are, once more, themselves—though they do not know what made this self-discovery possible. Demetrius tells the story of the night in terms of some "power" which helped him recover from "sickness" to "health." What they saw among the trees now seems to him "small and undistinguishable, / Like far-off mountains turned into clouds—" while Hermia, referring to their divided souls that could not distinguish between a dream-image and reality as long as they looked for and found shelter among the shadows and visions of the forest, remembers "these things with parted eyes, / When every thing seems double" (IV, 1, 195). Theseus alone, an image of human perfection, is at this moment in possession of a unified vision. It is he who leads them out of the wood into the temple where the marriage ritual will be performed.

Consciousness has been re-established as the only power that can guide men toward fulfillment of their own selves. The acorn has grown into an oak. The price they paid during the night was small in relation to the wisdom and happiness they obtained. Though for a time they seem to have eaten "on the roots / That takes the reason prisoner" (*Macbeth*, I, 3, 84), and had been held captives by the wood, their freedom is given back to them "from above." They do not have to fight for it. Their adventure is scarcely more than a psychological metaphor: Oberon, on the dream level, and Theseus, on the level of consciousness, re-establish order, first in their visual perception, and then by restoring to them their "reason" which they lost in the confusion of the forest. The wisdom they have achieved during that night is never hinted at when the play ends. Possibly it is the kind of insight that can grow only in the dark, enabling them to realize the limits of their strength and the measure of their "frailty." The temple, they now know, lies "beyond the wood": their exile into unreason has purged their "blood" and made them ready for the ritual. Only now will their judgment be joined to their blood in a celebration of consciousness regained.

[IV]

IN SHAKESPEARE'S ARCHETYPAL LANDSCAPE the tree and the cave can be found side by side. Both being maternal symbols they may either give shelter or hold the hero prisoner. At times protection from the vicissitudes of life can be provided only by a withdrawal, a voluntary imprisonment, indeed, a regression into a maternal unconscious where alone the hero can prepare his re-birth into consciousness. It is in the womblike cave, in the forest, on the seashore, or during his descent into the underworld, that the archetypal hero rediscovers his own identity or—if the introversion of his libido has progressed beyond cure—loses his identity for good. One of the most illuminating distinctions between comedy and tragedy appears to consist in the effect on the hero of this primordial setting: the final affirmation of life in comedy is synonymous with the hero's departure from the cave and the forest, from the isolation in which his unconscious held him captive, and his acceptance of love; conversely the denial of life's values in tragedy is symbolized by the all-enclosing darkness of cavé and forest, the labyrinthian nature of cavern within cavern when the unconscious first disintegrates and finally vanquishes the principle of love.

In Shakespeare's plays this "landscape" may be quite real, existing, as it were, simultaneously on a naturalistic as well as on a symbolical level. The spectator in the theatre sees only the cave and the forest; the reader of the play may detach this "dramatic" setting from its merely outward form and conventional meaning, and perceive, beyond stage appearances the symbol which stands for a psychic reality. It is then only that it becomes an archetype of transformation and rebirth; for "anyone who gets into that cave, that is to say into the cave which everyone has in himself, or into the darkness that lies behind consciousness, will find himself involved in an—at first—unconscious process of transformation. By penetrating into the unconscious he makes a connection with his unconscious contents. This may result in a momentous change of personality in the positive or negative sense. . . ." [14]

Such personality changes fascinated Shakespeare no less than they do the modern psychiatrist, whose own attempt at understanding them may assist us in establishing an adequate response to what Jung here calls the "positive" and the "negative" effects of such a contact with one's unconscious. Thus the "motherless" young lover who withdraws into his cave in the forest will come forth revived and strengthened by his contact with the womb of the mother earth: Valentine, otherwise a very unheroic figure, yet bestows forgiveness on a faithless friend for no other reason, it appears, than that meditation in the forest and the self-knowledge consequent upon it have revealed to him a deeper truth than can be found in "vengeance." If the uninitiated reader finds Valentine's unexpected generosity at the end of the play dramatically quite unconvincing, the student of human nature may be less surprised. For Valentine, having been exiled from the presence of his beloved and the one he still considers his best friend, is in the position of one driven back upon himself and therefore compelled to transform his repressed psychic energy into new spiritual strength. For "the treasure which the hero fetches from the dark cavern is *life;* it is himself, new-born from the dark maternal cave of the unconscious." [15] Similarly Orlando and the exiled Duke withdraw into caves during their stay in the Forest of Arden. The meditative quality of their life there prepares them for a return of their libido in a newly creative form, the Duke to rule his country in wisdom, Orlando to forgive his brother and give back to Rosalind that love whose meaning and essential reasonableness she taught him in the Forest.

In *The Two Gentlemen* and *As You Like It* the cave and the forest are what Jung calls "positive" maternal symbols. Though they form part of an "exile" from normal living, they represent the rejuvenating effect of the mother-image when the hero's consciousness is found to be in need of this kind of nourishment. The exile of Belarius' and Cymbeline's two sons and their life in a cave, cut off from any social contact, is another and more extreme instance of regression into the unconscious. Here the two possibilities inherent in the symbol are more explicitly stated than in the two earlier comedies. On the one hand, life in the forest and the cave is described by Belarius as an *escape* from "th' art o' th' court" and

> . . . the toil o' th' war,
> A pain that only seems to seek out danger
> I' th' name of fame and honour, which dies i' th' search,
> And hath as oft a sland'rous epitaph
> As record of fair act. (*Cymbeline,* III, *3, 50*)

To one of his adopted sons, however, the cave is

> A cell of ignorance, travelling a-bed,
> A prison, or a debtor that not dares
> To stride a limit. . . . (III, *3, 33*)

while his brother is much more outspoken in his impatience to
leave the "pinching cave" behind in order to achieve a higher
form of humanity than is possible in the darkness of their present
dwelling-place:

> We have seen nothing.
> We are beastly: subtle as the fox for prey,
> Like warlike as the wolf for what we eat. (III, *3, 39*)

Freedom and bondage as experienced in the cave seem to
complement each other. The two brothers are like "prison'd
birds" that sing their "bondage freely." They are simultaneously
prisoners of a past of which they know nothing, and harbingers
of a future not yet born. Chosen by fate for the "heroic" life,
they have suffered regression and are compelled to hide within
the crevices of the earth. Out of the cave which is their home
in exile renewal or annihilation may come. They are quite unaware of any of these implications, leading their life of exile
as a matter of incomprehensible necessity rather than of free
choice. Yet they are freer in their present bondage in the cave
than others are at court.

Etymology, Jung says, bears out this twofold meaning of
"cave." Thus the root of the Greek word $\kappa \epsilon \nu \theta o s$ which means
the "innermost womb of "the earth" is related to *Hades* as well
as to *hoard,* while the Greek word $\kappa \upsilon \theta o s$ and its various deriva-
tives may mean a *cavity,* a *vault,* a *casket,* or any hollow vessel,
as well as *to be pregnant, to swell, to be strong.* The Latin word
cavea, similarly, is any *hollow, cavity, enclosure, assembly,* but
in its Indo-European origin—*kevo*—it meant *to swell, to be
pregnant.*[16] The "hollowness" of the cavern and the abundance
that issues from it for either good or evil, are symbolic of the
psychic content of the archetype: its "positive" effect upon the
hero produces a rejuvenated strength, its "negative" effect

weakens his resistance to evil. It swallows the hero into the darkness of his own unconscious, deprives him of the use of his reason, and confounds what he believes his eyes see with the chaotic images that his disordered imagination creates. It is then that the cavern becomes a symbol of hell, into which man is "exiled" when his consciousness fails to provide him with the criteria required to face the meaning of reality.

Macbeth's second meeting with the witches is Shakespeare's most frightening metaphor of the maternal archetype in action. This fateful encounter takes place "at the pit of Acheron," a dark cavern situated in that region of Macbeth's own unconscious where the active extraversion of his wife and his own passive introversion unite in one common urge, expressed in the desire to extract from the depths of the earth the hidden treasure of eternal renewal. What he *does* discover in the darkness of the cave is his own barrenness symbolized in terms of tree-apparitions such as that of "a child crowned, with a tree in his hand" which may be either Malcolm or Fleance (whose fathers Macbeth killed), while the sceptre is a well-known symbol of sexual power carried in the hand of the one whose royal attributes are beyond question. The prediction that he will never be defeated until "Great Birnam wood to high Dunsinane Hill / Shall come against him" (IV, 1, 93) is countered by Macbeth's argument that no one can "bid the tree / Unfix his earth-bound root." Malcolm's order to his advancing army "Let every soldier hew him down a bough / And bear't before him" (V, 4, 5) provides every one of his soldiers, as it were, with a "sceptre" under the shadow of which his army advances toward Dunsinane. It is, significantly, an army of young men who have only recently grown out of boyhood—"many unrough youths, that even now / Protest their first of manhood" (V, 2, 11). The boughs they carry before them have been cut from the forest that had given shelter to Macbeth's castle. The symbols of the maternal cave and the trees in the hands of children are here most wonderfully united in the image of Hecate (whom Macbeth addresses before he

murders Duncan), the goddess in whose honor cave-mysteries
used to be celebrated in Samothrace where she was worshipped
as "spirit-mother" whose domain was nightmare and madness,
the inundation of the conscious mind by "moon-sickness" or
lunacy. In these cave-mysteries, we are told, a wand used to be
broken in which "we recognize the motif of the sacred tree, the
mother who might not be touched." [17] This, once again, indicates the close symbolic relationship between cave and tree in
its "negative" effect on the hero's consciousness. For the symbolic
felling of trees or the cutting down of boughs appears in Shakespeare whenever the maternal image has failed to supply the invigorating nourishment that might have led to rebirth.

Thus Belarius (in *Cymbeline*) remembers the inevitable regression of his own libido when he was banished, in terms of a
tree exposed to the ravages of a storm—

> Cymbeline lov'd me. . . .
> . . . . then was I as a tree
> Whose boughs did bend with fruits. But in one night,
> A storm, a robbery (call it what you will)
> Shook down my mellow hangings, nay, my leaves,
> And left me bare to weather. (III, *3, 58*)

In the same way Timon compares his own failure to preserve
men's loyalty to the leaves of an oak which "have with one
winter's brush / Fell from their boughs and left me open, bare /
For every storm that blows" (IV, 3, 265). As if to bring home the
barrenness of his present way of life and his readiness to deprive
himself even further of any chance of renewal, Timon shortly
before his death speaks of the felling of a tree that grows in
front of his cave, not far from the sea. It must be felled "That
mine own use invites me to cut down" (V, 1, 211). Timon's grave
is found in the forest "Entomb'd upon the very hem o'th'sea"
(V, 4, 66). It is to his mother earth that he returns, seeking shelter
in the threefold symbol of the cave, the wood, and the sea. In
this way he expresses his Tolstoyan discontent with "the life of
the conventional world, recognizing it to be no life, but a parody

of life, which its superfluities simply keep us from understanding." [18] William James after quoting Tolstoy calls him "one of
those primitive oaks of men to whom the superficialities and
insincerities . . . of our polite civilization are profoundly un-
satisfying." [19] We remember the curious similarity between Tolstoy's death and that of Shakespeare's Timon. Thus the reference
to the felling of trees and the cutting down of branches acquires
a significance transcending the realistic level of meaning ordinarily associated with such "nature" imagery.

The parallel with primeval man is easily drawn. According
to Frazer's account of the ancient myth of Attis "he unmanned
himself under a pine-tree, and bled to death on the spot." The
ritual that was connected with his death and rebirth, and of
which descriptions exist, referring to Roman and Phrygian cere-
monies that originated in prehistoric Asia, consisted in the
cutting down in the woods of a pine-tree which was "brought
into the sanctuary of Cybele, where it was treated as a great
divinity. The duty of carrying the sacred tree was entrusted to a
guild of Tree-bearers. The trunk was swathed like a corpse with
woolen bands and decked with wreaths of violets, for violets
were said to have sprung from the blood of Attis . . . and the
effigy of a young man, doubtless Attis himself, was tied to the
middle of the stem." [20] The further back in time we follow the
myth, the more archetypically revealing are the customs associated with the sacred tree that symbolized Attis' rebirth. For
during the spring festival at Hierapolis in Syria "the excitement
spread like a wave among the crowd of onlookers" until, sur-
rendering to a collective unconscious that held them captive for
the duration of this festival, "man after man, his veins throbbing
with the music, his eyes fascinated by the sight of the streaming
blood, flung his garments from him, leaped forth with a shout,
and seizing one of the swords which stood ready for the purpose,
castrated himself on the spot." [21]

Apart from Belarius and Timon, three of Shakespeare's most
heroic figures are at one time or another compared to trees that

are cut down or broken by a storm, and are therefore prevented from bearing any more fruit. In each case this symbolic emasculation is the result of the hero's inability to come to terms with an anima figure that dominates his masculinity and ultimately defeats it. The oak, the cedar, and the pine are the trees most often alluded to. While the pine-tree, as in the Attis-myth, is a more clearly defined sexual symbol, the other trees may stand for pride, strength, and the superiority of the male hero over other less powerful human beings. Thus Coriolanus is first described as "the rock, the oak not to be windshaken" (V, 2, 118). When, however, he yields to his mother's entreaties, kneeling down before her in a symbolic gesture of surrender in order to prevent her from lowering herself before her son, he exclaims,

> Your knees to me! to your corrected son!
> . . . . then let the mutinous winds
> Strike the proud cedars 'gainst the fiery sun. (v, 3, 57)

Antony's love for Cleopatra, as perceived by outsiders, had always appeared to them as a defeat of his masculinity in order "to cool a gypsy's lust." Thus Caesar's perspective is strongly coloured by his belief that a man's psyche should remain unaffected by his sexual encounter with woman.

> [Antony] is not more manlike
> Than Cleopatra; nor the queen of Ptolemy
> More womanly than he, . . . (I, 4, 5)

says Caesar at the beginning of the play. Antony's love for Cleopatra is, more often than not, shown to be on the defensive, and the element of passive surrender—almost, indeed, of "frailty"— is evident. Fully realizing that "she is cunning past man's thought," he yet admits that "the beds i'the east are soft," and that, by implication, Octavius' judgment of him was basically correct. How correct, he himself formulates immediately after his defeat in the sea-battle where, he suspects, Cleopatra has betrayed him. The tree-image is once more used in connection with a man's yielding to an anima archetype quite beyond his rational comprehension—"and this pine is bark'd / That over-topp'd them all" (IV, 10, 36). And finally, when Macbeth returns from the dark cave where the witches have shown him a tree in the hand of a child, he himself is "ripe for shaking." The last glimmer of his consciousness shows him his "way of life" in terms of a rotten tree that "is fallen into the sere, the yellow leaf" (V, 3, 23). The hero, then, falls as a tree, cut to the ground, its branches lopped off and its leaves withered. The archetypal sacrifice to the maternal unconscious is thus accomplished.

If, as in all the preceding cases, the felling of the tree occurs in connection with an archetypal anima-image, the tree need not therefore be taken as an exclusively masculine symbol. Its bisexual nature has been mentioned before. It again becomes apparent when not only the tree but also its fruits form part of Shakespeare's imagery. For they may stand for masculine or feminine symbols according to the context in which they occur in the plays. The same Timon who is so anxious to fell the tree that stands before his cave in order the sooner to find his grave at the very "hem" of the sea and thus return to the primal element of all life, pronounces almost impassioned words on the "motherliness" of nature and its fruits:

> Behold the earth hath roots;
> Within this mile break forth a hundred springs;
> The oaks bear mast, the briers scarlet hips,
> The bounteous housewife nature on each bush
> Lays her full mess before you. (IV, 3, 423)

Certain kinds of fruits have, indeed, an explicitly feminine connotation—such as the medlar, a kind of brown-skinned apple that used to be eaten in Shakespeare's time when decayed to a soft pulpy state. Mercutio ridicules Romeo's dreaming that his mistress "were that kind of fruit / As maids call medlars when they laugh alone—" (II, 1, 35), while Lucio tells the Duke how he once got a wench with child, but never admitted it to the court, "they would else have married me to the rotten medlar" (*Measure for Measure*, IV, 3, 188). In *As You Like It* Rosalind, resenting Touchstone's remarks about the strange fruit that had been hanging from the trees, mockingly assures him that she will "graff" the fruit with him "and then I shall graff it with a medlar: then it will be the earliest fruit in the country: for you'll be rotten ere you be half ripe, and that's the right virtue for a medlar" (III, 2, 125). Lastly, in *Timon,* the two possible parallel meanings of medlar are used when Apemantus offers Timon one to eat and the latter indignantly refuses it:

T: On what I hate I feed not.
A: Dost hate a medlar?
T: Ay, though it look like thee.
A: And th'hast hated meddlers sooner, thou shouldst have loved thyself better now. (IV, *3, 306*)

A footnote in the Arden edition provides the information that there are at least three meanings of medlar or meddler: the fruit; a person who meddles or intrigues; one who overindulges in sexual intercourse. In Partridge's *Shakespeare's Bawdy,* however, the reader is, more specifically, told that "in Shakespeare 'medlar' means either pudend or podex or the pudend-podex area (the lower posteriors and the crutch)." [22]

As symbols of femininity these fruits are, metaphorically speaking, eaten by men for their sweet taste. Being rotten before any other fruit, they may indeed be called "the earliest fruit in the country." Yet they are easy to get and seem to be always "ripe for shaking." By implication, they infect with poison those who taste of them. The "poison" may refer to the sexual "knowledge" that the eating of the medlar confers upon the eater or, on the more realistic level on which Lucio uses the word, it may signify syphilis, the "felling of the tree," the emasculation of the hero as a result of having "meddled" too much with the forbidden fruit.

The image of the soul as a fruit hanging upon a maternal tree is, to the best of my knowledge, used only once in Shakespeare. In the most moving scene in *Cymbeline,* a play full of tree images, Posthumus returning from banishment, and rediscovering the innocence of Imogen whom he has suspected of womanly "frailty" during his absence, joins his soul to hers in a wonderfully affirmative gesture of renewal. When she embraces him after having been "dead" to the world for so long a time, he surrenders his being to her with these words,

> Hang there like fruit, my soul,
> Till the tree die. (v, 5, 264)

By returning the fruit to the tree to which it originally belonged, Posthumus re-establishes the primordial union of the masculine and feminine in all human nature. The soul as fruit, then, is both cause and effect of rebirth. As a symbol of immortality it will drop to the ground only when the tree dies. Now it is son, father, husband, all in one, while the tree having evolved from mother to wife, will again grow into daughter, when the fruit, having fallen, will take root in the soil and quicken into new life. What is, in addition, being symbolically enacted in this amazing scene is the final return of man's soul to the physical substance that gave birth to it. Bodily and psychic elements are here inextricably linked in a form of integration that stands for self-awareness on both a physical and spiritual plane. If the soul of man is indeed the "fruit," then the "tree" is the maternal source of all life. But the image as used by Shakespeare impels one to think of the fruit and the tree as one. This very synthesis of leaf, blossom, fruit, and bole, prevents too precise a distinction between the masculinity of the one and the femininity of the other. On the deepest level of meaning, Shakespeare's tree metaphors always seem to refer to that miraculous tree of life upon which the Phoenix-bird eternally renews itself without ever assuming either clearly defined masculine or feminine shape. It scarcely seems a matter of chance that Antony's soul should recall the image of the Phoenix, "O Antony, O thou Arabian bird" (*Antony and Cleopatra,* III, 2, 12), while Jachimo standing in front of sleeping Imogen becomes aware of the same Phoenix association—"She is alone th'Arabian bird" (*Cymbeline,* I, 6, 17).

The Phoenix-bird then is the most precious "fruit" borne by the tree: it also qualifies the tree's sexual symbolism. Its rootedness as well as its shape relate it to the male organ of procreation. Its fruits, its blossoms, and its leaves, its ability to "give birth" as part of the vegetation symbolism of its own "mother," the earth, make it a symbol of femininity.

In primitive myth and ritual this sexual ambivalence was taken for granted. For though the priest, in ancient Rome, who guarded the sacred tree and worshipped it, also "embraced it as his wife . . . kissed it . . . lay under its shadow [and] poured wine on its trunk . . . , the custom of physically marrying *men and women* to trees is still practised in India and other parts of the East." [23] On a more sophisticated level of ritual, and one that abolishes all merely sexual distinctions in an all-embracing vegetation myth, there is the legend of Osiris, the son of Isis, who was found by his mother, dead and enclosed in a tree trunk. Brought back from Byblos in Lebanon to Egypt, he was transformed into the "djed pillar" and worshipped "as a phallic tree fetish, as a symbol of the youthful lover." [24] Although the significance of the "djed pillar" in the Osiris ritual has never been fully understood, it is generally "taken to represent a tree-trunk with the stumps of branches projecting to either side at the top. In the cult, at all events, it was as bulky and heavy as a tree-trunk." [25] That this was taken to be a symbol of immortality representing man's longing for a unified personality outlasting the vicissitudes of time, is an interesting assumption. Considered as an intrinsic element in the formation of the Self as reflected in man's image-creating power, it may stand for the process of individuation itself which, on this particular level of self-awareness in the history of human consciousness, was represented by the various stages of growth and decay, the felling and the renewed blossoming of the tree: "This is seen in the raising of the body of Osiris upon the tree, in the symbol of tree birth, the lifting of the buried effigy, the placing of the sacrum upon the tree in the *djed* symbol, and above all in the erection of the *djed*

pillar. The *mystique* of erection and ascension is intimately connected with the mystery of wholeness and integration." [26]

The various stages of the Osiris myth show us first the "son"
enclosed within a tree trunk and later transformed into a tree.
It is the story of man imprisoned within the mother's womb, his
consciousness unawakened and therefore as yet incapable of ap-
prehending life, seeking the protective darkness of the maternal
"cave" and yet yearning for the freedom that consciousness will
give him. In mythological terms it is the story of the liberation
of the son from his mother, his ascent into individuation in
spite of the "maternal" resistance emanating from his own unconscious. It is, in many significant details, the story of Edgar
in *King Lear*.

Now Edgar is the son of a father who, throughout the play,
never once mentions his wife, though Edgar's bastard brother's
mother is referred to at least once. Gloucester himself speaks of
her as one who "grew round-womb'd, and had . . . a son for
her cradle ere she had a husband for her bed" (I, 1, 14). He also
informs Kent, in the presence of Edmund, that the latter's mother
was "fair" and that "there was good sport at his making" (I, 1,
23). These remarks—a middle-aged father swaggeringly recount-
ing the sexual exploits of his youth—do not pass unnoticed.
Edmund ridicules his father's foolish sexual boasting and expresses contempt for the latter's clumsy attempts at justifying the
present unsatisfactory condition of the world by an extravagant
reference to the influence of the stars, the moon, and the sun on
human life. Edmund knows that his father's relation to his
mother was a simple case of adultery, and therefore it is nothing
but "an admirable evasion of whoremaster man, to lay his goatish
disposition to the charge of a star!" Edmund therefore refuses
to see in his father anything more than a superstitious old hypocrite, and dismisses his own "nativity" as a deplorable accident
quite independent of any specifically "maternal" influence. For
though his mother was doubtless a loose woman and in all likelihood no virgin, "I should have been that I am had the maidenli-

est star in the firmament twinkled on by bastardizing" (I, 2, 147). The goddess to whom he addresses his prayer, then, is "Nature" who alone should be held responsible for the creation of illegitimate sons. His prayer, not without irony, ends with an invocation to the gods whom he asks to "stand up for bastards"—which may be taken to be just one more reference to "the lusty stealth of nature" which both gods and goddesses indulge in when they have "hot backs."

Edgar is motherless in quite a different sense. Having been conceived "within a dull, stale, tired bed" and therefore the "legitimate" son of a mother who will remain anonymous until the end of the play, he is left without the support of any abstract maternal principle (such as Edmund's goddess "Nature") when disaster threatens to overtake him. After his bastard brother has turned against him in order to "grow" and "prosper" with the assistance of the gods and goddesses who so freely and generously copulate "in nature," Edgar, finding himself proclaimed, looks for shelter—

> And by the happy hollow of a tree
> Escap'd the hunt. (II, 3, 2)

It is Shakespeare's most moving portrayal of regression into the maternal womb. There alone Edgar can "preserve" himself.

To primordial man the "cloven" or the "hollow" tree has always appeared as a symbol of rebirth. Numerous legends and parables tell us of such trees whose hollowness stood for the source of all life whether as fountain or vessel, as trough or shadow: "This ambiguity refers to the different aspects of the tree: as a 'stock,' the oak is the source of the fountain, so to speak; as the trough it is the vessel, and as the protecting tree it is the mother. From ancient times the tree was man's birthplace; it is therefore a source of life. The alchemists called both the vessel and the bath the 'womb.' The cloven or hollow trunk bears out this interpretation." [27]

Edgar sheltering inside the tree acquires a new identity. He does so in full consciousness. His new personality, which is that of a "Bedlam beggar," symbolizes a return to nothingness and the unconscious; since Edgar is aware of the consequences of putting on this mask of lunacy, he acts "in contempt of man." When Lear meets him in the nakedness of his body, he also starts tearing off his clothes. In Edgar, reduced to the apparently incoherent babbling of the unconscious, Lear discovers "the thing itself, unaccommodated man" who "is no more but such a poor, bare, forked animal as thou art" (III, 4, 110). That Edgar should have decided to assume this shape, half man and half beast, hiding in the hollow of a tree because he was accused of parricide, may explain his otherwise unintelligible reference to the Stygian lake and Nero's mad attempt to catch fish in the Lake of Darkness. The passage which Edith Sitwell in her *Notebook on William Shakespeare* calls "one of the keynotes of the play," occurs at the very moment when Lear, Edgar, and the Fool enter the farmhouse and Lear decides to bring his daughters to trial: "Frateretto calls me, and tells me Nero is an angler in the Lake of Darkness" (III, 6, 6).

Nero's madness is here related both to his mother and to the Alcyonian Lake through which Dionysus is supposed to have gone to Hell to fetch up his mother Semele, the moon-goddess. In Pausanias' *Description of Greece* the lake is described as bottomless: "I never heard of any one who was able to sound the depth. Nero himself made the experiment . . . but he could find no bottom. . . . I was told too, that smooth and still as the waters of the lake look to the eye, it yet has the property of sucking down any one who is rash enough to swim in it. The water catches him, and sweeps him down into the depths." [28] This bottomless lake, Edith Sitwell suggests, is human nature in which Nero, the matricide, finds "blackness after blackness, depth beneath depth." But she also quotes Higden's comment on Nero's matricide in the translation of Trevisa: ". . . he (Nero) let kerne his own moder wombe, for he wolde see the place that he was conceyved in." [29]

What is being suggested here is that Edgar, hiding behind his mask of lunacy, evokes a form of ultimate psychic anarchy where son and mother destroy each other in an uncontrolled urge toward mutual annihilation. This image of hell, with its bottomless lake shrouded in darkness, is related to the many symbols of the maternal unconscious that have already been encountered in Shakespeare's equivocal use of the image of the cave and the cavern, the forest and the sea, the pit of Acheron and the treasure buried underground, the womb that brings forth and the womb that swallows. That Shakespeare was, however dimly, aware of the association between the anarchic contents of the maternal unconscious and the dangers threatening man when these uncontrolled forces are let loose, is indicated in one of Lear's most revealing utterances when he realizes that he carries hell within and calls it "Mother":

> O! how this mother swells up toward my heart;
> *Hysterica passio!* down, thou climbing sorrow!
> The element's below. (II, *4, 56*)

That one may suffer from a malady called "the mother" the symptoms of which have been described in contemporary medical treatises, is alluded to in Elizabethan medical writings more than once. A footnote in the Arden edition quotes Edward Jordan's *Brief Discourse of a Disease called the Suffocation of the Mother,* 1605, where he writes on page 5: "This disease is called by diverse names amongst our authors, *Passio Hysterica, Suffocatio Priefocatio,* and *Strangulatus uteri, Caducus Matricis,* i.e. in English, the Mother or the Suffocation of the Mother, because, most commonly, it takes them with choking in the throat; and it is an affect of the mother or the wombe, wherein the principal parts of the bodie by consent do suffer diversely according to the diversities of the causes and diseases wherewith the matrix is offended." [30]

Lear's reference to this malady and his use of its name, "Mother," indicates where he thought its origin lay. That he should undergo the affliction of this particular "sorrow" relates it to Edgar's mention, a few scenes later, of Nero angling in the Lake of Darkness. "The element's below," murmurs Lear. But "below" is the realm of the mothers—"there's Hell, there's darkness, / There is the sulphurous pit. . . ."

Is it, one wonders, too farfetched to assume that when Shakespeare created Goneril and Regan, Gertrude and Lady Macbeth, Cressida and Cleopatra, he associated them with that "pit," symbolized by the cave where Hecate was worshipped in prehistoric times, and with the maternal lake of darkness and dissolution from which all being arose?

7

Hecate

HALF WITCH AND HALF GODDESS, associated with pre-Hellenistic fertility rites, the favorite of Zeus, and one of the queens of the underworld, Hecate is mentioned altogether six times in Shakespeare's plays. As a rule editors use footnotes to refer the reader to the Hecate-myth.

Contemporary depth psychology has revealed aspects of this myth that are full of bewildering ambiguities and contradictions. A study of the basic materials that constitute it indicates an archetype of evil basically matriarchal in nature, which Shakespeare alludes to in three of his tragedies. Hecate appears at midnight, an emanation of darkness, in the form of a curse, a poison, a dagger, to demand her offering. In the myth, men build altars to her and worship her in ecstatic self-abandonment. Her most insidious symbol is the snake: the tempter, the seducer, the poisoner.

In her twofold image as witch and goddess she is both destroyer and preserver. Related to the Egyptian Isis, the Canaanite Anath, and the Hindu Kali, her appalling blood-thirstiness is itself a symbol of her fertility. Blood shed by her is as the dew and the rain: the earth must drink it up in order to be fruitful. The myth joins birth to death, the masculine to the feminine, the lily to the weed. She is the Earth Mother, and yet dwells in the underworld. Human sacrifices are offered to her in rites that are meant to ensure the fruitfulness of men, cattle, and crops.

Shakespeare knew the myth in its most personalized form—after it had become part of classical literary tradition. In several instances, however, he made the myth his own, as if it no longer pertained to the literature of Rome where he found it. He incorporated it in his own poetry as a metaphor of evil closely associated with the tragic universe he created in these plays. No footnote can do justice to the archetype of witch and goddess, maid and mother, at times the eternal feminine and again a bisexual monster, standing watch at the crossroads where she dispenses eternal damnation, madness and death.

When Shakespeare alludes to the Hecate-myth in *Midsummernight's Dream* and *1 Henry VI* it is no more than a conventional literary device. Puck speaks of "triple Hecate's team. . . . Following darkness like a dream" (V, 2, 14), while Talbot (in a passage of doubtful origin) describes Joan of Arc as "that railing Hecate." He also calls her a "gad" and suspects her of surrounding herself with "lustful paramours" (III, 2, 53). Whenever Hecate appears in the world of Shakespeare's tragedies, she forms part of a prayer or invocation addressed to the powers of darkness to bring about the death of someone whose destruction would be the sacrifice required to ensure the victory of evil over good.

She is thus invoked in *Hamlet* by Lucianus, "nephew to the king," just before he pours the poison into the sleeping player-king's ear. The lines, we are given to understand, were written by Hamlet especially for this occasion. The poison—it may or may not be "Hebenon"—has been prepared according to a magic formula the core of which constitutes the threefold curse of Hecate:

> Thoughts black, hands apt, drugs fit, and time agreeing;
> Confederate season, else no creature seeing;
> Thou mixture rank, of midnight weeds collected,

> With Hecate's ban thrice blasted, thrice infected,
> The natural magic and dire property,
> On wholesome life usurp immediately. (III, 2, 270)

Hecate is twice mentioned in *Macbeth*. She also actually appears in Act III, scene 5, a scene which, in the opinion of some, is spurious,[1] while others again believe it to be an integral part of the *Macbeth* universe of evil.[2] The two invocations to Hecate that concern us here, were obviously written by Shakespeare himself. The first is spoken by Macbeth shortly before he murders Duncan, while the second occurs just after he has sent the murderers to kill Banquo. As in the poisoner's speech in *Hamlet*, the elements that lead up to the first invocation of Hecate belong to night, sleep, and violent death:

> Now o'er the one-half world
> Nature seems dead, and wicked dreams abuse
> The curtain'd sleep; witchcraft celebrates
> Pale Hecate's offering. (II, *1, 49*)

The second invocation is spoken in a spirit of even greater exaltation. Macbeth, almost beside himself with the anticipation of deliverance from Banquo and the witches' ambiguous prophecy to him, visualizes the coming murder as a kind of sacrifice at the altar of Hecate whose awe-inspiring presence broods over the whole scene:

> Ere the bat hath flown
> His cloister'd flight, ere to black Hecate's summons
> The shard-borne beetle with his drowsy hum
> Hath rung night's yawning peal, there shall be done
> A deed of dreadful note. (III, 2, *40*)

Lear's first frenzied outburst against Cordelia is centered upon an invocation to Hecate. He curses his daughter "By the sacred radiance of the sun / The mysteries of Hecate and the night. . ." (I, 1, 111) disclaiming all "propinquity and property of blood" and referring in particular to those "barbarous Scythians" who feed on the flesh of their parents.

From these four passages it is possible to reconstruct an archetypal Hecate as Shakespeare's creative imagination must have
visualized her in these three tragedies:

1. She possesses all the characteristics of either a witch or a
goddess.

2. Man prays to her for help in moments of spiritual crisis or
profound mental anguish.

3. She is on the side of evil, not an "instrument of darkness,"
but herself an embodiment of darkness.

4. The evil she stands for is clearly nonhuman. It works by
magic and is far beyond man's intellectual grasp.

5. She is associated in man's mind with violence of various
kinds, such as murder by poison or by stabbing, and the disrup-
tion of normal relationships between human beings.

6. She is invoked in an atmosphere of religious awe, her
name never being pronounced but in fear and trembling. Those
who make use of her name seem to be on the verge of insanity.
They are, as it were, possessed and no longer fully responsible
for what they are saying or doing.

7. Once Hecate has been addressed in prayer there is no return to normal living. In the play within the play the poisoner,
with whom Hamlet seems to identify himself, holds up the mirror to Claudius so that he may see himself as he really is, one
of Hecate's most faithful disciples, whose guilt will "unkennel"
itself only if and when he confronts the truth represented by the
image of the murder he has committed and which is now being
staged before him by Hamlet—the "nephew" of the play—for
his uncle's benefit. Macbeth, a dagger in his hand and an imaginary dagger floating before his already half-blinded eyes, realizes
pale Hecate's presence in his castle. He is no longer in full control of either his senses or his mind. A victim of his own hallucinations, he goes to Duncan's bedroom to murder sleep. In
order to survive in a world where "nothing is but what is not,"
he must provide Hecate with her "offering," the blood-sacrifice
that is going to be "celebrated" in an orgy of witchcraft. Lear's

curse implies the coming chaos of the storm on the heath. All blood-relationships will be abolished. The children of primeval times who gorged themselves on their parents' flesh will be nearer to his heart than are his daughters. For none of these three protagonists is there a return to spiritual conformity and to the acceptance of normal standards of conduct. Hamlet's uncle tries to pray in order to be forgiven, though he cannot repent. Realizing that the "primal eldest curse" is upon him, he naturally fails at prayer. Violence, Hecate's most characteristic attribute, joined to lust, has taken root in his soul. He is beyond redemption and knows it. So does Macbeth, for "returning were as tedious as go o'er" (III, 4, 137). There is indeed not blood enough to fill the "cistern of his lust." The image of the fly getting more and more "engaged" in a spider's web, used by Claudius in his prayer, is no less appropriate to Macbeth and Lear. Lear's predicament appears at first sight tragically more significant, because his "offering" to Hecate was made in all the innocence of his fatherhood, free of the moral evil that is implied in the invocations made in the other two plays. The redemption which the two usurpers, Claudius and Macbeth, fail to achieve, is given to Lear at the very moment of death, but only after he has passed through all the stages of suffering that seem to follow from Hecate's curse. For this is a poison which even Cordelia's "patience and sorrow" cannot undo.

8. The experience of human malignity which involves Hamlet, Macbeth, and Lear, is closely related to the lives of women whose unconscious is like "an unweeded garden that grows to seed." The evil they have cultivated has multiplied and has now come out into the open. For these women-figures are themselves emanations of Hecate, over life-size in their greed for power, or their corruption through lust, or both.

[I]

ONLY VAGUELY does Hamlet imply that his mother is the victim of an unscrupulous schemer, the "serpent" that is now her husband. It is not the "incest" itself that appalls Hamlet, but the to-him-incomprehensible intensity of her "compulsive ardour." Nor does Hamlet ever blame his father for the disaster that seems to have overtaken his marriage. Yet he implies on at least two occasions that something must have gone fundamentally wrong with a marriage where the husband was so loving a person "That he might not beteem the winds of heaven / Visit her face too roughly" (I, 2, 141), and yet was replaced by a rival whom Hamlet compares to a "mildew'd ear" and who—being doubtless "rank and gross in nature"—possesses all the qualities of a satyr and none of the divine attributes of Hyperion. That Hamlet should be so neurotically aware of the implications of the act committed by his mother and his uncle, whether in adultery or in legal marriage, characterizes his fantasy life in a manner which reflects elements of psychic instability in his own unconscious. His excessive grief for his dead father and his desire to kill his uncle are both compensatory manifestations of his own sense of unworthiness. The "mildew'd ear," by overcoming the "wholesome" brother, has proved the strength of the beast and the frailty of being merely human. The victory of the satyr over Hyperion leaves Hamlet without any meaningful mother-image. As the wife of his dead father, she is remembered as an idealized figure of purity and saintliness which in all likelihood she never was; as the wife of his uncle she represents sexual lust. Both images are creations of his unconscious. For "the underlying theme (of the play) relates ultimately to the splitting of the mother image which the infantile unconscious effects into two opposite pictures: one of the virginal Madonna, an inaccessible saint towards whom all sensual approaches are unthinkable, and the other of a sensual creature accessible to everyone. Indications of this dichotomy between love and lust . . . are to be found later in most men's sexual experiences. When sexual repression is highly pronounced, as with Hamlet, then both types of women are felt to be hostile: the pure one out of resentment at her repulses, the sensual one out of the temptation she offers to plunge into guiltiness. Misogyny, as in the play, is the inevitable result." [3]

"The killing of the uncle" is a necessary part of the son's final liberation from his mother. By identifying himself completely with his father whose death has to be "avenged," he recreates the masculine world of fatherhood in terms of a greatly purified self, symbolized by the sun and the emergence of consciousness. His uncle, by marrying his mother, has let loose the "cave-keeping" evils of their unconscious. Therefore Hamlet can never really forget himself when he remembers his uncle. His fate and that of the "adulterous beast" are inextricably bound up, in life no less than in death. By being his mother's lover, his uncle has accomplished in reality what has been buried in the deepest layer of Hamlet's own unconscious. Now to kill "the beast" is synonymous with killing himself. [4]

When Hecate is being invoked by the poisoner in the "Mousetrap," in words apparently written by Hamlet himself, the murder committed on the stage reflects Hamlet's own predicament. As a "nephew to the king" he appears to be killing his uncle, while in reality it is his father that is supposed to be murdered by his brother. Hecate's poison then is used for both father and uncle by a murderer whose compulsive act will lead to the marriage of a "nephew" with his "aunt" because, as Hamlet tells Ophelia, "the murderer gets the love of Gonzago's wife" who is now a widow but still a queen. Yet the supposed marriage between the murderer (who, by identification, is Hamlet himself) and the king's wife (who, after all, is his own mother) is not shown on the stage. Hamlet's choice of this play must have first originated in his *conscious* desire to perform his father's murder on the stage in order to test the conscience of the king, but later on, through unconscious identification, he sees himself—not as the nephew of a "damned villain"—but as the son of a beloved father whose wife he will marry, now that, at last, her widowhood would give him legal access to her. The situation thus created is not merely analogous to Oedipus' marrying his own mother, but can be found in numberless myths where the mother-goddess, uroboric, yet eternally feminine Hecate, endowed with the masculine attributes of the serpent, reveals symbolically significant aspects of her relationship with her son-lovers: "The Attis, Adonis, Tammuz, and Osiris figures, in the Near Eastern cultures are not merely born of a mother; on the contrary, this aspect is altogether eclipsed by the fact that they are their mother's lovers: they are loved, slain, buried, and bewailed by her, and are then reborn through her." [5] On the level of primeval mythology, Hamlet's "revenge," his killing both uncle and mother, may then be interpreted as one of the most significant events in a personalized history of the evolution of human consciousness: "In contrast to the passive, self-absorbed and narcissistic resistance to the mother, the fleeting defiance and self-destruction, this strengthening of masculine consciousness leads the ego to pit itself against the supremacy of the matriarchate." [6]

Hamlet's failure ever to become fully conscious of his entanglement with a Hecatelike *Magna Mater* and to free himself of it before it is too late, no doubt constitutes part of his "tragedy." Hamlet dies, as it were, in ignorance of the disease that caused his death. Yet he alone could have told the *complete* story of which Shakespeare gives us only the fragment that led to the killing of his uncle, the poisoning of his mother, and to his own death. Horatio being quite incapable of telling a story whose significance lies hidden in Hamlet's own unconscious, of which Horatio knows as little as anyone else in the play, Hamlet takes his secret along with him into the grave. As for his mother, there never really was anything that had to be hidden—being both "Niobe, all tears" and a "most pernicious woman," a symbol of the purest motherhood and at the same time a revolting monster, attractive and repulsive in equal measure—she is merely her maternal self in all the unconsciousness of her womanhood. It has, quite rightly, been pointed out that Gertrude is one of Shakespeare's least revealed women characters: it is her very indistinctness, the absence of any rationality about her, that deprives her of any conscious individuality and thus turns her into a symbolic representation of the power of the anima archetype over the lives of both husband and son.

Macbeth's consciousness is equally defeated by his wife, who, dedicated to "nature's mischief," looks like "the innocent flower" but is "the serpent under't." [7] Once more the myth of the Great Mother may help one to understand the significance of the psychological situation that makes the first two and a half acts of *Macbeth* the most harrowing in the play. According to the myth the respective development of the masculine and the feminine in human nature occurred regardless as to whether consciousness resided in the former or the latter. The myth may also provide us with an answer to the question whether Lady Macbeth is "conscious" of what she is doing or acts out of an irresistible impulse. For the relationship between Macbeth and his serpent-like wife can be understood only in terms of an increasingly ambiguous distribution of consciousness as the play progresses toward its inevitable conclusion. If one accepts the principle that "even in woman, consciousness has a masculine character" and that therefore "the correlation 'consciousness-light-day' and 'unconsciousness-darkness-night' holds true regardless of sex, and is not altered by the fact that the spirit-instinct polarity is organized on a different basis in men and women," [8] it is possible to arrive at an interpretation of Macbeth's tragic fall as a dissolution of personality and individual consciousness. Such a disintegrating process then leads to a form of insanity which, the myth never tires of telling us, "is an ever recurring symptom of possession by the emasculating, bewitching, deadly, and stupefying nature of the Great Goddess." [9] Lady Macbeth's prayer to the "spirits that tend on mortal thought" surely belongs to the domain of primeval myth rather than psychological drama. This element—the gradual but inevitable loss of consciousness in the "hero"—is even more obvious in Macbeth's descent into the cave, the underworld where Hecate and the witches are waiting to inflict upon him the final defeat by the apparition of the child with a tree in his hand and by the offerings thrown into the boiling cauldron.

Lear's two Hecate-like daughters, one of whom, at least, is called a "gilded serpent," revolt against his authority, and are driven by violence and lust to self-destruction. Yet Lear himself, Shakespeare's most patriarchal figure, comes to us out of the primordial darkness of myth. He represents all those irrational impulses that are commonly associated with a prehistoric culture based on the earliest taboos embodied in a primitive patriarchal code regulating human relationships.

There is, of course, the temptation to explain the ruthlessness and sexual revulsion which permeate the writing of *King Lear* in terms of the sources that Shakespeare used or, as some suggest, in terms of a personal sense of frustration that found an outlet in the writing of the play. On the other hand, one may see in *King Lear* the last and inevitable advance toward "ripeness," an advance of which Shakespeare was fully conscious when he created Edgar by the side of Edmund, and Cordelia by the side of Goneril and Regan. Even if all these are taken into account, a return to the myth and its primordial conflict between defeated fatherhood and fiend-like daughters, may prove illuminating. For the same fear of patriarchal disintegration can be observed in both the myth and Shakespeare. And though this fear may be expressed in a complex variety of ways, it consistently stresses the ominous threat to man's consciousness. The ambivalent femininity of the daughters imperils not merely a father's authority, but the very essence of all fatherhood.

The Greeks, in particular, supply us with a ready wealth of gods and goddesses whose pagan attributes pertain to the world of *King Lear*. For instance, one of the titans, Phorkys, called by Hesiod "the old one of the sea" [10] had three daughters, also mentioned by Hesiod, the Gorgons, by no means old women, but "rather similar to the masks that were set up to Hecate and also depicted her." [11] One of Phorkys' daughters was (again according to Hesiod) a goddess named Echidna: "She was born in a cave . . . with a masculine disposition and a gigantic frame resembling neither a human being nor an immortal god. In half of her body she was a beautiful-cheeked, bright-eyed young woman; in the other half she was a terrible, huge snake, thrashing about in the hollows of the divine Earth and devouring her victims raw. . . . In old vase-paintings she is indeed depicted as a winged and beautiful goddess with the body of a serpent from the hips downward." [12] Lear, in his adultery speech where "from the waist they are Centaurs / Though women all above," uses imagery that seems to be related to the ancient myth though there is no reason to assume that Shakespeare knew it.

To a patriarchal society, the only one that Shakespeare could take for granted, the revolt of the daughters against their father must have seemed a return to a barbarous matriarchal past where the dividing line between gods and men, on the one hand, and between men and beasts, on the other, had not yet been firmly established. The only fully integrated figure in *King Lear* is Edgar: it is through his eyes that we follow the violent growth of evil set in motion by the Hecate-like monsters, and the final return to a purified patriarchate based not on the absolute authority of a godlike tyrant, but on "ripeness" born of suffering and compassion. Cordelia, Shakespeare's own contribution to the original myth, sheds tears instead of blood. Her death, in the arms of her dying father, reconciles the warring elements: lust is turned into love, and barrenness into fertility.

Every one of these tragic heroes, then, lives under the shadow of a terrifying *Magna Mater,* a feminine projection of the collective unconscious, an anima-archetype symbolizing the as yet unrevealed chaos within. She transcends rational analysis. It is she who turns their life into a "tale told by an idiot." And the darkness which they follow is as remote from Puck's allegorical midsummer night's dream as it is closely related to the midnight orgies which early man celebrated in praise of Hecate around a boiling cauldron to pray for regeneration or accept the ineluctability of death.

What, then, is the meaning of this terrifying maternal symbol? What made Shakespeare transplant Hecate from her pre-Hellenistic habitat in the forests of Accadia to the remoteness of Hamlet's Denmark, inspire the cursed thoughts and bloody knives in medieval Scotland, and provide Lear's "darker purpose" with an even darker mystery in prehistoric England? The myth that preceded Shakespeare (and must have been well known to him in its personalized form) is confusing in its detailed explicitness. It seems to embrace the whole of man's unconscious life. Hecate is its main theme: the diverse manifestations of evil, in spirit and in substance, that man is heir to, are its main variations.

[II]

THE HISTORICAL APPROACH which attempts an analysis of this archetype in terms of influence, literary fashions and schools, uncovers obvious literary origins of the myth as used by Shakespeare. Many of his sources are found in the literatures of Greece and Rome. A good deal is known about the way Shakespeare adapted these sources for his own dramatic and psychological purposes. Medieval beliefs, legends and tales, as well as classical literature, also supplied Shakespeare with many of his references to witchcraft, magic, and various other forms of non-human evil which man has to fight in his struggle for survival.

Many of the medieval definitions of black magic made use of classical terminology. This may explain the psychological ambiguities resulting from the transmission of myths from one age to another. Thus we find in the English-Latin wordbook *Catholicon Anglicon* (1483) that an "Elfe" is defined as "lamia, eumenia" [13] while two centuries later (in 1650) in William Somner's Anglo-Saxon dictionary called *Dictionarium Saxonico Latino-Anglican* the following definition is given: "Hagesses. Larva, lamia, faria, Hecate, a hagg, a witch, a furie or a fiend, woman-Devill." [14]

In the specific case of Hecate Shakespeare had no need to consult dictionaries. Nor would Holinshed have been of any help, for Hecate is not mentioned there. The obvious source, then, is Ovid. In Books VII and XIV of his *Metamorphoses* Hecate appears a number of times as part of a pastoral civilization. Ovid's Hecate pertains to a more polite age than those that Shakespeare portrays in these three plays. Medea of Corinth invokes her whenever superhuman good or evil has to be accomplished. The ritual that Medea enacts on several occasions refers to a rejuvenation-cult with which Hecate was supposedly associated. First we hear of her "when her (Medea's) reason could not subdue her madness." [15] Trying to win Jason over to her love—"She went to Hecate's old altar, hidden / Deep in a shady forest. . . ." When Jason asks Medea to help him to add a few years to his father's life, she promises him to do so, "if only Hecate will stand by me." Her invocation to Hecate which follows immediately after, describes her as a kind of nature-goddess controlling all "natural" magic, which, incidentally, includes both good and evil:

> O Night, most true to mysteries, O stars
> Whose gold with the moon's silver shines and follows
> The fires of day, O Hecate, triple goddess,
> Witness and helper of magic art and charm,
> O Earth, provider of the herbs of magic,
> O winds, O little breezes, O streams, O mountains,

O lakes, O groves, O gods of the groves, O gods
Of night, come, help me, help me, help me!

. . . .

You have seen me . . . still the angry oceans,
Rouse the calm waters, drive the clouds away
Or marshall them together, exile winds,
Recall them . . .

. . . .

. . . I can make the moon
Darken, the car of the Sun turn pale at my singing,
The Dawn turn pale at my poisons. . . .[16]

That the first part of Medea's prayer reminds us of Prospero's
description of his "so potent Art," while the last lines evoke
Lady Macbeth's "black" magic when she asks "thick night" to
pall her "in the dunnest smoke of hell," is one more proof of
Shakespeare's astounding ability to adapt his sources to the exigencies of his various plots.

The ritual of rejuvenation is performed with the help of a
cauldron, a fertility-symbol in the ancient myth of Hecate. The
"boiling cauldron" is used by Shakespeare as a parody of the
original symbolic process by which human consciousness is shown
to develop out of an alchemical mixture of fire and water which
makes "the seed of consciousness" grow. Thus Jung refers to a
series of European mandala drawings "in which something like
a plant seed surrounded by its membranes is shown floating in
water. Then, from the depths below, fire penetrates the seed,
makes it grow, causing a great golden flower to unfold from the
germinal vesicle." Shakespeare is, of course, not aware of the
parallel; yet the "boiling cauldron" produces precisely the opposite effect of the alchemical process described by Jung: "Darkness gives birth to light; out of the 'lead of the water-region,'
grows the noble gold; what is unconscious becomes conscious in
the form of a living process of growth. . . . In this way the union
of consciousness and life takes place." [17]

Shakespeare exploits the possibilities of ambiguity inherent in the symbol. The knowledge Macbeth acquires is the result of a perversion of the ancient cult: while his despair, defeat, and death are implied in his final nightmare-vision of Banquo's sons, Medea's prayer for rejuvenation above the boiling cauldron is granted by Hecate. Aeson, Jason's father, is given back his youth by "natural" magic:

> Under the open sky
> She built twin altars of turf, the one on the right
> To Hecate, the one on the left to Youth. . . .
>
> . . . .
>
> And all the while the brew in the bronze cauldron
> Boiled and frothed white; in it were root-herbs gathered
> From Thessaly's lonely vales, and seeds and flowers,
> Strong juices, and pebbles from the farthest shores
> Of oceans east and west, and hoar-frost taken
> At the full of the moon, a hoot-owl's wings and flesh,
> A werewolf's entrails also, and the fillet
> Of a fenny snake, the liver of a stag,
> Long-lived, the eggs, the head, of the crow whose years
> Run for nine generations. All of these
> Were in the cauldron, and a thousand others,
> Things without names, out of the world of mortals . . . [18]

That "natural" magic may equally well be used for evil purposes is shown in the episode where the daughters of Pelias ask Medea to rejuvenate their father. Once more Medea "builds a quick fire under another cauldron" [19] and puts in only "clear water, no powerful herbs at all." Her magic spells and incantations make Pelias fall asleep, "a sleep like death." This is Duncan asleep as seen through Lady Macbeth's eyes after her matter-of-fact preparations for his murder. She has asked her husband to put "this night's great business into my dispatch" (I, 5, 67). Now that he hesitates, she ironically refers to his hope for kingship, as having been "drunk" in the past and now looking "green and pale" with fear. Medea addresses the daughters of Pelias in very similar language:

> You sluggish creatures,
> Why do you dawdle now? . . .
> Draw your swords, let his old blood out. . . .
>
> . . . .
>
> Where is your devotion?
> Where are you silly hopes? Perform your duty!

Love having changed into hate, Hecate's fertility-rite is turned
upside down. Instead of rejuvenation there is cold-blooded murder. Sight is replaced by blindness and the hands that kill become the true "instrument of darkness." Ovid's description

> Never a one
> Could watch the blow strike home; each turned her eyes;
> Blind girls with cruel hands, they struck. . . .

inevitably reminds us of the innumerable references to hands and
eyes in *Macbeth,* and Shakespeare's haunting insistence that such
a deed could only have been committed "in blindness" or must
ultimately lead to blindness—"What hands are here! Ha! they
pluck out mine eyes" (II, 2, 59), or Lady Macbeth's prayer for
darkness "That my keen knife see not the wound it makes" (I,
5, 53). When Medea transforms "sleep like death" into real
death, she herself becomes an embodiment of the Great Goddess.
Fertility changes into barrenness, nature as a symbol of the affirmation of all life is turned into a life-denying mockery. Hecate's cauldron is filled with "nature," dissected and deformed,
"things without names." When, in *Macbeth,* the witches, under
Hecate's guidance, prepare the cauldron for a final ceremony in
confirmation of Macbeth's sterility and in honour of Banquo's
"royal nature," they tell Macbeth that what they are doing is
"A deed without a name" (IV, 1, 49).

Hecate appears in Book XIV in an equally relevant context.
When Circe transforms Odysseus' men into beasts, it is only by
invoking Hecate's help that her success is assured. Once more
"natural" magic is used for purposes of evil. The following
lines[20] are full of associations pertaining to the *Macbeth*-universe:

But she [Circe] sprinkled
Poisonous juices on them, and called forth
Night and the god of Night from Hell and Chaos,
Wailing to Hecate in long-drawn crying,
And *the woods leaped from their place,* and *the ground rumbled,*
The trees grew white, and the grass was clotted red
Where the drops of poison fell, and *stones, it seemed,*
Made hoarse and bellowing sounds, dogs bayed, and the ground
Crawled loathsome with black snakes, and the thin phantoms,
The silent dead, fluttered around. The men
Trembled and wondered, and she touched their faces,
Trembling and wondering, with her wand; no man
Was any longer man; they all were beasts,
All different, all horrible.

In Macbeth's second monologue, where the invocation to Hecate first occurs, he prays to "the sure and firm-set earth" not to divulge his secret, "for fear / Thy very stones prate of my whereabouts" (II, 1, 57). And when Macbeth descends into the underworld, the cavern where the witches will tell him the future, we hear of trees "leaping from their places," while at the time of Duncan's murder "the earth was feverous and did shake."

Hecate, in Ovid as in the ancient myth, has the power to project the animal nature of man beyond the boundaries of his consciousness. She is frequently called the Mistress of Wild Animals and is represented on a number of monuments flanked by wild beasts. Shakespeare was fully aware of the psychological implications of a "magic" that holds such a mirror up to human nature. His use of the man-beast metaphor lights up the human condition in terms of a dichotomy which, in the tragic context of these plays, frequently reduces the "paragon of animals" to the status of a beast. Hamlet indeed speaks of his own oblivion as "bestial" and compares his mother to a "beast that wants discourse of reason." In his overwrought imagination both mother and uncle are transformed into beasts and he describes their love-making as the loathsome accouplement of animals "over the nasty sty." Similarly, in the Macbeth-universe animal images predominate. Lady Macbeth asks her husband after he has insisted that he "dare do all that may become a man"—

> What beast was it then that made you break
> This enterprise to me? (I, 7, 47)

Birds and beasts, throughout *Macbeth,* inhabit a darkness as profound as that of the human unconscious. They await Hecate's summons to be her messengers of death. They lurk in "fog and filthy air," ready to pervert nature or to offer themselves up as a sacrifice to the goddess whom they serve.

When Lear curses Cordelia "by the mysteries of Hecate," he reverses the natural order of things. Once more, in Edgar's words, man is "brought near to beast." The correlation between man and beast is constantly made: for "man's life is as cheap as beast's" (II, 4, 270). And Edgar knowing no less than Hamlet what the embodiment of the unconscious, the serpent's perversion of reason, can do to man, describes himself, with the desperate logic of lunacy, as having been "hog in sloth, fox in stealth, wolf in greediness, dog in madness, lion in prey" (III, 4, 94).

[III]

OVID'S USE of the Hecate myth provides a domesticated version of the archetype. By letting Medea (or Circe) invoke her for human good or evil, Ovid "personalizes" the myth. It is, therefore, a comparatively "tame" Hecate who is here associated with human love or hate, and who will, finally and without any rational motivation, further the one or the other. She is merely a supernatural agency in mythological garb, transformed into a literary device, which is used by the poet to convey an atmosphere of dread and mystery to the sophisticated Roman reader. Herein Ovid follows the polite fashion of the day. About a hundred years after him we find a similar treatment of Hecate in Apuleius' *Golden Ass* where she is called "the natural mother of all things . . . the initial progeny of all the worlds, chief of the powers divine, queen of all that are in Hell. . . ." [21]

Shakespeare's adaptation of the myth—as a mirror of life rather than as part of a literary fashion—implies a return to the archetypal content of the image created by primeval man in the "dark backward and abysm of time." In attempting to follow Shakespeare beyond Ovid, we may have to disregard historical continuity for a while. For the archetypal image is always with us and conventional division of time into past, present, and future becomes meaningless. What we are concerned with here are various levels of meaning that encompass a specific form of man's psychic reality, a spiritual tension which, unconsciously at first, found its original expression in myth and ritual. Shakespeare's modified use of both myth and ritual in these three tragedies dramatizes the tension and reveals implications that point beyond the text of the individual plays.

For the archetype, transformed into metaphor, adds a dimension of meaning that transcends the psychological or realistic validity of the experience represented on the stage. Once the pattern has been made clear, significances will relate to deeper layers of the unconscious than are accessible to conventional literary investigations on sources and historical background. The metaphysical nature of the Hecate myth, including the ritual associated with it, however elusive it may appear today, characterizes the archetype. The myth as dramatic metaphor has become a communicable symbol which the reader shares with the poet because it constitutes a timeless pattern made use of by Shakespeare as if it were, indeed, a religious rather than a literary formula.

It is, of course, doubtful whether an average Elizabethan audience—not having read Ovid as carefully as Shakespeare seems to have done—could "place" Hecate in any significant way. On the other hand, Shakespeare's three invocations to Hecate, in *Hamlet, Macbeth,* and *King Lear* (none of which deals with a specifically Greek subject or has a Greek background) may well have been an unconscious projection of certain passages from Ovid's *Metamorphoses,* a "sleeping image" out of the deep well of memory, for which there is no rational explanation, creating that magical synthesis which finds a place for the Hecate of the Greek myth in Hamlet's Denmark, Macbeth's Scotland, and Lear's England. The prayer to Hecate in these three instances is not necessarily even addressed to this or that goddess of the Greek myth, but to the speaker's own unconscious urge to identify himself with one of nature's archetypal emanations of darkness. In the idiom of today it might well be called a projection of their death wish into a universe peopled by powers of evil which are, very largely, of their own making. In that sense Shakespeare's Hecate is not the one we meet in Ovid: Shakespeare "de-personalizes" her again; instead of dispensing a merely human evil whenever it pleases her, she is present in the shadow of her primeval and nonhuman existence which hovers over these plays.

The prehistoric myth, as Ovid himself must have known it, is fairly explicit as regards Hecate's genealogy. Most of it comes from Hesiod's *Theogony,* written in the eighth century B.C., a poem dealing with the creation of the world, the gods, their origin and their relationships to one another. The names of several folk-gods mentioned by Hesiod are of Sanskrit origin and date from Indo-European times. The emphasis throughout is religious, not literary. Hecate has a hymn all to herself. The most detailed account of the part played by Hecate in Greek mythology is given by the imaginary narrator in Kerenyi's *The Gods of the Greeks*: "Hecate . . . was always closest to us—although her name perhaps means 'the Distant one'. It is not only her name that links her with Apollon and Artemis, who are also named Hekatos and Hekate, but also her family origin—if Hesiod is right in his account of it. She is elsewhere supposed to have been one of the Daughters of Night. . . . Hesiod, however, gives us the following genealogy: the Titan couple Phoebe and Koios had two daughters—Lete, the mother of Apollon and Artemis, and Asteria, a star-goddess who bore Hecate to Persaios or Perses, the son of Eurobia. Hecate therefore is the cousin of Apollon and Artemis, and at the same time a re-appearance of the great goddess Phoebe whose name poets often give to the moon. Indeed, Hecate used to appear to us carrying her torch as the moon-goddess. . . . She was therefore a true Titaness of the Titans, even though this is never expressly stated. On the contrary, she is said to be that Krataiis, that 'strong one' who bore to Phorkys the female sea-monster Skylla. Tales are told of her love-affair with gods of the sea: with Triton, in particular, whom Hesiod calls Eurybias, 'of wide force'. On the other hand, it was also said that Hecate was mistress of the Underworld and every night led around a swarm of ghosts, accompanied by the barking of dogs. She was even called Bitch and She-wolf." [22]

Her name has led to a good deal of confusion. She was sometimes called Prothyraia—the goddess who helped women in childbed (or sometimes cruelly oppressed them), while at other times she seems to be identical with Persephone who was also called Kore, the "Maiden." Both Hecate and Persephone were their mother's only daughters—a characteristic which they again share with Pandora and Protogeneia. Greek myths tell us that Persephone was ravished by Hades and fell victim to the god of death. Yet it is Hecate who is supposed to be queen of the realm of the dead.

The sacred number three was always associated with her— possibly because she ruled over the three elements of heaven, earth and hell. Shakespeare, incidentally, makes much of it. Puck speaks of "triple Hecate's team." In *Macbeth* the number three is constantly used in magic invocations. The witches dance to the rhythm of

> Thrice to thine, and thrice to mine,
> And thrice again to make up nine. (I, 3, 35)

"Magic" time is measured by the threefold mewing of the brinded cat and the threefold whining of the hedge-pig. The first witch curses the captain of the "Tiger" in very similar terms:

> Weary sev'n-nights nine times nine
> Shall he dwindle peak and pine. (I, 3, 22)

The poisoner in *Hamlet* describes the poison as having been "thrice blasted, thrice infected" with Hecate's ban. The sacred number three is part of the ambiguity which constitutes the Hecate myth. On the one hand, the trinity form is confined to women goddesses only: the Great Goddess' "tripartite sacred year"[23] was created when the powers of the underworld came to preside over agriculture and divided the seasons into three, symbolizing each season by an animal—lion for spring, goat for summer, serpent for winter. The dead themselves were invoked thrice: "Sacrifice was offered to them on the third day; the mourning in some parts of Greece lasted three days; the court of the Areopagus, watched over by the deities of the underworld, sat on three days; at the three ways the threefold Hecate of the underworld was worshipped."[24] Statues or images of Hecate were set up at the crossroads of three ways, "three wooden masks upon a pole, or a threefold statue with three faces looking in three directions."[25] She has, indeed, "three bodies and three heads—lion, dog and mare."[26] The number of her companions, the Erinyes, was also three. They were supposed to be "personified pangs of conscience after the breaking of a taboo—at first only the taboos of insult, disobedience, or violence to a mother."[27] Shakespeare's three witches in *Macbeth* are no less archetypal than their mistress Hecate. The Thessalian witches were Hecate's servants, whenever she was invoked in clandestine rites of black magic, especially where three roads used to meet. The place and time of the meeting of the witches at the beginning of *Macbeth* establish the relevance of the archetype for the rest of the play. It is not only "in thunder, lightning, or in rain," and "upon the heath": the constant references to darkness, night, hell, and death forever recall the fact that Hecate's dominion is with us throughout the play.

As an archetype, the Great Mother in the myth simultaneously destroys life and gives birth to life. The tree that is sacred to Hecate (as well as to Circe and Persephone) is the willow: both the willow and the yew are trees of death. The juice of the yew tree, Hebenon, is poured into the ear of Hamlet's father. His mother also dies poisoned. So does Hamlet himself. His uncle is forced to "drink off this potion" which is indeed "a poison temper'd by himself" (V, 2, 342). Hecate's cauldron contains "slips of yew / Sliver'd in the moon's eclipse" (IV, 1, 28). Macbeth as well as his wife inhabit a universe made barren by poison. He speaks of the "poison'd chalice" that he will have to drink though he prepared it for Duncan; Lady Macbeth has "drugged" the two chamberlains' possets "That death and nature do contend about them / Whether they live or die" (II, 2, 8). Lear, at the moment of greatest anguish, "bound upon a wheel of fire" asks Cordelia—"If you have poison for me, I will drink it" (IV, 7, 72). The myth helps us to enlarge our vision of Shakespeare's archetypal universe of evil in terms of poison made by men or nature. When Hercules, during his Twelfth Labour tries to capture Cerberus, the creature resists, "averting his eyes from the sunlight, and barking furiously with all three mouths; his slaver flew across the green fields and gave birth to the poisonous plant econite, also called Hecareis, because Hecate was the first to use it." [28] It is both a poison and a paralysant and is used by the Thessalian witches in the manufacture of their flying ointment. The death element in the Hecate universe is further emphasized by Hecate's messenger, the owl. In *Macbeth,* at the very moment the murder is being committed:

> It was the owl that shrieked, the fatal bellman,
> That gives the sternest good-night. (II, 2, 4)

When the northern tribes invaded Greece, they must have found Hecate established there since primeval times as a fertility goddess rather than as goddess of death—involving ideas and practices contrary to their own beliefs and customs. Her cult was far too powerful and deeply rooted to be ignored by them. She became one of the Chthonioi—spirits who live in the dark recesses of the earth, providing men with their means of subsistence and taking them back into the earth when they die. To offer up sacrifice to the dread underworld-goddess, Hecate, was an action fraught with great danger: for she might cast a spell on you for either good or evil, life or death. Hesiod gives us the only connected account of the instructions given for the performance of a sacrifice to Hecate: "Waiting for the mid-moment of the night's dividing, having washed thyself in the flood of the unwearied river, alone and apart and clad in sombre hues, dig thee a pit well-rounded. And within slay a she-lamb, and lay it raw and whole on a pile which thou hast heaped together in the pit. Then pray to Hecate the sisterless, who is called Perseis, pouring from a cup of honey of the hive-bee. When thou hast thus mindfully propitiated the goddess, get thee away back from the pyre; and let neither thud of feet nor howl of dogs tempt thee to look back, lest thou bring all to nought and thyself return not to thy comrades in any seemly wise." [29]

The cauldron in *Macbeth* is a repetition of the same sacrificial ritual. The fertility prayed for in the ancient rite, at all times of a questionable nature, has here been infected by the poison within and without. It is a distorted picture of the Thesmophoria, the great festival of Demeter and her daughter Kore—and, by implication, of Hecate, the great Earth Mother. The ritual is today known fairly well. A deep cleft was dug in the earth. Into it women threw certain magic charms, fir cones, snakes, live pigs, and various other sexual symbols. There they remained until they were collected and scattered over the fields to ensure fertility. The Sacred Sow is indeed the only animal in Greek religion that actually had sacrifice made to it: "The heretical image of the sky-woman as a sow, which shows her star-children going into her mouth in the manner of a sow eating her young, is to be found in a linguistically very early dramatic text preserved in the false tomb of Seti I, in the temple of Osiris at Abydos. . . . Isis, like Nut, the Kore Kosmu, appears as a white sow and the head of the old god Set has been interpreted as that of a pig. In Troy, Schliemann found the figure of a pig dotted with stars, evidently representing the sky-woman as a sow, and the cult of the sow as a mother-goddess has left numerous traces. . . . It is important to remember that when Eleusis was permitted to make its own coinage, the pig was chosen as a symbol of the mysteries. . . . The pig, then, symbolizes the female, the fruitful and receptive womb. As the 'uterine animal,' it belongs to the earth, the gaping pit, which, in the Thesmophoria is fertilized by pig sacrifice. . . ." [30] That Shakespeare was aware of the sacredness of the sow as a symbol of fertility when he wrote *Macbeth,* appears from the cauldron scene itself. When the first witch asks Macbeth "If thou'st rather hear it from our mouth / Or from our masters?" and Macbeth wants to see those "masters," the witch applies the ancient fertility-rite in order to deceive him the more—"Pour in sow's blood, that hath eaten / Her nine farrow" (IV, 1, 64). In this connection one remembers the second witch's reply to the question "Where hast thou been sister?"—"Killing swine" (I, 3, 2). These fertility-rites with their symbolic cleft in the earth and the pig-sacrifice associated with it are far removed from the civilized pastoral invocations we find in Ovid. Women appeared at these festivals dressed as men, and men as women wearing veils. These orgies were called "Hysteria" because of their close association with the pig and the womb. Those who participated were indeed obsessed by divine madness: "In the celebration of these anniversaries, the priestesses of Aphrodite worked themselves up into a wild state of frenzy, and the term Hysteria became identified with the state of emotional derangement associated with such orgies. . . . The word Hysteria was used in the same sense as Aphrodisia, that is, as a synonym for the festival of the goddess." [31] Some of Hecate's masculine attributes, the snake, the dagger, and the torch, occur in significant contexts in *Macbeth.*

The bisexual nature of the worship and of the Great Goddess herself also reminds us of Shakespeare's constant references to the confusion of sexual elements in *Macbeth*. Obviously masculine elements are associated with the Weird Sisters. Lady Macbeth wishes to be "unsexed" while her husband is "too full of th'milk of human kindness." It is she who repeatedly expresses doubts as to Macbeth's manhood while he, appalled at what he considers to be an unnatural absence of tenderness in her, exclaims—

> Bring forth men-children only;
> For thy undaunted mettle should compose
> Nothing but males. (I, 7, 72)

It is an androgynous universe in which we move with the twofold symbol of the sow that farrows and the wolf that kills.[32]

The original Hecate myth appears to be the result of a clash of mighty spiritual forces that called for reconciliation. Gilbert Murray formulates the clash in terms of religious and cultural setting when he speaks of "the tradition of a Northern conquering race, organized on a patriarchal monogamous system vehemently distinct from the Matrilinear customs of the Aegean and Hittite race, with their polygamy and polyandry, their agricultural rites, sex-emblems and fertility-goddesses."[33]

Can this conflict between patriarchal and matriarchal systems of culture which is at the very core of the Hecate myth, reveal anything new to the reader of Shakespeare's plays? How, indeed, can the myth of the Great Mother reaching back thousands of years into nonhistoric, indeed preconscious times, be reconciled with the creative impulse that made Shakespeare write tragedies at the beginning of the seventeenth century? Surely, the artist who created Gertrude, Lady Macbeth, Goneril and Regan, as well as their male counterparts, indeed their "victims"—the son, the husband, and the father—was not conscious of using an archetype? He introduced the archetype into his vision of the perils of the soul, and gave dramatic significance to the fear and the worship of the Great Mother leading to self-sacrifice and self-immolation at the altar of "pale Hecate." Yet, Shakespeare through the medium of his art which created mother and son, wife and husband, father and daughters, made a rebirth into consciousness possible—which is no longer part of the myth— through suffering, insanity and annihilation.

The Hecate figure, may, indeed, be interpreted as a primordial image. It speaks with a thousand voices. When Shakespeare restores it to its ancient, prehistoric context "he enthralls and overpowers, while at the same time he lifts the idea he is seeking to express out of the occasional and the transitory into the realm of the ever-enduring. He transmutes our personal destiny into the destiny of mankind, and evokes in us all those beneficent forces that ever and anon have enabled mankind to find a refuge from every peril and to outlive the longest night." [34]

[IV]

THE MYTH AND THE PLAY have this in common: they spring from the same source though their mode of expression differs. The one creates the psychological archetype, the other gives it a human face. What is vague, confused, indistinguishable in the myth, acquires form and structure in the artistic vision. The poet, a creator of symbols, transmutes the archetype into a condition of the human soul. Man's tortuous pilgrimage from the unconscious, its instinctual drives and orgiastic frenzies of self-abandonment, to self-hood, the purposeful delineation of values and the consequent ability to create universally valid symbols, corresponds to man's gradual deliverance from the Great Mother, and his deepening of consciousness and self-realization. In this context, Shakespeare's use of the Hecate figure outgrows the limitations of his source material and enlarges the range of his tragic vision.

The hero, be he son, husband, or father, is, in terms of the archetypal symbol, always in danger of losing his masculine independence, of being first "blinded" and then swallowed by the "maternal unconscious." The threat comes from without as well as from within. All the uncontrolled affects and primeval impulses, all the evils that have their origin in the unconscious, are the progeny of the *Magna Mater*. She is the archenemy of the hero, the symbol of the tamer of instincts, the destroyer of the dragon. He, the hero, "is the bringer of light, form, and order out of the monstrous pullulating chaos of Mother Nature." [35] Both in the prehistoric myth and in Shakespeare's tragedies, the symbolism points clearly enough to the victory of the masculine, conscious spirit over the powers of the matriarchate. The mother, the wife, and the daughter have to be overcome so that order and consciousness may be re-established. Hamlet's realization that the "readiness is all"; Macbeth's final resignation before the "brief candle" which is his life; and Lear's discovery of "patience," take place when the fight is already over, the anima-archetype vanquished, and the need for order made conscious. Each of these plays has its secondary hero whose primary function it is to let us perceive the psyche behind the symbol, the light-giving integrity of the self piercing the darkness of unconscious violence and lust. Fortinbras, Malcolm, and Edgar— though by no means the main protagonists in their respective plays—show us the evolution in Shakespeare's own awareness of the symbolical content of the archetype: while Fortinbras is "of unimproved mettle hot and full" and no doubt remains so to the end of the play; and Malcolm, though certainly a bringer of light, argues the justice of his cause politically and therefore lacks the innocence of the archetypal hero, Edgar, who alone, almost literally, makes others "see," and teaches them, and us, to be "pregnant to good pity" (IV, 6, 227). His "ripeness" is that of human consciousness, not that of the womb. Yet all the three alike belong to the same archetype: they are young and aware of the strength that youth gives; they return from exile where they lived in defeat and humiliation; they do not acknowledge any significant family relationship. Though they are all three sons, their fathers have died violent deaths, slain in battle, murdered in sleep, annihilated in blindness. Their will is all their own: their natural element is fighting. Their triumph is "masculine" in the literal and symbolic sense of the word. Gertrude, Lady Macbeth, Goneril and Regan are dead. The monster has swallowed itself. The "time is free," because the sacrificial ritual to Hecate has come to an end. The emphasis on fertility has shifted from the "sulphurous pit," the farrowing sow, the three-headed beast, to Miranda's brave new world, Shakespeare's utopia of the reign of man's consciousness over the unconscious.

When Shakespeare writes *The Tempest* he is as aware as ever of man's craving to satisfy his lust and his desire for power. The Hecate-myth still haunts Shakespeare in the figure of Sycorax, the witch, her god Setebos, and her son Caliban. The story of Ariel's liberation from the cloven pine in which he was held captive by Sycorax—just as Edgar's "preservation" in a hollow tree—is indeed the story of man's deliverance from the evil of the unconscious. Sycorax has her magic charms as Hecate had hers—"toads, beetles, bats" (I, 2, 340)—animals belonging to the *Macbeth* universe of the Great Mother. Hecate, incidentally, like Sycorax, also had an island of her own, Hekatesnesos, near the island of Delos, where she was worshipped in ancient times. The power of Sycorax also extends over the sea, the earth and the sky. Once more, adapting Ovid for his own purpose, Shakespeare tells us that she was

> One so strong
> That could control the moon make flows and ebbs,
> And deal in her command, without her power. (v, *1, 269*)

As a moon-goddess she could impose her will on the spirits of darkness and death: her art like Hecate's was black magic. For this she was banished from Argier. Prospero speaks of "Mischiefs manifold and sorceries terrible / To enter human hearing" (I, 2, 264). Her "grand hests" are too horrible to be named. Ariel being too delicate "To act her earthy and abhorr'd commands"

(I, 2, 273), was confined "in her most unmitigable rage" into a cloven pine. She did this with the help of "her most potent ministers." The spirits of the underworld serve her no less faithfully than they did Hecate.

The dividing line between myth and metaphor disappears when we apply the criterion of the archetype. The very name of Sycorax, though not found elsewhere, may be derived from the Greek συς (sow) and κοραξ (raven). Circe whom we have already met in a similar context, is an even more likely source. It is she who (in Ovid) invokes Hecate to reduce men to beasts by working on their senses. Is this Sycorax' "grand hest" which Ariel is either unwilling or unable to fulfill? Her son Caliban, the fruit of her womb, appears to us the ultimate symbolic manifestation of the beast in man, whose consciousness has failed to free itself from the sulphurous pit. He acts out his passions in the calculating violence of his various lusts, and basically unaware of the validity of moral distinctions, incapable therefore of sympathy and compassion. And yet Prospero endowed with a "beating mind" which makes him choose the "rarer action" of forgiveness rather than vengeance, acknowledges Caliban as his: this "thing of darkness" is impervious to Prospero's "art."

Caliban is the price that Prospero has to pay for having overcome the anima-archetype. By freeing Ariel he integrates the unconscious, imposes a newly acquired discipline upon the mind, indeed "makes conscious" his own striving for independence from the orgiastic ritual of sacrifice and fertility, while at the same time he becomes aware of the limitation of his own ego in more profound anguish than any Fortinbras, Malcolm, or even Edgar can ever realize. By controlling the elements of nature and the mind of man, his "art" prepares a redeemed world of civility and learning, in every sense the antithesis of the unholy power of Sycorax. The Masque which he performs for the benefit of the two young innocents, though clearly in imitation of ancient fertility rites, but within the context of a pastoral civilization which upholds the principles of honor and chastity, is therefore merely an "insubstantial pageant," and the vision that he creates, a "baseless fabric" doomed to dissolve into nothingness.

Hecate, then, has been overcome only for the time being, civilized values upheld, man's spirit freed. The archetype of unreason no longer exercises her mighty fascination over men, filling them with a frenzied desire to offer themselves up to her in senseless self-immolation. Out of the waves of the unconscious arises Miranda, the maid and the virgin, whose chastity and honour are inviolable and who looks at life with the innocent eyes of childhood. She is no longer aware of the curse, the poison, or the dagger because her father by his "rarer action" has exorcised the evil and has substituted compassionate intelligence for violence and lust.

Ferdinand and Miranda cannot help Prospero carry his burden of despair. For the agony of consciousness is his alone. Having disposed of his Art by throwing it away, he now returns to ordinary humanity. It is not "brave"; neither is it new or innocent. Looking at his unredeemed brother Antonio and remembering Caliban, he realizes that Nature and Man have not been, in any fundamental way, chastened or redeemed. He may well ask himself what price man must pay to uphold the stability of a patriarchal civilization (of which he is Shakespeare's most convincing—because most conscious—representative). If Caliban cannot be "nurtured" in the arts of civilization, is man not then condemned to live under Hecate's ban forever, even though he may, if only for a time, succeed in covering it up by the discipline of Art and the conscious exercise of compassion?

PART THREE

The Self

8

Prometheus

T HE *Self,* in Jung's theory of archetypes, is an invisible component of the unconscious. Like other archetypes, it cannot be defined except through symbols. The language used in
such definitions must, thus, necessarily be metaphorical. Since
the Self is an indispensable ingredient in the process of individuation, it comprises both what the ego "knows," that is man's
consciousness, and what it is ignorant of. The Self stands for
whatever totality a man may achieve in his striving for integration. As an archetype of wholeness, the Self stresses the need for
an enlarged consciousness which has succeeded in integrating the
unconscious without dissolving itself in it.

Being an image of totality the symbols of the Self most nearly
corresponding to its "personality" are those which contain elements of brightness and darkness, unity and division, form and
formlessness. In a passage dealing with the mana-personality,
Jung describes it as being "strange to us and yet so near, wholly
ourselves and yet unknowable, a virtual centre of so mysterious
a constitution that it can claim anything—kinship with beasts
and gods, with crystals and with stars—without moving us to
wonder, without even exciting our disapprobation. . . . I have
called this centre the *Self.* . . . It might equally be called "the

God within us.' " ¹ As it can be known only through myths, dreams, and fantasies, its symbolism is of a primordial nature. It may, for instance, appear as a single star, sun, or eye, or assume the shape of a mandala. It is implied in the concept of quaternity as well as that of the circle. Although the "shape" of the *Self* may be sensed, nothing can be said about its contents. For though "the ego is the only content of the Self that we do know . . . [it] is itself a transcendental postulate which, although justifiable psychologically, does not allow of scientific proof." ²

What has already been said about the anima-archetype with regard to Shakespeare is equally applicable to the Self. Insofar as it is an archetype and not a "character," it appears on the stage as a projection only. Within the context of a dramatic action it serves as a principle regulating the interaction between the ego and the contents of the unconscious. As it pertains to the process of individuation, the Self is thus a symbol of integration, the *daimon* of the ancient Greeks, the very opposite of what makes men "selfish" or "individual."

The Prometheus figure, as interpreted by Jung, is doubly relevant in a study of Shakespeare, first, as it furnishes a revealing analogy to the tormented attempts of some of Shakespeare's heroes to reach individuation through consciousness alone, and secondly, as an archetypal image of human excellence. These two apparently contradictory interpretations of the Prometheus archetype supplement each other. As a bringer of consciousness he reveals the pitfalls that stand in the way of complete integration of the ego through too great a reliance on the elements of rationality in the human psyche, while at the same time he alone, through the exercise of the power of consciousness for the good of others, can point the way toward psychic wholeness. Like all other archetypes, the Prometheus figure embodies a choice between two contradictory and mutually exclusive forms of existence. On the human plane this choice frequently determines the preponderance of good over evil, or the conquest of the fair by the foul. The archetype thus represents no clear-cut ethical

principles of conduct. It is, like the unconscious from which it
springs, morally ambivalent.

The "suffering" of Prometheus, Jung implies on several occasions, is related to his usurpation of consciousness. By achieving
the "new knowledge" he has raised himself above the level of
ordinary mortals and thereby has alienated himself from humanity. Now he is, as the myth says "chained to the lonely cliffs of the
Caucasus, forsaken of God and man." [3]

The conquest of consciousness may lead to either liberation
or captivity. In civilized society it stands for what Jung calls "a
Promethean freedom"; for this reason it "also partakes of the
nature of a godless hubris." [4] Each new advance toward a greater
consciousness causes "a kind of Promethean guilt" at having substituted man's knowledge for knowledge derived from nature,
and the values of civilization for the authority of primordial
experiences. It may well be because of this alienation from the
divine, the human, and the natural that Prometheus "suffering
his 'godlike' state . . . is preparing a work destined to alleviate
the sufferings of mankind." [5]

The stories woven around Prometheus in the original Greek
myth illumine the diverse manifestations of consciousness as they
appear in some of Shakespeare's plays. As a dual being, he is one
of the gods of Olympus and yet takes the side of mankind when
its survival is threatened by the gods. His "crooked thoughts" and
devious ways help him to steal the fire from heaven. Some ver-
sions of the myth even go so far as to assert that he himself
created man in opposition to the autocratic rule of Olympus.
Having given life to the body, the myth continues, he, like Pyg-
malion, fell in love with his own creation. Not satisfied with
being an artificer of beautiful forms, he felt the need to create
consciousness which alone would infuse life into inanimate
matter. This, indeed, is what he is supposed to have done, either
alone or with the help of some other gods: "Certain late-period
sarcophagi in Rome are adorned with reliefs, showing how
Prometheus fashioned man: in the form of a small statue, on

which Athene is bestowing a soul, by bringing to it a butterfly which in our (i.e. Greek) language is called *psyche,* like the soul." [6]

By giving consciousness to man he became a bringer of freedom and made man's survival possible and, indeed, desirable. As his name implies, he is also "the foresighted" and "the provident." In a recent study of Prometheus as "an archetypal image of human existence" he is described as being "compelled by his own shortcoming to offend against his environment and his companions in growth; who in so doing employs devious, crooked thinking (for in the world of growth the pathways are naturally crooked); inevitably a wounder and a wounded one." [7]

The most distinctive feature of this archetype as he appears in the primordial myth is his willingness and ability to help others in distress. Though his wisdom seems to be of divine origin, the means he employs to translate this wisdom into action are human. Symbolically, he is a figure dispensing light and warmth among those who live in darkness. To raise these desperate and lost souls to a level where survival, be it in body or in mind, is an aim worth pursuing, is his main function. He has much in common with the "wise old man" of dreams and fairy tales, the product of a collective unconscious reappearing in different shapes and situations, as "magician, doctor, priest, teacher, grandfather, or any other person possessing authority . . ." but always when he is most needed to hold up an ideal image of wholeness that "compensates [man's] state of spiritual deficiency by contents designed to fill the gap." [8]

The "wise old man" of folk legends and dreams appears as a symbol of moral and spiritual forces that lie beyond man's conscious thought. At times, indeed, he acquires a valid existence only when "thinking" is no longer possible and the hero finds himself in the desperate situation of having to make a decision without having the inner resources to do so. Whenever the archetype appears, the hero is compelled to make a choice for better or for worse. Though the wisdom of this archetype may assume a healing virtue, it may equally well possess all the attributes of an affliction. Among primitives the medicine man is generally taken to be a healer and helper, though he may be responsible for the poison that kills, if the patient is unwilling to be cured. Whatever the ultimate function of the "wise old man" in myth or dream, he is always a mediator between man's ego-centered consciousness and his unconscious. As a lightbearer he may show the way to affirmation or to denial, to heaven or to hell. He may therefore appear as a divine tutor or as a satanic seducer. Thus he becomes an embodiment of psychic polarity dispensing good or evil, "but it depends upon man's free—i.e. conscious—decision whether the good also will be perverted into something satanic. Man's worst sin is his unconsciousness." [9]

The archetypal healer as he appears in Shakespeare, therefore, must first wound in order to cure. The devious ways he employs to help the hero in his growth are part of the process of individuation which he helps to bring about. By adjusting himself to the "naturally crooked" ways of men, he symbolically acquires the characteristics of the darkness he is supposed to disperse. He in no way resembles the romantic Promethean figure as Goethe conceived it, the solitary and "immortal prototype of man as the original rebel and affirmer of his fate: the original inhabitant of the earth, seen as an anti-god, as Lord of the Earth." [10] Nor does he foretell the coming of ultimate harmony and liberation of Shelley's prophetic vision. He is far more Greek than "modern," a revitalized archetype rather than a re-interpretation of the ancient mythologem in terms of nineteenth-century liberalism and belief in human progress. As a mediator between the human and the divine, he is both savior and seducer, providing men with fire either to create life anew or destroy it. An antithetical figure in terms of his half-human, half-divine nature, he belongs to Olympus no less than to Hades. The realm where he feels most at home, however, is darkness. It is this archetype of the mediator that Shakespeare resurrects in some of his plays.

His healers exhibit the mature wisdom of middle age. He uses some of them in quite a casual manner, though without them the hero would have been unable to extricate himself from a perplexing situation brought about by his own lack of awareness or insight. Such a figure is Friar Francis in *Much Ado*. Others again are an intrinsic part of the play's dramatic texture. Their wisdom, however, is impersonal and uninvolved. They dispense the fruits of their maturity, as it were, "from above."

The common denominator that characterizes such different figures as Theseus, in *Midsummer Night's Dream*, Vincentio, in *Measure for Measure*, and Prospero, in *The Tempest*, is their ability to mediate between the conflicting trends in human nature and to impose a principle of order on the chaos that inevitably results when the unconscious threatens to win the upper hand. Their apparent aloofness from human strife, emotional bias, and intellectual confusion, hides a profound awareness of the destructiveness of uncontrolled impulses. This awareness is translated into action in a variety of ways. Survival is rendered possible only after disguise, make-believe, or even "magic," have re-established the normal function of consciousness as a regulating principle in the human psyche. In this sense, Theseus appears to be a preparatory sketch for Vincentio who, in turn, paves the way for the coming of Prospero. Yet it is Friar Francis, in the earlier comedy, a relatively insignificant figure in the play, who first makes use of the "devious" formula for survival which pertains to the Promethean archetype. Though Hero's death is "real" only insofar as Claudio's "study of imagination" is concerned, it constitutes the only true cure for his defective insight. Where that other priest, Friar Laurence in *Romeo and Juliet*, one more mediator between light and darkness, so lamentably fails because his formula is determined by the material properties of nature only, Friar Francis succeeds. He is the first of Shakespeare's "wise old men" who replaces medical prescription based on man's fragmentary knowledge of curative chemistry by the "magic" of spiritual healing.

Vincentio carries the application of this esoteric remedy a step further. The "old fantastical duke of dark corners" is an expert in devious ways. To save others, he must indeed first save himself. By putting on the garb of a priest he is able to apply "craft against vice," and only by forcing others into various disguises can he re-establish some form of primeval innocence (however crookedly arrived at). Friar Francis's individual treatment through spiritual rebirth is here applied to a whole group of people: deceit and artifice become instruments of truth, while a semblance of authority is the pathway that leads to a greater coherence in living. The very shortcomings of the archetypal figure [for Vincentio, in spite of obvious "divine" analogies, is, if anything, human indeed, "one that, above all other strifes, contended especially to know himself" (III, 2, 226)] guarantee the survival of Angelo. For since the repressed contents of man's unconscious are most subject to corruption, he has to be saved through his own unconscious, and in "crooked" ways, from the chaos created by incompatible impulses striving for fulfillment.

Prospero turns the "priestly" prescription into the magic of his art. The figure who comes nearest the ideal of human wholeness in Shakespeare's work, he controls the forces of nature, and disciplines the supernatural. The "fire" that he brought to men is in part stolen from heaven, but it also has all the attributes of the fires of hell. For both Ariel and Caliban are necessary to make his world. The political opportunist and the moral misfit, the ignorant young and the smug middle-aged, the innocently unaware and the consciously corrupt, are all equally shown to be in need of guidance. By directing the action from afar and imposing the highest moral criteria on himself as on others, his own defective awareness is relegated to the past, while the present reveals him as a redeemer and healer of wounds. Though Shakespeare never explicitly relates Prospero's past lack of insight to his present integrated personality, one is made to understand that the twelve years spent on the island have been devoted to this process of individuation. Only now does he begin to understand himself and others. From the seclusion of his cell to which he retired to improve by his "Art" what "Nature" had failed to accomplish, he frees men—even if only temporarily—from despair and suffering. The ideal image of human existence he wishes to re-create is a reflection of his own psyche. It lies in the nature of the archetype that this image should contain an unbridgeable polarity. The very validity of survival, in the company of Caliban —and perhaps even in his service—is, by implication, questioned. Prospero may well ask himself whether his own completeness provides sufficient moral justification for the redemption of mankind. For can what he has achieved by "Art" be communicated to those whose nature has left them incomplete? Shakespeare, in *The Tempest,* leaves his archetypal tale unfinished. Having brought forgiveness to men, Prospero realizes his own integration. Yet he seems to suggest that the end of "healing" art may still be despair, unless he takes the ultimate step from magic to prayer, and from forgiveness to compassion.

To approach these three figures in terms of "characterization" would burden the archetype with historical and psychological formulas, without revealing its essentially dual nature. More than half a century ago, for example, in a scholarly edition of *Measure for Measure,* an attempt was made to apply psychological criteria to Vincentio's moral conduct. Considered as a character taken from life, which here means nineteenth-century middle-class behavior patterns, Vincentio failed to please the average theatre-goer: "The Duke hardly seems to be a personage to delight in. It is not merely his didactic platitudes and his somewhat over-done pompousness that get upon one's nerves, but his inner character. We first meet him too timid or too irresolute to enforce his own laws and deputing his duty to another, while he himself plunges into a vortex of scheming and intrigue; concluding by falling in love with a votary. . . . And was not his a very shifty way of bringing [Angelo] to justice, instead of a straight prosecution? . . . I imagine Shakespeare was not in love with his Duke. . . ." [11] Yet Vincentio, just as Theseus before him or Prospero after him, eludes this kind of character analysis. For their function in the plays is symbolic rather than dramatic. There could have been little hope for man's survival, on the individual or the social plane of existence, no renewal of life, no spiritual rebirth, without the archetypal teacher, guide, and healer. They occur in Shakespeare's plays wherever he requires a symbol of initiation, mediating between the conscious ego and the contents of the unconscious, finally leading the action of the play to a meaningful conclusion. Such a Promethean figure represents the "recognized archetype of the mighty man in the form of hero, chief, magician, medicine-man, saint, the ruler of men and spirits, the friend of God." [12]

The psychic integrity of the mana-personality is beyond the range of modern man's increasingly restricted field of imagination. Such an ideal image of human perfection must necessarily remain a psychological abstraction to those whose minds have been infected by a belief in scientific progress as the sole criterion of the good life. Accustomed as we are to think of human completeness exclusively in terms of the social adaptability of the individual, conformism to the lowest average is regarded as the most desirable of all virtues, while any form of conscious nonadaptation to evil is likely to be looked down upon as eccentric willfulness or moral self-conceit. The mana-personality is, by definition, nonconformist. For its integrity can have no dealings with the average. Its dual propensity for good or for evil, to dispense blessing or damnation, to heal or to infect, is therefore always subject to popular suspicion. In our own time it has, as a rule, been liquidated in a monotonous brutality of ways. For today, as in the primordial past and still so in Shakespeare's time, "the mana-personality is always in possession of the secret name, or of some esoteric knowledge, or has the prerogative of a special way of acting . . . in a word, it has an individual distinction." [13]

Anthropology corroborates the findings of depth psychology. The "wise old man" that emerges out of the collective myth, reappears in the shape of the priestly king, as the incarnate human god who by sympathetic magic or apprehension controls the destiny of men. According to Frazer, ancient man's faith in the king as a mediator between him and the gods was encouraged by his conviction that the king was "frequently a magician as well as a priest; indeed he appears to have often attained to power by virtue of his supposed proficiency in the black or white arts." [14] Now, upper-class conduct at the court of Messina, in *Much Ado,* in the Vienna of *Measure for Measure,* and at the courts of Naples and Milan, in *The Tempest,* is the very opposite of archaic man's simple trust in divine or kingly providence. It is on purpose shown to be highly sophisticated and subtly civilized. It is also fully aware of the existence of strict codes of conduct intended to guide members of this upper class in their dealings with one another, be it in politics or war, love or marriage. In each of these societies moral uncertainty prevails. The young, the ignorant, and the corrupt require the guidance of some "wise old man" who also would have the power of preventing them from losing their moral bearings. Claudio without the support of Friar Francis, Angelo without Vincentio's compassionate understanding, Antonio and Sebastian deprived of Prospero's intervention, would have brought about increased suffering and irremediable evil on themselves as on others. Their civilization is merely skindeep. The predominance of the unconscious creates a susceptibility to the contagion of evil. This, in turn, makes the ideal counter-image indispensable: Claudio's blindness could only be healed by Friar Francis' all-seeing wisdom, Angelo's loss of self-control by the all-controlling knowledge of Vincentio, Antonio's and Sebastian's compulsive urge toward absolute political authority by Prospero's all-embracing insight.

In this sense Friar Francis, Vincentio, and Prospero stand outside and beyond the civilization to which all the other characters in these plays belong. Friar Francis, a holy man coming from nowhere to officiate at a wedding ceremony, uses the cruel expedient of Hero's pretended death to compel Claudio to reevaluate his situation in the light of his expanded consciousness. He plays the part of the ancient wonder worker, the primordial medicine man, within a make-believe civilization symbolized by the pleasing, though frequently shallow, intellectual fireworks of Beatrice and Benedick. After the miracle has been successfully performed, Friar Francis, true to his archetypal function as a light-bearer, promises to tell them all about the miracle. "Meantime let wonder seem familiar," he adds, thereby implying that the miracle of self-knowledge will eventually be revealed and will not be beyond the comprehension of even the most artificial civilization.

Vincentio chooses voluntary exile in order the better to observe the one whose psychic stability in the exercise of political power he wants to test. His perspective is no longer determined by the absurd prohibitory laws of Vienna, but by patterns of insight which he alone can uphold. Once again miracles are performed which are nothing but deceptions practiced in the name of some suprapersonal power. What appears to be magic is added to strengthen kingly rule. When Vincentio's aim has been accomplished, Angelo's unconscious integrated, and true authority re-established in the name of consciousness, Vincentio returns to the society over which he rules and to which he is, in truth, a stranger; yet he is still a redeemer of men, having saved them from that very evil of uncontrolled impulses which civilization had created. For when Vincentio asks Angelo to enforce those preposterous laws punishing with death premarital sexual relationships, he compels him to confront his own unconscious. It is a far more perilous experiment than the one that Friar Francis performs when he lets Hero die an artificial death. Yet in both cases it is in the depth of the unconscious that the initiation to self-knowledge takes place. Like Friar Francis, Vincentio also promises to explain all, to let the past, as it were, interpret the future:

> So bring us to the palace, where we'll show
> What's yet behind that's meet you all should know. (v, *1, 540*)

By trying to let wonder seem familiar, Vincentio no less than Friar Francis wishes to reduce the miracle of self-knowledge to the proportion of a historical civilization (that of Messina and of Vienna). Throughout these two plays Shakespeare takes for granted that this civilization, through corruption and make-believe, has done all it could to prevent the miraculous return of insight with which the two plays end.

Prospero's spiritual exile is, as it were, voluntary, as is in the same sense Vincentio's withdrawal from life in order to guide it from afar. Prospero's exile has been inherent in the shortcomings of his previous self-centered existence as a ruler. Possibly, Vincentio was no better ruler. The civilizations over which each presided before exile, directed men's minds away from the wonder of self-realization and toward an increasing dependence on courtly Renaissance values of *savoir vivre*, expressed in looseness of moral conduct and a cynical attitude toward power politics. While Prospero was "all dedicated / To closeness and bettering of [his] mind" (I, 2, 89), and retired from the affairs of state, his dukedom was taken away from him by force and cunning. Yet his loss of political power is compensated by spiritual awareness which he calls his Art, but which to unconscious, unregenerated man can but appear as magic. It is this conscious mastery over man and nature that enables Prospero to understand the significance of his brother's evil which originated in his own lack of awareness. When he returns to civilization, he does so as a healer rather than as a magician. The various miracles he performs accomplish their purpose, that of partially freeing man's unconscious from a repressed sense of guilt and shame, so closely linked to that same society of which Prospero before his exile has been, after all, a most deficient ruler. Like Friar Francis and Vincentio before him he promises to explain all, at least insofar as the insight he has gained in solitude is at all communicable to the imperfectly initiated and the excessively and perhaps incurably self-centered. He still appears to believe, against all evidence to the contrary, that the total range of his consciousness can be fruitfully transmitted to those who continue to be attached to the negative attributes of their unconscious: greed, envy, and ambition. Thus he visualizes a time, after they have all returned to "real" as opposed to "magic" existence, when

> . . . at pick'd leisure
> Which shall be shortly, I'll resolve you,—
> Which to you shall seem probable,—of every
> These happen'd accidents. (v, *1, 247*)

What explanation, one wonders, will they give of Claudio's unbelievable obtuseness, Angelo's demonic lust and Antonio's uninhibited greed for power? And will the cure which in each case is of a spiritual nature seem convincing when all that can be seen is the magic solution to a complex human situation fraught with treachery, violence, and murder? Yet the explanation is itself an indispensable part of the healing process in spite of the fact that, as Jung remarks in connection with the role of the "wise old man" in fairy tales, "the resultant enlightenment and untying of the fatal tangle often has something positively magical about it—an experience not unknown to the psychotherapist." [15]

We may call Friar Francis, Vincentio, and Prospero symbolical representations of the "wise old man," reappearing in the shape of a Prometheus-like image of human existence. Their nonattachment to material possessions is their most distinctive common characteristic. In such plays as these, the archetype "represents knowledge, reflection, insight, wisdom, cleverness, and intuition, on the one hand, and on the other, moral qualities such as good will and readiness to help. . . ." And if the assumption is granted that this as any other archetype "is an autonomous content of the unconscious" [16] it fulfills a basic function in Shakespeare's plays, not, as has so often been argued, that of a character "taken from life," but of a universalized symbol of the transcendence of consciousness over the unconscious, of awareness over mere sense perception, of compassion over self-centeredness.

9

Orpheus

THE PROCESS OF INDIVIDUATION as portrayed by Shakespeare puts an increasing emphasis on the need for harmonious integration of all the disparate elements in the psyche. Spiritual healing is frequently associated with the effect that music has over the minds of men.

Shakespeare knew the Orpheus myth from Ovid where the music of his lyre, heard among the "buried ghosts" in the underworld, dispersed the shades of Hell and "made the pale phantoms weep." After the loss of Euridice, Orpheus withdrew to a wide treeless plain. As his fingers ran over the strings of his lyre, "the shade came there to listen" and the plain was all at once covered with trees. Ovid tells the legend of Orpheus' death as a story of musical antagonism and war. When disharmony rises against harmony, the sweetness of Orpheus' mournful lyre is defeated by the harsh discords of the instruments of war—

> Flutes
> Shrilling, and trumpets braying loud, and drums,
> Beating of breasts, and howling, so the lyre
> Was overcome.[1]

The Orpheus myth is explicitly mentioned by Shakespeare in only three of his plays. It is, however, dramatically and psychologically present in the polarity of contradictory forces that fight for predominance in man's unconscious. Once, in *The Two Gentlemen,* Orpheus' music is compared to the poet's art "For Orpheus' lute was strung with poets' sinews" (III, 2, 78). The poet's verse has the same effect on nature and man as the music played on Orpheus' lyre—it softens, tames, and civilizes. In *Henry VIII* the song sung by the gentlewoman to disperse the troubles with which the Queen is afflicted refers to Orpheus' music as liberating nature from the darkness and the freezings of winter while at the same time, on a human level, making

> Killing care and grief of heart
> Fall asleep, or hearing, die. (III, *1, 13*)

An equally conventional use is made of the Orpheus myth in *The Merchant of Venice.* Beasts are tamed by "the sweet power of music," the wild raving of the senses is transformed into modesty, fury into mildness, war into peace. Once more it is music that civilizes all things, animate or inanimate, for even stones are charmed by its magic power.

Wilson Knight's assumption that "the heart of the Shakespearian mystery" can be found in "the opposition, throughout the plays, of 'tempests' and 'music'," attempts a helpful formula of what he considers to be the unifying principle according to which Shakespeare's imagination is seen to work. It is only in the Final Plays, concludes Wilson Knight, that "the marriage of tempest and music" is consummated.[2] The priest that officiates over this marriage is the musician, Shakespeare's symbolic representation of the healer-archetype who, by playing on his "lyre," quiets the tempest in the mind and prepares the ground for the attainment of an integrated personality.

This is implied in the Orphic attitude according to which "the empirical world is wretched, confused, tormented . . . but through music, contemplation, love, man is given the possibility of liberating himself from the sphere of sensory experience."[3] As a form of psychic healing music may effectively counteract emotional instability caused by uncontrolled impulses such as greed, envy, ambition, or lust. As part of an "alchemy of the mind" the musician provides Shakespeare with a symbol of the unconscious curing the emotionally disturbed of their disease by merely participating in their suffering.

The encounter between the musician and the mentally afflicted is therefore very much like the meeting between the analyst's unconscious and that of the sick man. The doctor being faced with the same task as his patient, it will therefore be "his own hurt that gives the measure of his power to heal." [4] The miracle of healing through shared suffering applies equally to the doctor and to the musician: the cure effected will result in an attitude of detachment and patience in the face of suffering which is analogous to the harmony experienced by both musician and listener.

Music, as a curative drug to assist the sick man in his attempt at integrating his divided mind, may, however, act as a poison no less than as a remedy. This it has in common with many other magic devices employed by primordial man and of which an echo can be found in many references to musical cures in Shakespeare. The dual nature of the remedy itself is a prerequisite of life: it cures by killing. And as light can be perceived only against a background of darkness, so a sense of harmony can be aroused only in relation to some previously existing discord. What is true of light and music, is applicable to the various layers of the soul. The deeper the music penetrates, the more lasting its effect on the unconscious. Therein also lies the danger that the cure may fail. The effect of discord upon a divided personality may produce greater dissociation. Orpheus' music, instead of curing, may also be regarded as a threat to integration.

Shakespeare is fully aware of this possibility. Vincentio, himself a healer of souls, though not a musician, finds Mariana listening to a song in which her divided soul reflects itself in "displeased" mirth and "pleased" woe. The Duke's comment is general enough to be applied to any emotionally charged situation such as the one in which he finds Mariana. For, says he, "music oft hath such a charm / To make bad good, and good provoke to harm" (IV, 1, 16). What Vincentio implies is that there is little, if any, likelihood of music appealing directly to man's consciousness and his power of discrimination. It may, on the contrary, induce sleep (as indeed it very often does in Shakespeare) and encourage submission to trans-personal powers over which the mind has no control. Then its alchemy will have the opposite of the desired effect (and psychotherapists who have ever used music as a means to cure mental disturbances know this): instead of relieving the psychic disorder, it may increase it—by deepening the feeling of helplessness in the face of it. This is what King Richard means when—though thankful for the present of music that is being played outside his prison cell, he exclaims,

> This music mads me: let it sound no more;
> For though it have holp madmen to their wits,
> In me it seems it will make wise men mad. (*Richard II*, v, 5, 62)

Shakespeare frequently associates playing and listening to music with psychic processes. Two passages, both referring to Hamlet's mind, concern the fragile relation between man's unconscious impulses and his awareness of an orderly universe with which he has to live in harmony. In both passages Hamlet's apparently disintegrating mind is compared with discordant music. Ophelia, herself deeply disturbed at the time these lines are spoken, describes a Hamlet the spectator has never seen on the stage, an ideal image of human excellence in whom "a noble mind" was joined to the dignified bearing of the courtier, the eloquence of the scholar, and the courage of the soldier. As "the observed of all observers" he symbolized for her—and undoubtedly for the whole court of Denmark—an ideal of completeness, as his father had indeed been before him. At one time, it appears, Hamlet had been—"take him for all in all"—a man endowed with "king-becoming graces." The disintegration that followed

is expressed in significantly musical terms. For Ophelia now hears
in Hamlet's words the echo of an inner discord, "That noble and
most sovereign reason / Like sweet bells jangled, out of tune and
harsh" (III, 1, 166). This, she assumes, is the result of "ecstacy," a
word used by Shakespeare to indicate any violent disturbance
of the mind bordering on insanity. It is this same word that
Hamlet's mother uses when she sees her son bending his eye on
vacancy and behaving in a way she suspects to be the effect of
ecstacy. Yet, Hamlet replies in musical language, disproving
Ophelia's assumption that it is "madness" that has thus transformed him:

> Ecstacy!
> My pulse, as yours, doth temperately keep time,
> And makes as helpful music. . . . (III, *4, 139*)

The two women who mean most in Hamlet's life suspect him of
having lost his reason. Its "nobility" gone, it is no longer in
control of those unconscious impulses that drive him still deeper
into madness. Hamlet's musical defense confirms Shakespeare's
belief in music as a form of mental discipline as long as its time-
keeping is temperate—the opposite of which would be musical
"ecstacy."

On an earlier occasion, Hamlet, comparing his soul to a
musical instrument, questions the ability of those who want to
play on it to extract all the latent harmony that could be found
if only the musician knew his art. It is Shakespeare's subtlest
allusion to the sick man's need of a physician who would be a
musician, and who by playing upon his soul would share his
suffering. Neither Rosencrantz nor Guildenstern, to whom this
passage is addressed, have the gift or the willingness to share the
discord in Hamlet's soul:

> You would pluck out the heart of my mystery; you would sound
> me from my lowest note to the top of my compass; and there is
> much music, excellent voice in this little organ, yet cannot you
> make it speak. (III, 2, *387*)

In *The Merchant of Venice* occurs Lorenzo's description of "the man that hath no music in himself." It may appear doubtful whether Lorenzo, an unimpressive and morally ambiguous figure, refers to the human soul, Hamlet's "little organ." It is an earlier, less mature, Shakespeare that speaks. But the assumptions on which Lorenzo's generalizations on the nonmusical man are built are the same as Hamlet's. For the absence of music in a man's spiritual make-up would indicate an unhealthy predominance of conscious ego-centered forces, and therefore a strong, possibly irresistible, inclination to do evil merely for evil's sake. The man "that hath no music in himself" is the repressed personality *par excellence,* the Shylock in each one of us. Cassius's rare and equivocal smiles are related to the observation, made by Caesar, that he "hears no music." It may be assumed that, for the same reason, Iago is not naturally given to smiling, nor Lady Macbeth, nor Hamlet's uncle. "There's daggers in their smiles," instead of music. Lorenzo's generalization about the man who is not "mov'd with concord of sweet sounds" should be quoted in full. For such a man, he says (and one remembers Hamlet's astonished comment "that one may smile, and smile, and be a villain")—

> Is fit for treasons, stratagems, and spoils;
> The motions of his spirit are dull as night,
> And his affections dark as Erebus:
> Let no such man be trusted. (V, *1, 85*)

The most revealing instance of music being used as a remedy in a case of violent mental disturbance occurs in *King Lear* where the doctor prescribes music to cure Lear's "untun'd and jarring senses." Prospero, similarly, restores the disordered minds of his enemies by "a solemn air and the best comforter / To an unsettled fancy" (V, 1, 59). Repeatedly, in *The Tempest,* music is employed as a cure to mental anguish, emotional distress, or psychic unbalance. Thus Ferdinand, listening to the music that Ariel plays for him, finds that it allays both the fury of the water and his own passion "with that sweet air." Orsino also requires the "sweet air" of music to alleviate his anguish. Having listened to it once, he wants to listen to it again. For "Methought it did relieve my passion much." It must have helped him to restore that regulating principle which, at least temporarily, harmonizes one's unconscious drives with one's conscious aspirations.

Shakespeare's plays are filled with vocal and instrumental music, both as reflection of a social convention and as a fulfillment of various characters' intense personal need. Such musical experience opens the way to complete spiritual restoration. Its strength lies in making conscious what has been repressed and thereby establishing a solid foundation upon which integration may be built. At times it provides relief, most frequently provoking sleep and causing forgetfulness. Its healing power, however partial it may be, lies in the harmony it communicates. Ariel, in the service of Prospero's maturing mind, is the ideal image of the healer as a musical being. His music has such potency that it leaves its curative effect even on Caliban. For not even this "thing of darkness" is impervious to the healing power of musical concord:

> The isle is full of noises,
> Sounds and sweet airs, that give delight, and hurt not.
> Sometimes a thousand twangling instruments
> Will hum about mine ears; and sometimes voices,
> That, if I had then wak'd after long sleep,
> Will make me sleep again: and then, in dreaming,
> The clouds methought would open and show riches
> Ready to drop upon me; that when I wak'd
> I cried to dream again. (III, 2, 146)

10

Asklepios

THE ARCHETYPAL HEALER is as remote from the modern university-trained physician as the latter's cure is from the primordial miracle of healing. Yet all cure in Shakespeare is founded on "wonder," all remedy derives from a trust in the efficacy of the human spirit to heal. Diseases of the body are thus frequently taken to be symptoms of specific psychic dispositions. Therefore the cure of the sick body requires the completely integrated strength of a healer's mind. At times it is by an effort of consciousness that the disturbance originating in the unconscious can be cured. At other times, the diseased unconscious is made to heal itself with the aid of the very instruments that the disease has put at the sufferer's disposal. By encouraging the repressed impulses to come to the surface and thereby become part of the process of individuation, the healing process impels the patient to come to terms with what, till then, has been an unacknowledged aspect of his personality.

The most effective antidote for the cure of repressed or uncontrolled impulses is shared suffering. This is true both of psychotherapeutic treatment, as envisaged by Jung, and of the relationship established between sufferer and healer in a Shakespeare play. The psychologist as well as the dramatist acknowledges the existence of the unconscious. Throughout the psychic process of healing both sufferer and healer are mutually exposed to the transforming impressions and influences emanating from their encounter. It is in the course of such an encounter that they "share" the same psyche, it being both subject and object of observation, the place where the disease originates as well as the principal source of the cure. The aim of such shared suffering should, first of all, be to "help [the patient] acquire steadfastness and philosophic patience in face of suffering." [1]

A recent study of Asklepios as an archetypal image of the physician shows that this element of participation in the sick man's suffering was discovered in ancient images and descriptions of the god. The art of healing consisted then of two aspects: on the one hand, "techne" or the knowledge and skill of the professional physician, and on the other, the divinely inherited gift of healing involving miracle and mystery beyond the intellectual grasp of common mortals. It was the latter aspect that was considered to be a true *religio medici*. All healing, then, was rebirth, a kind of *incubation* during which the physician remained in the background and the patient sought out the deity "to bring out the cure whose elements he bore within himself." [2] But this deity appeared to the patient in human shape, himself a wounded one, a co-sufferer whose pain, however, was not centered in the body but in the spirit. However "individual" the sickness of the patient appeared to be, the remedy against suffering was of universal application. Thus, in an early fragment of a statue of Asklepios, the eyes seem "to look upwards and into the distance without definite aim. This combined with the vivid movement gives us an impression of a great inner emotion, one might almost say of suffering . . . he is assailed as it were by the suffering of men which it is his vocation to assuage." [3] Furthermore, in a picture at the sanctuary of Epidaurus, the face of Asklepios is shown to be "grave, virile, cognizant of human suffering." [4] The god's special gift of healing may indeed be described as "a spark of intuitive knowledge about the possibilities of rising from the depths." [5] Ultimately, the cure he performs is related to the ambiguously dual faculty of being "at home in the darkness of suffering and there to find germs of light and recovery." [6]

Jung's reference to the psychotherapist whose healing power may, and often does, seem to the patient a form of magic, indicates the close relationship between the exercise of spiritual control over the minds of men and any possible cure that may be effected. The curative formula that a charismatic personality in a Shakespeare play applies is not only anti-scientific in its reliance on a responsive spiritual disposition on the part of the patient (as has already been observed in the instance of music as a remedy against sickness), but consistently nonmedical. The best example for such healing through "grace" rather than medical science is found in *Julius Caesar* where Brutus' apparently undivided personality is shown to be the best remedy against sickness. Ligarius, one of the fellow-conspirators, "discards" his bodily affliction when he finds Brutus leading the conspiracy. The cure is, indeed, a kind of *religio medici,* for Ligarius appeals to the gods to witness it:

> By all the gods that Romans bow before
> I here discard my sickness. Soul of Rome!
> Brave son, deriv'd from honourable loins!
> Thou, like an exorcist, hast conjur'd up
> My mortified spirit. (II, *1, 320*)

The patient's willingness and readiness to be cured is essential for the performance of the exorcist's miracle. It is significant that Ligarius should speak of his spirit rather than of his body as being "mortified." Brutus' power as healer can thus be compared to the spiritual remedies employed by Vincentio and Friar Francis. For both Angelo and Claudio are shown to be sick men in need of spiritual assistance. The true miracle then, consists in the spiritual upheaval that accompanies the healing and makes the patient conscious of his disease. Yet the healing factor in all

these cases is the "doctor's" personality rather than the means
he employs to cure a sick soul or a diseased body. What distinguishes such a doctor's consciousness from others is his acceptance of a spiritual frame of reference which gives meaning
to his own life as well. Brutus' conception of personal and national honor upon which his leadership of the conspiracy is based
provides such a framework. Vincentio's conscious search for a
guiding moral principle that would determine individual conduct within society, is another. Friar Francis's "study of imagination" supplies a universal psychological setting with the aid
of which not only Claudio but all that are blind like him can
be cured. Such a frame of reference need not be built on religious
belief. The gods are invoked to provide help or to witness. Their
presence merely serves the purpose of some trans-personal evidence to support the magic cure. If Jung thinks of the ideal
psychotherapist as a "philosophic doctor" and of his work as a
"religion *in statu nascendi*," [7] he no doubt refers to such a
spiritual framework within which the doctor's work is carried
on. It alone guarantees his own integration—insofar as, indeed,
it is at all possible to imagine a fully individuated human being.
Jung's portrait of the doctor's personality closely resembles the
ideal image of human existence: ". . . the art of psychotherapy
requires that the therapist be in possession of avowable, credible,
and defensible convictions which have proved their viability
either by having resolved any neurotic dissociation of his own
or by preventing them from arising." [8]

Jung's use of the word "convictions" may prove to be a serious limitation imposed upon Shakespeare's concept of the healer.
Do Friar Francis, Vincentio, Prospero, possess any such viable
convictions? Their healing power comes from within and acts
as a projection upon the soul of the sick man. Brutus, who holds
very strong convictions, can cure Ligarius' "mortified spirit" by
offering him "honour," but he cannot prevent his own "state of
man" from "suffering the nature of an insurrection." His convictions, it has rightly been pointed out, are his tragic flaw.

Though they are "defensible," they are not "viable." His gift of healing the sick spirit of individuals has never before been applied to a wider social frame of reference. The moment he applies them, his convictions become dissociated from his self. He dies, a victim of his own split consciousness. He thus corresponds to the earthly counterpart of the divine physician: though a bringer of light and a healer of men, he is himself doomed to darkness, and like Machaon, one of the sons of Asklepios, he belongs as much to death as any other mortal. For, according to these legends, "the best physician on earth is a hero who wounds, heals, and is fatally smitten." [9]

The least problematic of these healers in Shakespeare is Camillo, in *The Winter's Tale*. His most significant gift seems to be an insight enabling him to see "with thine eyes at once . . . good and evil / Inclining to them both" (I, 2, 303). This inclination, however, is no conviction: he is clearly on the side of goodness. Like all healers in Shakespeare he is the first in this particular play to recognize the existence of the disease. It is also he alone who attempts to make the patient realize the perils to his soul should he refuse the remedy. Camillo considers Leontes' frantic and quite irrational jealousy to be a violent disturbance of the mind, requiring the immediate attendance of a "physician"—

> Good my lord, be cur'd
> Of this diseas'd opinion, and betimes,
> For 'tis most dangerous. (I, 2, *296*)

Yet Leontes' cure is not effected by Camillo. The doctor's services are rejected. He has to flee the country. Only when the king is ready for the cure is the physician called back. The evil of uncontrolled affects followed by suffering and repentance are the successive stages that Leontes has to go through until he himself *wishes* to be cured. Such a healing process is possible, Leontes seems to realize, only in the presence of the one who first attempted, though unsuccessfully, to make the sick man confront his own diseased unconscious. Camillo senses this need of his former master when he asks Polixenes to permit him to return to Sicilia: "Besides, the penitent king, my master, hath sent for me; to whose feeling sorrows I might be some allay (or I o'erween to think so) which is another spur to my departure." (IV, 1, 7)

It should be noted that during the whole process of Leontes' individuation, the "doctor" has been living in exile. No transference has taken place. Other therapeutic factors have played their part. Most of them, like the Delphic oracle, are of great symbolic significance. But what Shakespeare stresses is not the miraculous aspect at all, but Leontes' newly acquired insight expressed through his "feeling sorrows."

Both as physician and archetypal "wise old man" Camillo uses the devious ways that human nature compels him to employ as a means of salvation. Young Florizel realizes that Camillo, though human, possesses divine healing graces. When Camillo plans his return to Sicily, which will involve nothing more serious than a bit of fairly obvious disguise, Florizel exclaims,

> May this, almost a miracle, be done?
> That I may call thee something more than man
> And after that trust to thee? (IV, 3, 547)

Yet Camillo possesses only one qualification to heal "feeling sorrows," his insight into the suffering of others, and his gift of sharing it. Florizel addresses Camillo as a divine physician, the one and only healer of both royal houses,

> Camillo,
> Preserver of my father, now of me,
> The medicine of our house. . . . (IV, 3, 598)

One somehow wishes Shakespeare had told us more about this healing mediator as an ideal image of human existence. Camillo's attitude to Leontes' cure, of which he is merely a remote instrument, is practical rather than spiritual. The means he uses are neither medical nor metaphysical. His mere presence, both in Sicily and in Bohemia, allays the "feeling sorrows" of two fathers.

His service consists in compassionate awareness. His only conviction is his goodness; Polixenes says as much when he refuses to let him go back to Sicily: "The need I have of thee, thine own goodness hath made; better not have had thee than thus to want thee . . ." (IV, 2, 13). A few lines later, Polixenes indeed uses the word "service." The archetypal image of the healer as reflected in the Greek myth and in Shakespeare involves an element of mystery in the service of man. Whether as god or as mortal, the physician merely assists at the miracle. He is "the fountainhead. . . . His manifestation is the cure or, to put it the other way round, every cure is his epiphany." [10]

There are no physicians in Shakespeare's history plays. Yet sickness throws its shadow over the land and no remedy is in sight. The king who should have been a healer is himself the victim of disease: it is his shadow that falls on the mighty and the humble alike. Richard II seen through the eyes of the dying John of Gaunt is the chief "patient" who is most in need of cure. Yet he rejects any suggestion to be treated with the contempt of one who would rather "kill [his] physician and [his] fee bestow / Upon the foul disease." [11] John of Gaunt diagnoses the king's illness as the true cause of his land's disease:

> Now He that made me knows I see thee ill
> Ill in myself to see, and in thee, seeing ill.
> Thy death-bed is no lesser than thy land,
> Wherein thou liest in reputation sick,
> And thou, too careless patient as thou art,
> Commit'st thy anointed body to the cure
> Of those physicians that first wounded thee. (II, *1, 93*)

Bolingbroke, Richard's successor, inherits the disease from the former king. Though an abler politician, he lacks the spiritual wholeness of the healer. National division and civil strife reflect his own divided mind. In the absence of any curative miracle, the king can no longer uphold the divine principle of rebirth, but himself stands for the disintegrating element of the unconscious, symbolized by the sickness of his country:

> Then you perceive the body of our kingdom
> How foul it is, what rank diseases grow,
> And with what danger, near the heart of it. (2HIV, III, *1, 38*)

Warwick, to whom Henry addresses these words, suggests the obvious cure with the assistance of medical science. His comparison between the "body" of the kingdom and the body of a sick man, both in need of medical attendance, hints at the scientist's foredoomed attempts to cure the spirit by "prescriptions." Thus he rationalizes the disease in the true tradition of the professional doctor:

> It is but as a body yet distempered,
> Which to his former strength may be restor'd
> With good advice and little medicine. (III, *1, 41*)

As Shakespeare's art grows more mature, his disbelief in the efficacy of medical advice and treatment increases. This is particularly evident in the three doctor scenes in *Macbeth*. The political situation there is not dissimilar from that in the earlier history plays. Macbeth, like Henry IV, is both a murderer and a usurper of the crown. Both are in need of a "physician" to restore their kingship and their land to health. Yet it is into the latter play only that the symbolic figure of the healer—as opposed to the doctor—is introduced. He is part of the pattern of Macbeth's personal tragedy as well as of the national disaster caused by the evil he commits. Without the symbol of the healer there would have been no rebirth.

The two physicians in the play, one at the English court where we meet him in the company of Malcolm, the future king of Scotland, and the other, later on, in Macbeth's castle in Dunsinane, admit their own ignorance as regards the mysterious relationship between the sick body and the sick mind. Accordingly they are concerned with bodily health rather than with "grace" or shared suffering. They are aware of the possibility of miraculous cure, but consider all psychic treatment beyond their scope.

They have indeed no wonders to perform. They freely acknowledge that their medical knowledge, sometimes also called an
"art," is limited to what little they know of the human body.
They, however, confess that there may be cases where physical
remedies prove ineffective. This is why one of them, observing
Lady Macbeth walking in her sleep and re-experiencing through
her repressed unconscious all the horrors of the past, concludes,
"More needs she the divine than the physician" (V, 1, 81).

Friar Francis, Vincentio, Prospero, and even Camillo, are
healers of the soul. The devious remedies they sometimes have
to use to accomplish the wonder of healing, may well seem to
those on whom they are applied, the result of divine interference.
In *Macbeth* such a miraculous cure is described by one who has
witnessed it. The English doctor first, and then Malcolm, tell
Macduff how the king of England habitually cures those among
his subjects afflicted with a disease called "the Evil." The reference is evidently to the "royal touch," the king's grace projected
on to the sick man. It is not merely a symbol of sanctity but of
spiritual wholeness as well. The king, though we never see him
on the stage, is himself an ideal image of human perfection. The
nature of the disease is left in doubt. Its name may equally refer
to the body as to the mind. The sick are described as "swoln and
ulcerous," which lays the emphasis on the body. Yet only a "good
king" could cure the illness from which they suffer. The doctor
admits that "their malady convinces / The great assay of art"
(IV, 3, 142), medical science being incapable of providing any
relief, while Malcolm calls the illness "the mere despair of surgery." The impression that the whole passage leaves on one's
mind is, in effect, that what these "wretched souls" are most in
need of is "the philosophic patience in face of suffering" rather
than the assistance of a medical practitioner:

> A most miraculous work in this good king
> Which often, since my here remain in England,
> I have seen him do. How he solicits Heaven,

Himself best knows; but strangely-visited people,
All swoln and ulcerous, pitiful to the eye,
The mere despair of surgery, he cures;
Hanging a golden stamp about their necks,
Put on with holy prayers: and 'tis spoken,
To the succeeding royalty he leaves
The healing benediction. With this strange virtue
He hath a heavenly gift of prophecy;
And sundry blessings hang about his throne,
That speak him full of grace. (IV, 3, 147)

In contrast to the evil that has vanquished Macbeth's unconscious, the English king's curative blessing seems to be an
attribute of grace, possibly itself the result of a psychic equilibrium that the uninitiated may well call "divine". Shakespeare,
indeed, claims for it a religious and specifically Christian frame
of reference which throughout the play is opposed to Macbeth's
diseased mind. At the same time he also insists on the purely
intuitive psychotherapeutic nature of the cure performed by the
king.

The doctor who, in Macbeth's castle, realizes the need of a
priest rather than a physician to cure Lady Macbeth of her mental affliction, is humble enough to confess that psychic disorders
require the patient's cooperation to render any cure effective.
Thus when Macbeth asks him,

Canst thou not minister to a mind diseas'd
Pluck from the memory a rooted sorrow,
Raze out the written troubles of the brain? (V, 3, 40)

the doctor no longer even mentions the possibility of a "divine"
curing Lady Macbeth, but stresses the required willingness of
the mentally afflicted to be cured without which even the priest
would fail: "Therein the patient / Must minister to himself."
Macbeth's angry exclamation, "Throw physic to the dogs; I'll
none of it," serves as an ironic comment, possibly Shakespeare's
own, on the average man's belief in the progress of contemporary

medical science and the rationality that he assumes to be the foundation of all medical knowledge.

In *Macbeth,* then, Shakespeare introduces on two occasions a physician's failure to cure the diseases of the body or of the mind. Throughout this play the existence of unconscious motivations directing man's action toward evil or toward good, determines Shakespeare's attitude to sickness and health. Holinshed, Shakespeare's obvious source, mentions Edward the Confessor, who was thought to have been "inspired with the gift of prophesie and to have had the gift of healing infirmities and diseases." [12] Yet reference to Holinshed may be as little relevant to our understanding of Shakespeare's attitude toward the archetypal healer as Frazer's ironic reminder that "perhaps the last relic of such superstitions which lingered about our English kings was the notion that they could heal scrofula by their touch. The disease was accordingly known as the King's Evil. Queen Elizabeth often exercised this miraculous gift of healing." [13]

Shakespeare's use of the symbolism of wholeness and grace in the passage from *Macbeth* and his frequent references to the figure of the physician as an embodiment of ignorance and unawareness, indicates a conscious acceptance of what Frazer calls "superstition." Shakespeare evidently considered that the evil that emanates from the sick man's unconscious can only be cured by a healer's consciously disciplined charity. The king's "healing benediction" corresponds, very largely, to Jung's own conception of the *religio medico,* not in terms of any specialized medical science but on the contrary, in terms of "universalism and . . . the complete overcoming of the specialist's attitude, if the totality of body and soul is not to be just a matter of words." [14] What is being re-enacted at the court of England, before the astonished eyes of a medical scientist, is the mythologem of the healer, "the proclamation of a miraculous birth in death." [15] That such miraculous healing was common enough in the Middle Ages and during Shakespeare's own lifetime is of mere historical relevance. Shakespeare's use of this mythologem within the tragic context of Macbeth's own sick mind indicates his vivid preoccupation with the healer-figure as archetype rather than as incidental character.

Shakespeare's portrait of the English king as a priestly healer performing miraculous cures on those that are afflicted in mind or body, adds an essential feature to the ideal image of human perfection. A savior-figure conferring health and spiritual restoration is naturally related to the archetypal mana-personality of myth and dream. It commonly originates in a sense of loss and alienation, caused by man's awareness that nature has not provided him with the instruments of moral control that might enable him to master his impulses. As a projection of the collective unconscious it counteracts emotional upheavals or failure of judgment in the young and immature, such as Claudio or Angelo. When it appears in human form, as priest, wise old man, healer or king, it blesses him that takes and him that gives. And though its trans-personal powers to cure may at times terrify, it is the most humane of all archetypes.

Its most significant feature is that it symbolizes a mature form of consciousness and insight, far beyond the confines of the historical period in which it happens to exercise its power. Within the human context of Shakespeare's plays the healer archetype stands for a projection of consciousness upon those contents of the personal unconscious that have to be subjected to a principle of order and integration before complete spiritual disorientation sets in. In accordance with the archetypal situation evoked by Shakespeare, man, in order to merit survival, has first to descend into the darkness of nonbeing, that is, of the unconscious. There could be no attempt at resurrection without the experience of dying. Shakespeare, both in comedy and in moments of the most intense tragic suffering, seems to conform to a primordial image of human existence according to which "it is possible for a man to attain totality, become whole, only with the cooperation of the spirit of darkness; indeed the latter is actually a *causa instrumentalis* of redemption and individuation." [16]

Such an interplay of darkness and redemption characterizes the psychological pattern of the *Macbeth* universe. The rapidly deteriorating consciousness of the·protagonist is counteracted by the healing power of the archetype. When the instruments of darkness take over, Macbeth's mental and moral balance suffers defeat. His ability to think and make moral distinctions is being undermined from the first scene of the play, until neither reality nor appearance provide valid criteria for action. Thinking itself is turned into a projection of Macbeth's unconscious. Instead of establishing a clear dividing line between right and wrong, being and seeming, it confounds the thinker and compels him to delve even deeper into the darkness of his own unconscious. It is there that he discovers that in his thought the murder has already been committed, a revelation that

> Shakes so my single state of man
> That function is smother'd in surmise
> And nothing is but what is not. (I, *3, 140*)

In the realm of the unconscious where "nothing is" but what "surmise" creates, illusion becomes reality, and division appears as unity. Macbeth sees only one dagger, but surmises that there are two. His divided consciousness even supplies a pseudo-scientific explanation. Possibly, he surmises, one of the daggers is merely "A dagger of the mind, a false creation / Proceeding from the heat-oppressed brain (II, 1, 38). This attempt at explaining away the illusions created by his unconscious, is in keeping with Shakespeare's later comment on the helplessness of any merely scientific knowledge in the face of violent spiritual division such as the one Macbeth and his wife are afflicted with. Their disease is not due to their "heat-oppressed brain," nor have they eaten "on the insane root / That takes the reason prisoner." Theirs is a disease that "convinces the great assay of art": the only remedy lies in an impossible return to spiritual wholeness.

Malcolm, the son of the murdered king, inherited some, at least, of the healing grace of his father. Trying to comfort Mac-

duff for the loss of his wife and children at the hands of Macbeth,
he uses an image taken from the language of medicine:

> Let's make us med'cines of our great revenge
> To cure this deadly grief. (IV, 3, 214)

The student of the healer archetype will find this image singularly apt. For corruption, on the level of the body no less than
of the mind, can be cured only by a process of purification which
may, and indeed often does, involve the sacrificial shedding of
blood. Malcolm at the end of the play is shown to be a symbol
of this kind of cure acting by physical means toward a spiritual
end. The country, to be restored to its pristine health, will, literally as well as symbolically, be "watered" by the blood of those
who redeem the evil committed by Macbeth and his queen by
their death. His own followers, turning away from him, rightly
call Malcolm "the medicine of the sickly weal." Together with
him they will "dew the sovereign flower and drown the weed"
(V, 2, 30). The sacrifice of the young and innocent, such as
Siward's son, will restore the dynamics of healthy growth again.
The miracle of healing and rebirth that is being enacted in
Macbeth, involves not one man, but a whole nation. "By the
grace of Grace" wholeness has been brought back to the land.
"The time is free," because the healer has applied his art to a
nation's destiny. In addition, instead of the one priest, magician,
medicine-man, or exorcist, the collective unconscious has re-
created the archetype under several guises. There are "gracious"
Duncan and the divinely inspired King of England, representing
the old, the wise, and the good. On the other hand, there are the
future healers and bringers of light whose individuation does not
form part of the play and who, either because they are still too
young or because they are killed by Macbeth, are merely "primordial children" and never reach full manhood in the play.
Apart from Duncan himself, Banquo, Macduff, Siward, are all
fathers of sons. Macbeth, we remember, has no children.

[II]

IN ONLY ONE INSTANCE is the failing health of a sick ruler ever fully restored. In *All's Well,* as in the preceding plays, "good advice" and "little medicine" prove to be of no avail. The innocence of a young girl succeeds with "sympathetic magic" where all physicians failed before her. She performs the miracle of healing and renewal against all dictates of medical practice. Shakespeare, more emphatically than ever before, stresses the "specialist's" preoccupation with the diseased body, and his helpless ignorance in face of a suffering soul. The afflicted king "hath abandon'd his physicians . . . under whose practices he hath persecuted time with hope, and finds no other advantage in the process but only the losing of hope by time" (I, 1, 11). When Helena tells Bertram's mother of her intention to cure the king, the countess replies,

> He and his physicians
> Are of a mind; he, that they cannot help him;
> They, that they cannot help. . . . (I, *3, 245*)

The king himself is even more explicit as to the hopelessness of his condition, and warns Helena not to be overcredulous,

> When our most learned doctors leave us, and
> The congregated college have concluded
> That labouring art can never ransom nature
> From her inaidable estate. I say we must not
> So stain our judgment or corrupt our hope,
> To prostitute our past-cure malady
> To empirics, or to dissever so
> Our great self and our credit, to esteem
> A senseless help, when help past sense we deem. (II, *1, 119*)

It might be instructive to draw a modern parallel to the king's naive trust in the "labouring art" of the medical practitioner. The average patient's credulity in the benefits invariably bestowed by medical science—as long as the disease is kept under control with the aid of drugs—is matched by the physician's own belief in the infallibility of his prescriptions. Jung's comment on the "congregated college" of learned doctors runs as follows: "Of all the professionals, the medical man has the least opportunity of developing the function of *thinking*. So it is no wonder that even psychologically trained doctors have the greatest difficulty in following my reflections if they follow them at all. They have habituated themselves to handing out prescriptions and mechanically applying methods which they have not thought out themselves." [17] The king, in *All's Well,* like so many modern patients, evidently misunderstands the nature of his sickness and the sort of cure that Helena might be able to perform. He suspects her of being a quack and of going to use "senseless" (that is, magical, and therefore ineffectual) remedies. He and his physicians, like their modern counterparts, are fanatical believers in medical prescriptions: if these fail, death alone can supply the ultimate cure. Yet Shakespeare hints at spiritual no less than physical infirmities the king is afflicted with. Medically speaking, he is suffering from a kind of ulcer, called a "fistula." This, one is given to understand, may be a symptom or one of the effects of his spiritual ailment. Having at the beginning of the play abandoned all hope of cure, the king now gives way to despondency. Just before Helena appears before him to offer her services as a healer, he considers himself "near death." When she attempts to persuade the sick king to trust her "art" because her father on his deathbed had transmitted to her a secret curative formula transcending all accepted medical knowledge, the king's will to live has already been sapped by the disease and he can only respond reluctantly to her startling offer.

Spiritual succession from father to child is part of Shakespeare's portrayal of the ideal image of human existence. Frequently the wisdom of the old is handed on to the young at the very moment of dying. Virtues that have been acquired in the course of a long and selfless life are communicated to the immature and the as yet uncomprehending, when the time for renewal has come. For if, as Vincentio tells Angelo, our virtues "did not go forth from us, 'twere all alike / As if we had them not," there could be no rebirth, and the accumulated wisdom of the past would lose its validity in the present. The father-figure as a "wise old man" may or may not be a physician. His wisdom when transmitted to the young acquires a "magic" quality. This is certainly true of Portia's father (in *The Merchant of Venice*) who on his deathbed made her the somewhat bewildered recipient of an "inspiration" which determined her future happiness as Bassanio's wife. As for Helena's father, he seems to have been less concerned with her future as a wife than as a healer. For his "inspiration" was clearly of a medical nature. Though a physician by profession, he possessed some secret gift in addition to his professional knowledge as a doctor. For his medical skill was, in some mysterious way, connected with his moral character. His grace as a human being and his scientific knowledge, joined together, raised him far above the level of those physicians whose only remedy against disease was medicine for the body but who were ignorant of the "art" of healing an afflicted mind. Had his medical skill been as infinite as his moral integrity, Bertram's mother suggests, it "would have made nature immortal, and death should have played for lack of work" (I, 1, 23).

The healing principle, once more, is symbolized by integration and spiritual completeness rather than founded on medical proficiency. When Helena attempts to convince the countess that she should be permitted to cure the ailing king, she first meets with disbelief. The medical qualifications of an "unlearned virgin" to apply remedies when the Royal College of Physicians "embowel'd of their doctrine, have left off / The danger to itself" (I, 3, 249), must needs be put to doubt. Helena defends her qualifications point by point. The story of her father's in-

spired "prescription," the manner in which it was given to her,
and the reason she believes it to be applicable to the king's disease, are given by her in full:

> You know my father left me some prescriptions
> Of rare and proved effects, such as his reading
> And manifest experience had collected
> For general sovereignty; and that he will'd me
> In heedfull'st reservation to bestow them,
> As notes whose faculties inclusive were
> More than they were in note. Among the rest
> There is a remedy, approv'd, set down,
> To cure the desperate languishings whereof
> The king is render'd lost. (1, 3, 229)

The "inclusive faculties" which were part of her father's "prescription" evidently refer to certain nonmedical properties that
had to be employed when translating her father's "notes" into
the actual practice of the healer. This is also what Helena hints
at in reply to the countess' scepticism:

> There's something in't
> More than my father's skill, which was the great'st
> Of his profession, that his good receipt
> Shall for my legacy be sanctified
> By th'luckiest stars in heaven. (1, 3, 250)

The king at first disapproves of "divine" and trans-personal
interference in the curative process. Man's intellectual faculties,
he believes, are doomed to failure when "nature" frustrates his
knowledge. Having made up his mind that the present state of
medical information cannot "ransom nature," the king looks
upon Helena's suggestion through the spectacles of a worldly-
wise science that has already condemned him to death. Helena
accepts the challenge. Nature then will have to be defeated by
nonnatural means. For her father's prescription is "inclusive"
in a way the king does not and cannot understand. The real
remedy, she implies, lies in a combination of knowledge and

grace. What is required is an act of faith rather than a medical formula however esoteric. The paradox of faith accomplishing its task rather than science is strengthened by the choice of "the weakest minister" to carry out the healing. That Helena, whose grace is merely inherited, should have been chosen as a healer, may indeed seem to the king an unnatural and unintelligible choice. Yet, says she, the most insignificant causes have at times produced the greatest wonders, especially "when miracles have by the great'st been denied" (II, 1, 140). The king's pragmatic denial of miracles then *is* his disease. His spiritual stagnation and his lack of faith have to be cured first. The "fistula" which he thinks is the cause of all the trouble, can be taken care of last. The magic she is going to use to cure the king is "sympathetic" in more than one sense. It is the wonder of insight and compassion that she has stored up as if it were her "triple eye" until she finds an opportunity of executing the miracle. With this "triple eye" she will make the king "see" beyond his bodily affliction and thereby enable him to discover the nature of his true self.

Feeling that a divine healer is on her side inspiring her with a knowledge that is no longer restricted to what science has taught her father, she asks the king: "Of heaven, not me, make an experiment" (II, 1, 154). Thus her father's deathbed inspiration is projected onto the dying king and, just as in the earlier play, Bassanio chooses the leaden, the most humble, of the three caskets, the king no longer hesitates in *his* choice of remedy:

> Methinks in thee some blessed spirit doth speak
> His powerful sound within an organ weak. (II, *1, 178*)

The choice, Shakespeare implies, *is* the cure. Beyond this moment of inspiration, this deliberate insistence on the intuitive in preference to the "sensible" and "natural," Shakespeare refuses to supply any additional information. We are not present at the time the miracle is being performed—if indeed there was any need at all for any more "wonders" after the king has made his choice.

The only reference to the actual curing of the king occurs in the next scene when Lafeu and Parolles, neither of them blessed with grace, express their amazement at the spectacular healing of the king, apparently without the help of any known medical prescription. The performance of miracles in an enlightened society contradicts their most cherished belief in rationality and civilized progress:

> Lafeu: They say miracles are past; and we have our philosophi-
>   cal persons to make modern and familiar things super-
>   natural and causeless; hence it is that we make trifles
>   of terrors, ensconcing ourselves into seeming knowl-
>   edge when we should submit ourselves to an unknown
>   fear.
> Parolles: Why, 'tis the rarest argument of wonder that hath
>   shot out in our latter times. (II, 3, I)

The king, having been restored to health, calls Helena "my preserver," without ever alluding to the particular kind of inspiration that enabled Helena to cure him. He, in all likelihood, agrees with Lafeu who just now has called medical science "seeming knowledge" implying that the king's submission "to an unknown fear" might have led to his cure.

There are then at least two kinds of "knowledge" at work supplementing each other in the healing of the king. The "magic" recipe that has been transmitted to Helena by her dying father to which must now be added the ritual of rejuvenation which was not necessarily part of the original prescription, but which only she, being chaste and a virgin, could make effective. What she has received from her father in old-age wisdom she passes on to the king as the primordial knowledge of youth. For the healing of the king is undertaken by Helena with the express purpose of winning a husband: curing the king is the only remedy for the "disease" she is afflicted with, her unrequited love for Bertram. Whatever the recipe her father gave her, its efficacy must be tested by divine as well as human standards:

> Our remedies oft in ourselves do lie,
> Which we ascribe to heaven; the fated sky
> Gives us free scope. . . . (I, *1*, *235*)

she says, implying that by raising the king from his deathbed,
she might eventually succeed in "knowing" Bertram, and making him, willingly or unwillingly, her sexual partner, not merely
her legal husband. Having been "wounded" by Bertram, she
now cures the king to make her own wound heal. Lafeu, before
even the cure is accomplished, introduces Helena to the king
in language full of sexual *double-entendre*. Remarking jokingly
that the real disease the king is suffering from must be sexual
impotence, he symbolically hints at the "noble grapes" which
"my royal fox" pretends to ignore because he cannot reach them.
Becoming even more explicit he speaks of Helena as a physician
(he uses the word "medicine" instead)—

> That's able to breathe life into a stone,
> Quicken a rock, and make you dance a canary
> With sprightly fire and motion; whose simple touch
> Is powerful to araise King Pippen, nay,
> To give great Charemain a pen in's hand
> And write to her a love-line. (II, *1*, *76*)

The broadest hint of all occurs when Lafeu calls himself Pandarus and compares Helena to Cressida who comes to keep her
assignment with Troilus. This sounds like a clearly stated invitation to lechery. It is scarcely surprising to find the same Lafeu
describing the king's appearance after his cure again in explicitly
sexual language:

> Lustique, as the Dutchman says. I'll like a maid the better whilst
> I have a tooth in my head. Why, he's able to lead her a coronto.
> (II, *3, 48*)

Helena's never divulged remedy with which she heals the king
is only tenuously rooted in the past, her father's deathbed in-

spiration: its efficacy is psychologically bound up with her own future.

The ideal image of human excellence, the healer who in devious ways makes human survival possible, here acquires a new dimension. In the plays previously discussed here, a masculine figure, himself unmarried or a widower, intervened in the life of others who were in need of conscious guidance, as in the cases of Claudio, Angelo, Ferdinand, or Leontes. In spite of the ignorance, malice, and vice the healer had to fight against, his intervention had always tended to produce the desired end, marriage or reconciliation. This was made possible by a voluntary submission to a principle of integration. In *All's Well* the process is reversed. The king who himself should be a healer has lost his curative power and has to be restored to health. The instrument with the help of which the cure is accomplished is a young girl, an anima-figure who, in the words of Jung, "becomes creative when the old king renews himself in her. . . . The apotheosis of the king, the renewed rising of the sun, means . . . that a new dominant of consciousness has been produced and that the psychic potential is reversed. . . . It is primarily the feminine element in man, the anima, that becomes visible. . . . At a certain level, therefore, woman appears as the true carrier of the longed-for wholeness and redemption." [18]

What then distinguishes Helena from previous healers is not merely her sex, but her performing of a fertility rite which is followed by the king's restoration as well as the fulfillment of her own love. With the king's cure, society itself appears resurrected, and the play which began with the nostalgia of the weary and the sick for the good old days, ends with Helena herself restored to her natural function as wife and mother. For "Dead though she be, she feels her young one kick" (V, 3, 296).

Apart from obvious Christian analogies,[19] Helena's archetypal healing of the king appears to be an Elizabethan version of an ancient father-daughter mythologem. According to the original myth, twice told by Hesiod,[20] Prometheus, himself a savior-figure, had a daughter, Pandora, whom he created to share man's life on earth. It was, also according to the myth, Prometheus himself who animated her with the aid of the fire he had stolen from the gods. They, in turn, presented her with beneficial as well as harmful gifts and thus created the archetypal image of woman, both beautiful and evil, as symbolized by Pandora. Conveyed to earth by Hermes, she was accepted as a wife by Epimetheus, Prometheus's brother, and thereby became the mother of all women. It is she, Hesiod pessimistically remarks, who was responsible for the spread of diseases and vices among mankind by opening the fateful vessel which contained an infinite variety of evils that immediately flew away and infected alike men and women. The vessel, however, also contained Hope which was prevented from escaping and remained imprisoned in what has been described as a "huge earthenware storage jar . . . large enough to serve as a receptacle for the dead or . . . a shelter for the living." [21]

Other less prejudiced accounts of the Pandora legend, tell a very different story. For the archetype of the "mother of all women" originating among the primitive matriarchal Greeks, was a real goddess risen from the earth and worshipped by men as "the giver of all gifts." She was the Mother of Life; men did sacrifice to her: for her "vessel" (which never was a "box" but a symbolic representation of the grave as a place of burial as well as resurrection) contained all the divine gifts generously distributed among men who turned them into the humane arts and sciences, thus making civilization possible on earth. The shift from matriarchal to patriarchal interpretation of the original myth of the "first wife" and the "first mother," may not appear to be a real advance in human civilization. Yet "matriarchy gave to woman a false because a magical prestige. With patriarchy came inevitably the facing of a real fact, the fact of the greater natural weakness of women. . . . The future held indeed a time when the nonnatural, mythical truth came to be apprehended, that the stronger had a need, real and imperative, of the weaker." [22]

With Pandora, then, love came into the world and a humanizing of the affections. In an ancient vase-painting "an Eros flits above her head, with his troop of joyful heralds of marriage. Hermes is hastily approaching with a flower. . . ." Pandora, the all-giving, was not the frivolous handiwork of jealous gods, as Hesiod implies. Even Prometheus would have been unable to make this second gift to men "had not Mother Earth been willing to bestow upon them her own image." [23] The archetype contained in the Pandora-myth, then, stands for a peculiarly feminine kind of perfection, the ideal image of woman as a healer, supplementing the gifts of her primordial father by civilizing men and "thereby charming us into submission to more feminine habits"; it is due to her beneficial influence that "we acquired all kinds of artifices, sophistication, the supererogatory invention of all the other arts, and the readjustment of a hard and simple life to softer and more effeminate standards; all of which may be designated as 'the woman Pandora'." [24] According to a Neoplatonic exegesis of the Pandora myth she was identified with "the eternally feminine" or the "irrational life force," or simply "the irrational part of the soul." Goethe, who at the age of twenty-four, in 1773, wrote a Prometheus play which remained unfinished, must have known of such interpretations of the Pandora myth. In his dramatic fragment she is Prometheus' favourite daughter. Far from being deified, she is a lovely, innocent girl who understands her father so well that he confides to her the secrets of life and death. These secrets contain a wisdom that may be summed up in the Greek phrase, "the cause of life, however, is death." Prometheus standing before Pandora's image addresses to it an eloquent hymn of praise: "And you, Pandora, sacred vessel of all gifts that are delightful under the broad sky, on the infinite earth—all that which has ever revived me with joyful feelings, which has poured relief on me in the cool of the shadow . . . all that which I have ever tasted as a pure radiance of heaven and a calm pleasure of the soul—all this, all this, my Pandora." [25]

Shakespeare's Helena, the daughter of a holy and inspired father, from whom she inherited the miraculous gift of healing rejuvenation, contains those very features that have turned Pandora into the positive archetype of the anima in men. Whatever vessel it was that she opened, whether it was a gravelike jar or a basket called a "helene," filled with phallic emblems,[26] it must have contained a very special medicine for the ailing king to cure him of his old-age weariness (and his fistula). The same prescription was used for young Bertram to open his eyes and know her for what she really was. By bringing the gift of love to a sceptical, dying society she humanized their way of life, resurrected hope (so cruelly absent at the beginning of the play) and ensured that the "third eye" that had been bestowed upon her by her father should be transmitted to her children. In a more humane sense than in the ancient myth, Helena reveals herself as "the first wife" and the "first mother" of man: by hazarding all, she gives all—including her virginity. Not merely a "beautiful evil" created to tempt primordial man into tasting of forbidden knowledge, but an all-giving and therefore all-forgiving healer of souls. No longer in need of the magical prestige that matriarchy had in the past bestowed upon women, but herself a fateful vessel still containing the most precious recipe of all, Hope, which she now offers to man as the most curative of all prescriptions.

The artificer disguised as priest, the wise old man, the virgin, all of them healers of the mind, come to us out of a collective unconscious that gave shape to the Christian and pre-Christian symbolism of these plays. The darkness and exile imposed upon them by their human fate, at times almost defeat them. What makes human survival possible is the wonder of their spiritual healing, which they perform at a moment of miraculous perfection that is theirs and that they can transmit to the anguished soul of men threatened with extinction. The ambiguity with which Shakespeare endows these representatives of spiritual excellence lies in their awareness of being human and not divine, yet existing on a transpersonal level of intuition and prescience, quite beyond the confines of limited time and space as represented on the stage.

Works Cited

ALEXANDER, F. "A Note on Falstaff," *Psychoanalytical Quarterly*, II, (1933)

APULEIUS. *The Golden Ass*, translated by Robert Graves, Harmondsworth, Penguin Books, 1950

ARNHEIM, Rudolf. *Towards a Psychology of Art*, London, Faber and Faber Ltd., 1967

AUDEN, W. H. *Selected Essays*, London, Faber and Faber Ltd., 1964

AUERBACH, Erich. *Mimesis. The Representation of Reality in Western Literature*, Princeton, New Jersey, Princeton University Press, 1953

BARBER, C. L. *Shakespeare's Festive Comedy, A Study of Dramatic Form and its Relation to Social Custom*. Meridian Books. The World Publishing Company, Cleveland and New York, 1963

BETHELL, S. L. *Shakespeare and the Popular Tradition*, London, P. S. King and Staples Ltd., 1944

BODKIN, Maud. *Archetypal Patterns in Poetry. Psychological Studies in Imagination*, London, Oxford University Press, 1951, first published 1934

BOWDEN, William R. "The Human Shakespeare and *Troilus and Cressida*," *Shakespeare Quarterly*, VIII (Spring 1957)

BRADBROOKE, M. C. *Themes and Conventions of Elizabethan Tragedy*, Cambridge, Cambridge University Press, 1952

BRADBROOKE, M. C. *The Growth and Structure of Elizabethan Comedy*, London, Chatto and Windus, 1954

BRADLEY, A. C. *Shakespearean Tragedy: Lectures on Hamlet, Othello, King Lear, Macbeth* (1904) London, Macmillan & Co., Ltd., 1950

BRYANT, J. A. *Hippolyta's View, Some Christian Aspects of Shakespeare's Plays*, University of Kentucky Press, 1961

BULLOUGH, Geoffrey. *Narrative and Dramatic Sources of Shakespeare*, London, Routledge and Kegan Paul, 1958

CAMPBELL, Joseph. *The Hero with a Thousand Faces*, New York, Bollingen Foundation, Pantheon Books, 1949

CAMPBELL, Oscar James. *Comicall Satyre and Shakespeare's "Troilus* and Cressida," San Marino, California, The Huntington Library, 1938

CAMPBELL, Owen. "*Troilus and Cressida*. A Justification." *The London Mercury*, IV (1921)

CHARLTON, H. B. *Shakesperean Comedy*, London, Methuen and Co., 1938

DANBY, John F. *Shakespeare's Doctrine of Nature. A Study of "King Lear,"* London, Faber and Faber, 1949

DAVID, Richard. "Shakespeare and the Players," In: *Studies in Shakespeare, British Academy Lectures,* London, Oxford University Press, 1964

DICKEY, Franklin N. *Not Wisely But Too Well. Shakespeare's Love Tragedies,* San Marino, California, The Huntington Library, 1951

ELIOT, T. S. *The Use of Poetry and the Use of Criticism,* London, Faber and Faber, 1933

EMPSON, William. *Seven Types of Ambiguity* (1930), Norfolk Connecticut, New Directions Book, 1953

EMPSON, William. *The Structure of Complex Words,* London, Chatto and Windus, 1951

FARNHAM, William. *Shakespeare's Tragic Frontier* (1950), Berkeley and Los Angeles, University of California Press, 1963

FERMOR, Una Ellis. *The Frontiers of Drama* (1949), London, University Paperbacks, Methuen, 1964

FRAZER, J. G. *The Golden Bough* (1922), Abridged Edition in one volume, London, Macmillan & Co., Ltd., 1963

FREUD, S. *On Creativity and the Unconscious. Papers on the Psychology of Art, Literature, Love, Religion and the Unconscious.* Selected with Introduction and Annotations by Benjamin Nelson, New York, Harper Torchbooks, 1958

FRYE, Northrop. *Anatomy of Criticism, Four Essays,* Princeton, New Jersey, Princeton University Press, 1957

FRYE, Northrop, *Fables of Identity. Studies in Poetic Mythology,* New York, A Harbinger Book, Harcourt, Brace and World, 1963

FRYE, Northrop. *A Natural Perspective. The Development of Shakespearean Comedy and Romance,* New York and London, Columbia University Press, 1968

GILLET, Louis. "Shakespeare: Les femmes de son theatre." *La Revue Hebdomadaire,* XXIX (1930)

GODDARD, H. C. *The Meaning of Shakespeare,* Chicago, Illinois, Phoenix Books, The University of Chicago Press, 1951

GORDON, G. *Shakesperian Comedy and Other Studies,* London, Oxford University Press, 1944

GRANVILLE-BARKER, H. "From Henry V to Hamlet," *Studies in Shakespeare, British Academy Lectures,* Selected and Introduced by Peter Alexander, London, Oxford University Press, 1965

GRAVES, Robert. *The Greek Myths,* Harmondsworth, Penguin Books, 1955

GRAVES, Robert. *The White Goddess—A Historical Grammar of Poetic Myth,* London, Faber and Faber, 1961

GUTHRIE, W. K. C. *The Greeks and their Gods,* Boston, Beacon Press, 1950

HANNAH, Barbara. "*All's Well That Ends Well.* Studien zur Psychologie C. G. Jungs." *Festschrift zum 8o. Geburtstag von C. G. Jung.* Zurich, 1955

HARRISON, Jane. *Prolegomena to the Study of Greek Religion* (1903), New York, Noonday Press, 1955

HAZLITT, William. *Characters in Shakespeare's Plays* (1817), London, Oxford University Press, World's Classics, 1934

HEILMAN, Robert B. *Magic in the Web, Action and Language in "Othello,"* Lexington, University of Kentucky Press, 1956

HEMINGWAY, S. B. "On Behalf of Falstaff," *Shakespeare Quarterly,* III, (1952)

HOLLAND, Norman N. *Psychoanalysis and Shakespeare,* New York, McGraw-Hill, 1964

HUNTER, Robert Grams. *Shakespeare and the Comedy of Forgiveness,* New York, Columbia University Press, 1965

HYMAN, Stanley Edgar. *The Tangled Bank,* New York, New York Book Co., 1962

JONES, Ernest. *Hamlet and Oedipus,* New York, Doubleday Anchor Books, Doubleday & Co., Inc., 1949 edition

JONES, Ernest. *Sigmund Freud, Life and Works,* London, The Hogarth Press, 1957

JUNG, C. G. The following individual volumes and essays were found to be of special relevance for this study; they are here arranged in chronological order:

Symbols of Transformation, 1912, revised edition 1952, *Collected Works (C.W.)* vol. V

Psychological Types or The Psychology of Individuation, 1921, London, Pantheon Books, 1964 (12th impression). Translated by H. Godwin Baynes

"On the Relation of Analytical Psychology to Poetry," 1922, *C.W.* vol. XV

"Spirit and Life," 1926, *C.W.* vol. VIII

"The Structure of the Psyche," 1927, *C.W.* vol. VIII

Contribution to Analytical Psychology, 1928, London, Kegan Paul Trench, and Trubner & Co., translated by H. G. and Cary F. Baynes

"On Psychic Energy," 1928, *C.W.* vol. VIII

"Commentary on *The Secret of the Golden Flower,*" 1929, *C.W.* vol. VIII

"Psychology and Literature," 1930, *C.W.* vol XV

"The Stages of Life," 1930, *C.W.* vol. VIII

"The Meaning of Psychology for Modern Man," 1933/4, *C.W.* vol. X

"Archetypes of the Collective Unconscious," 1934, *C.W.* vol. IX, part I

"The Development of Personality," 1934, *C.W.* XVII

"The Soul and Death," 1934, *C.W.* vol. VIII

"Conscious, Unconscious, and Individuation," 1936, *C.W.* vol. IX, part I

"Psychology and Religion," 1938/40, *C.W.* vol. XI

"The Spirit of Mercurius," 1943, *C.W.* vol. XIII

Psychology and Alchemy, 1944, *C.W.* vol. XII

"On the Nature of Dreams," 1945, *C.W.* vol. VIII

"On the Nature of the Psyche," 1946, *C.W.* vol. VIII

"The Ego," "The Shadow," "The Syzygy: Anima and Animus," "The Self," 1951, *C.W.* vol. IX, part II

Two Essays on Analytical Psychology, New York, Meridian Books, 1956 (*C.W.,* vol. VII, 1953)

"The Personification of Opposites," 1955/6, *C.W.* vol. XIV

Memories, Dreams, Reflections (1961), New York, Vintage Books, 1965

Analytical Psychology, Its Theory and Practice, The Tavistock Lectures (1935) London, Routledge and Kegan Paul Ltd., 1968

KERÉNYI, C. *The Gods of the Greeks,* New York, Grove Press, Inc., 1960, translated from the German by Norman Cameron

KERÉNYI, C. *Asklepios, Archetypal Image of the Physician's Existence,* New York, Bollingen Series LXV/3, Pantheon Books, 1959, translated by Ralph Manheim

KERÉNYI, C. *Prometheus, Archetypal Image of Human Existence,* London, Thames and Hudson, 1963, translated by Ralph Manheim

KERÉNYI, C. and C. G. Jung. *Essays on a Science of Mythology, The Myth of the Divine Child and the Divine Maiden,* New York, Harper Torchbooks, Bollingen Foundation, 1963, translated by R. F. C. Hull

KING, Walter N. "Much Ado about Something," *Shakespeare Quarterly,* XV/3, (Summer 1964)

KIRSCH, James. *Shakespeare's Royal Self,* New York, G. P. Putnam's Sons, published for the C. G. Jung Foundation for Analytical Psychology, 1966

KNIGHT, G. Wilson. *The Wheel of Fire* (1930), London, Methuen & Co., Ltd., 1949

KNIGHT, G. Wilson. *The Shakespearean Tempest,* London, Oxford University Press, 1932

KNIGHT, G. Wilson. *Principles of Shakespearean Production* (1936), Harmondsworth, Penguin Books, 1949

KNIGHTS, L. C. *Some Shakespearean Themes,* London, Chatto and Windus, 1959

KOTT, Ian. *Shakespeare our Contemporary,* London, Methuen & Co., Ltd., 1964

KRIS, Ernst. *Psychoanalytical Explorations in Art,* New York, International Universities Press, Inc., 1952

LAWRENCE, W. W. *Shakespeare's Problem Comedies* (1931), Harmondsworth, Penguin Books, 1969

LEAVIS, F. R. *The Common Pursuit,* London, Chatto and Windus, 1952

LEGOUIS, Emile. "La Contesse de Rousillon, *English* I (1936/7)

MASEFIELD, John. *Shakespeare,* London, Home University Library, 1911

MACULLEN, Joseph T. "Brother Hate and Fratricide in Shakespeare," *Shakespeare Quarterly,* III/4 (1952)

MORRIS, Brian. "The Tragic Structure of *Troilus and Cressida,*" *Shakespeare Quarterly,* X/1 (Autumn 1959)

MUIR, Kenneth. *Shakespeare's Sources, vol. I, Comedies and Tragedies,* London, Methuen & Co., Ltd., 1957

NEUMANN, Erich. *The Origins and History of Consciousness,* New York, Harper Torchbooks, The Bollingen Foundation Inc., 1962, first published in English in 1954 by Pantheon Books, Inc., New York; translated from the German by R. F. C. Hull, 2 vols.

NEUMANN, Erich. *Amor and Psyche, The Psychic Development of the Feminine. A Commentary on the Tale of Apuleius.* Translated from the German by Ralph Manheim, New York, Harper Torchbooks, Bollingen Foundation, Inc., 1962; first published in 1956

OVID. *Metamorphoses,* translated by Rolphe Humphries, Bloomington, Indiana, Indiana University Press, 1955

PANOFSKY, Dora and Erwin. *Pandora's Box. The Changing Aspect of a Mythical Symbol,* New York, The Bollingen Library, Harper Torchbooks, 1965

PARTRIDGE, Eric. *Shakespeare's Bawdy, A Literary and Psychological Essay and a Comprehensive Glossary,* London, Routledge and Kegan Paul, 1961

PETTET, E. C. *Shakespeare and the Romance Tradition,* London, Staples Press, 1949

PHILIPS, William ed. *Art and Psychoanalysis,* New York, Criterion Books, 1957

QUILLER-COUCH, Arthur. *Shakespeare's Workmanship,* Cambridge, Cambridge University Press, 1918

RAGLAN, Lord. *The Hero, A Study of Tradition, Myth, and Drama,* New York, Vintage Books, 1956, first published 1936 by Methuen & Co., Ltd., London

RANK, Otto. *The Myth of the Birth of the Hero,* New York, Vintage Books, 1959

RAMSAY, A. W. "Psychology and Literary Criticism," *Criterion,* XV (1936)

SCHNEIDER, Daniel A. *The Psychoanalyst and the Artist* (1950), New York, A Mentor Book, The New American Library, 1962

SCOTT, W. I. D. *Shakespeare's Melancholics,* London, Mill and Boon Ltd., 1962

SITWELL, Edith. *A Notebook on William Shakespeare* (1948), London, Macmillan and Co., Ltd., 1962

SPIVACK, Bernard. *Shakespeare and the Allegory of Evil, The History of a Metaphor in Relation to His Villains,* New York, Columbia University Press, 1958

SPURGEON, Caroline. *Shakespeare's Imagery and What It Tells Us* (1935), Cambridge, Cambridge University Press, 1965

STEWART, J. I. M. *Character and Motive in Shakespeare,* London, Longmans, Green and Co., 1949

SUTTIE, Ian D. *The Origin of Love and Hate* (1935), Harmondsworth, Penguin Books, 1963

TILLYARD, E. M. W. *Shakespeare's Problem Plays,* London, Chatto and Windus, 1950

TINDALL, W. Y. *The Literary Symbol,* Bloomington, Indiana, Indiana University Press, 1955

TOOLE, William B. *Shakespeare's Problem Plays, Studies in Form and Meaning,* London, Mouton, 1966

TRAVERSI, D. A. *An Approach to Shakespeare* (1938), New York, Doubleday Anchor Books, 1956

VYVYAN, John. *Shakespeare and Platonic Beauty,* London, Chatto and Windus, 1961

WELLEK, René and WARREN, Austin. *Theory of Literature,* New York, Harcourt, Brace and World, Inc., 1942

WHEELWRIGHT, Philip. *The Burning Fountain,* Bloomington, Indiana, Indiana University Press, 1968

Notes

─────────

(Complete bibliographical information is provided in the preceding section herein, entitled "Works Cited.")

Introduction

1. Herbert Read, as quoted in A. Q. Ramsay, "Psychology and Literary Criticism," *Criterion*, XV (1936), 631
2. S. L. Bethell, *Shakespeare and the Popular Tradition*, p. 115
3. J. I. M. Stewart, *Character and Motive in Shakespeare*, p. 36
4. Ibid., p. 55
5. Ibid., p. 9
6. T. S. Eliot, as quoted in René Wellek and Austin Warren, *Theory of Literature*, p. 72
7. T. S. Eliot, *The Use of Poetry and the Use of Criticism*, pp. 118–119
8. Ibid., p. 148n.
9. Ibid., p. 155
10. T. S. Eliot, from the Introduction to S. L. Bethell
11. S. Freud, "The Aetiology of Hysteria," 1896. Quoted in Stanley Edgar Hyman, *The Tangled Bank*, p. 306
12. S. Freud, "Construction in Analysis," 1937. Quoted in Hyman, p. 419
13. S. Freud, *Interpretation of Dreams*, 1900. Quoted in Norman N. Holland, *Psychoanalysis and Shakespeare*, p. 60
14. Letter to James S. H. Branson, 15–3–1934. Quoted in Holland, p. 61
15. 15–10–1897. Quoted in Holland, p. 59
16. Quoted in Holland, p. 61
17. Ernest Jones, *Hamlet and Oedipus*, p. 22
18. Ernst Kris, *Psychoanalytical Explorations in Art*, pp. 285 and 287 ("Prince Hal's Conflict")
19. W. I. D. Scott, *Shakespeare's Melancholics*
20. Ibid., p. 165

21. C. G. Jung, "On the Relation of Analytical Psychology to Poetry," 1922, *Collected Works*, XV, 67/100. Compare this with the conclusion arrived at by William Philips, the editor of an anthology, *Art and Psychoanalysis*: "The work of neurotic writers can be characterized as neurotic only by reducing its total meaning to its seemingly neurotic components—which, in turn, are assumed to be identical with the neurosis of the author."

22. C. G. Jung, "Psychology and Literature," 1930, *C.W.*, XV, 104/161. Some dreams may, indeed, reverse the generally accepted relationship between ego-consciousness and the unconscious, with the result that the unreality of the dream image may then appear to the dreamer the only true reality worth preserving. In his old age Jung saw himself in a dream, dressed as a Yogi and in deep meditation. When he woke up, he thought, "Aha, so he is the one who is meditating me. He has a dream, and I am it. . . . Our unconscious existence is the real one and our conscious world a kind of illusion, an apparent reality as long as we are in it . . ." (*Memories, Dreams, Reflections*, New York, Vintage Books, 1965, pp. 323–4). This is an experience familiar to the reader of Shakespeare's plays. Their impact is as direct and immediate as a vision seen in a dream. The personality of the dramatist, indistinct at all times, recedes into the background when the curtain rises. Invisible at last, it is to the play we turn with a sigh of relief. Here alone, be it in the book or on the stage, can reality be found. We are ready to repeat with Jung, "Shakespeare had a dream—and we are it."

23. C. G. Jung, "On the Nature of Dreams," 1945, *C.W.* VIII, 282/532

24. ——"The Structure of the Psyche," 1927, ibid., 157/339

25. —— "On the Nature of Dreams," ibid., 293/558

26. —— "Psychology and Literature," *C.W.* XV, 90/141

27. Philip Wheelwright, *The Burning Fountain*, p. 81

28. C. G. Jung, "On Psychic Energy," 1928, *C.W.*, VIII, 48/92 This is what W. B. Yeats, in his *Autobiography*, calls "the great memory"—"an embodiment of disembodied powers" which, he says, repeat themselves endlessly "in dreams and visions." Thus, in the creative process, some "passing scene" is seized upon and molded into "an ancient symbol without help from anything but that great memory." Northrop Frye calls these symbols archetypal or universal, and adds "that some symbols are images of things common to all men, and therefore a communicable power which is potentially unlimited" (*Anatomy of Criticism*, Princeton, New Jersey, Princeton University Press, 1957, p. 118). The attempt to combine the new insights arrived at in anthropological and psychological research and to apply them to the study of literature is frequently suggested in Northrop Frye's writings: "The work done on the ritual basis of naive drama in Frazer's *Golden Bough*, and the work done on the dream basis of

naive romance by Jung and the Jungians are of most direct value to [the archetypal critic]" (*Anatomy of Criticism,* p. 108). Some years later Frye is even more explicit, "But the fascination which the *Golden Bough* and Jung's book on libido have for literary critics is not based on dilettantism, but on the fact that the books are primarily studies in literary criticism and very important ones." (*Fables of Identity, Studies in Poetic Mythology,* New York, a Harbinger Book, Harcourt, Brace & World, Inc., 1963, p. 17).

29. C. G. Jung, "Spirit and Life," 1926, *C.W., VIII,* 336/644

30. —— "Conscious, Unconscious, and Individuation," 1939, *C.W.,* IX, part I, 286/517

31. —— "On the Nature of the Psyche," 1946, *C.W., VIII,* 199/396

32. —— *Mysterium Coniunctionis, C.W.,* XIV, 207/271

33. —— *Aion. Researches into the Phenomenology of the Self, C.W.,* IX, part II, 13/24

34. Ibid., p. 17/34

35. Ibid., p. 40/73

36. C. G. Jung, "Spirit and Life," 1926, *C.W., VIII,* 326/619

37. An example taken from the history of art illustrates this dependence of a unified vision on psychic polarity. In Rudolf Arnheim's recent inquiry into the psychology of art, Jung's various statements regarding the identity of image and meaning in archaic symbols are applied to a Taoistic symbol, the T'ai-chi-tu, "a well-known ancient emblem symbolizing the yin-and-yang principle in Chinese philosophy." The most striking feature in the design is its structural simplicity. Close analysis of this simplicity, however, reveals the complexity of underlying thought expressed in "the kind of symbolism psychiatrists, anthropologists, and philosophers are concerned with." What the emblem stands for is the principle of polarity where two antagonistic forces interact and then balance each other. "The yang is the male principle, it stands for light, warmth, and dryness. The yin is female and represents darkness, cold, moisture. By being opposites, the two principles generate the phenomena of Nature." (*Towards a Psychology of Art,* London, Faber & Faber, Ltd., 1967, pp. 222 ff.) A detailed inspection of the various forms of interaction reveals the mutual dependence of art and philosophical thought, of form and content. In this instance, polarity merging into unity, is a basic ingredient of all visual perception. It is also a way of life. It originates in a primordial experience which the artist, the philosopher, and the primitive share. Jung himself refers to this Chinese emblem as a symbol of "the primordial condition of things, and at the same time a most ideal achievement, because it is the union of elements eternally opposed. Conflict has come to rest, and everything is still or once again in the original state of indistinguishable harmony." (*Analytical Psychology. Its Theory and Practice,* London, Routledge & Kegan Paul, Ltd., 1968, p. 133. The

quotation is from "Lecture Four" in a series of five lectures delivered by C. G. Jung at the Institute of Medical Psychology, Tavistock Clinic, London, between September 30 and October 4, 1935.)

38. C. G. Jung, "On the Nature of the Psyche," *C.W.*, VIII, 224/430

39. —— *Psychological Types* (London, Pantheon Books, 1964), "Individuation," p. 562. (First published in English translation in 1923.)

40. —— "The Soul and Death," *C.W.*, VIII, 407/800

41. —— "The Stages of Life," *C.W.*, VIII, 402/792

42. —— *Symbols of Transformation*, 1912, revised 1952, *C.W.*, V, 285/432

43. —— *Two Essays on Analytical Psychology* (New York, Meridian Books, 1956), p. 187. (This edition will be used throughout. It was originally published as volume VII in the *Collected Works* of C. G. Jung in 1953.)

1 / *The Mask*

1. C. G. Jung, "Archetypes of the Collective Unconscious," *C.W.*, IX, part I, 122/221

2. *Ibid.*, p. 20/43

3. C. G. Jung, *Two Essays*, p. 167

4. —— *Analytical Psychology, Its Theory and Practice*, p. 21

5. —— "Psychology and Religion," *C.W.*, XI, 84/141

6. —— *Mysterium Coniunctionis*, *C.W.*, XIV, 308/424 ("Rex and Regina")

7. W. Hazlitt, *Characters in Shakespeare's Plays*, "Henry IV," p. 167

8. John Masefield, *Shakespeare*, p. 112

9. Arthur Quiller-Couch, *Shakespeare's Workmanship*, chapter VII

10. S. L. Bethell, *Shakespeare and the Popular Dramatic Tradition*, p. 69

11. W. H. Auden, *Selected Essays*, "The Prince's Dog," pp. 65–66

12. Erich Auerbach, *Mimesis. The Representation of Reality in Western Literature*, "The Weary Prince," p. 324

13. Ernest Jones, *Hamlet and Oedipus*, p. 89

14. Ernst Kris, *Psychoanalytical Explorations in Art*, p. 282

15. F. Alexander, "A Note on Falstaff," *Psychoanalytical Quarterly*, II (1933), 592–606

16. John A. Barish, "The Turning Away of Prince Hal," *Shakespeare Studies*, I (1965), 9 ff.

17. H. C. Goddard, *The Meaning of Shakespeare*, vol. I, p. 171

18. S. B. Hemingway, "On Behalf of Falstaff," *Shakespeare Quarterly*, III (1952), 310

19. J. I. M. Stewart, *Character and Motive in Shakespeare*, p. 139

20. Much useful material will be found in Lord Raglan, *The Hero. A Study in Tradition, Myth, and Drama*, pp. 205–217

21. C. Kerényi, *The Gods of the Greeks*, p. 179

22. C. G. Jung, *Psychological Types*, pp. 590–1

23. —— *Two Essays*, p. 203

24. Ibid., pp. 203–4

25. Ibid., p. 204

26. Ibid., p. 167

27. Ibid., p. 206

2 / *Appetite*

1. C. G. Jung, *Two Essays*, p. 173

2. Ibid., p. 174

3. —— "Structure and Dynamics of the Psyche," *C.W.*, VIII, 393/764

4. —— "The Development of Personality," *C.W.*, VII, 173/292

5. This is true of both men and women, though in Shakespeare's plays a woman's appetite is most often seen and judged through man's eyes. For, in Jung's words, "What man has found to say about feminine eroticism, and especially about the feeling-life of women, is derived for the most part from the projection of his own anima and is accordingly distorted." (*Contribution to Analytical Psychology*, 1928, translated by H. G. and Cary F. Baynes, London, Kegan Paul, Trench, Trubner & Co., p. 200). What Orsino implies in *Twelfth Night*

> Their love may be call'd an appetite,
> No motion of the liver, but the palate, (II, *4, 100*)

becomes desperately explicit in Othello's agonising belief

> That we may call these delicate creatures ours,
> And not their appetite. . . . (III, *3, 270*)

Hamlet's ambiguous remark about his mother's love for her former husband,

> Why she would hang on him
> As if increase of appetite had grown
> By what it fed on. . . . (I, 2, *144*)

is supplemented by Enobarbus's observation about Cleopatra,

> Other women cloy
> The appetites they feed, but she makes hungry
> Where most she satisfies. (II, 2, *239*)

Iago expanding this into a comment on women in general provides it with an ominous significance, "When the blood is made dull with the act of sport, there should be again to inflame it, and to give satiety a fresh appetite. . . ." (II, 1, 231), while Lear's compulsive imagination visualises "Yond simpering dame" in terms of animal lust,

> The fitshew nor the soiled horse goes to't
> With a more riotous appetite. . . . (IV, *4, 125*)

6. "Troilus and Cressida," *Harper's Monthly Magazine,* CXV (Oct. 1907) 659

7. R. K. Root, *The Poetry of Chaucer,* pp. 104–5, quoted in Hyder E. Rollins, "The Troilus and Cressida Story from Chaucer to Shakespeare," *PMLA,* XXXII (1917) 383

8. Agnes M. Mackenzie, *The Women in Shakespeare's Plays,* p. 199

9. Oscar James Campbell, *Comicall Satyre and Shakespeare's "Troilus and Cressida,"* pp. 194 and 232

10. Una Ellis Fermor, *The Frontiers of Drama,* p. 72

11. C. G. Jung, *C.W.,* V, 137/197

12. *Turculan Disputations,* book IV, vi, 12, quoted in Jung, *C.W.,* V, 128/185

13. Achilles refers to this appetite for killing in an ambivalent erotic context. Patrocles had just warned him,

> A woman impudent and mannish grown
> Is not more loathed than an effeminate man
> In time of action. (III, *3, 218*)

A few lines later Achilles, assuming the part of an "effeminate man," tells Patrocles,

> I have a woman's longing,
> An appetite that I am sick withal
> To see great Hector in his weeds of peace. (III, *3, 238*)

14. Compare this with Agamemnon's reference to Achilles, "He that is proud eats up himself." (II, *3, 165*)

15. Achilles, however, is not the only "fool" in the play. There are many more if we are to believe Thersites. According to him, "Agamemnon is a fool to command Achilles; Achilles is a fool to be commanded of Agamemnon; Thersites is a fool to serve such a fool; and this Patrocles is a fool positive" (II, 3, 67). When Cressida calls herself a "fool," she adds one more dimension to Cicero's definition:

> See, we fools!
> Why have I blabbed? Who shall be true to us
> When we are so unsecret to ourselves? (III, *2, 131*)

16. C. G. Jung, "Psychology and the Unconscious," *C.W.,* V, 335/519

17. "It would seem fair to argue that Shakespeare's extreme sensi-

tiveness about the quality, cooking, freshness and cleanliness of food developed rather later—possibly after experience of more delicate fare than that of Stratford, at the tables of his London friends. . . . From thirty onwards there is increasing evidence of fastidiousness of sensitive digestion, of disgust at over-eating . . . which translated itself into terms of physical appetite and its disgust." (C. Spurgeon, *Shakespeare's Imagery and What It Tells Us*), p. 121

18. Ibid., p. 322

19. C. G. Jung, *Two Essays,* p. 37

20. Ibid., p. 107

21. Ibid., p. 234

22. Twentieth-century sensibility is less easily shocked by Pandarus than was that of earlier readers: "I must in passing protest against the traditional excess of contempt for this tenderhearted and fanciful snob." (I. A. Richards, *The Hudson Review,* Fall 1948, reprinted in *Speculative Instruments,* 1955, p. 205). Or, "We must not be repelled by Pandarus' lax morality in helping these two to illicit love: since, in so far as we regard their love as illicit, we are clearly missing the whole point of this theme." (G. Wilson Knight, *The Wheel of Fire,* p. 60, "The Philosophy of *Troilus and Cressida*")

23. C. G. Jung, *C.W.,* V, 155/220

24. D. A. Traversi, *An Approach to Shakespeare,* p. 70

25. C. G. Jung, "The Secret of the Golden Flower," *C.W.,* XIII, 41/60

26. Here are some estimates of Cressida written in the nineteenth century and more recently:

a. "A wily profligate. . . ." (Jusserand, *A Literary History of the English People,* vol. III, p. 253)

b. ". . . a stain in the gallery of Shakespeare's heroines." (Gervinus, quoted in P. Stapfer, *Shakespeare and Classical Antiquity,* 1880)

c. ". . . a shallow, frivolous, sensual, pleasure-loving coquette." (G. Brandes, *William Shakespeare, A Critical Study,* 1898)

d. "The villain of the piece . . . a woman without heart, without will, and without charm." (Owen W. Campbell, *"Troilus and Cressida, A Justification," The London Mercury,* IV (1921) 48–59)

e. ". . . she is born, not made a wanton. In the polite language of the day she is 'over-sexed'." (John Palmer, *Saturday Review,* CXIV (1912) 732–3)

f. "There is not the least trace of feeling in this little schemer. Needless to say she is another Dark Lady." (Louis Gillet, "Shakespeare: les femmes de son théâtre," *La Revue Hebdomadaire,* XXIX (1930), pp. 70–94)

27. William Empson, *Seven Types of Ambiguity,* pp. 178–9

28. I. A. Richards, *Speculative Instruments,* p. 204

29. D. A. Traversi, *An Approach to Shakespeare,* p. 68

30. John Vyvyan, *Shakespeare and Platonic Beauty,* p. 197

31. C. G. Jung, *Two Essays,* p. 199

32. —— *C.W.,* XVII, 198/339

33. Joseph Campbell, *The Hero with a Thousand Faces,* p. 120

34. G. Wilson Knight, *The Wheel of Fire,* p. 70

35. Brian Morris, "The Tragic Structure of *Troilus and Cressida,*" *Shakespeare Quarterly,* X (Autumn 1959) 488

36. William R. Bowden, "The Human Shakespeare and *Troilus and Cressida*" *Shakespeare Quarterly,* VIII (Spring 1957) 177

37. C. G. Jung, *Two Essays,* p. 58

38. —— *C.W.,* V, 274/421 ff.

39. —— *C.W.,* V, 216/315

3 / *The Shadow*

1. C. G. Jung, *Mysterium Coniunctionis, C.W.,* XIV, 98/117

2. —— "Archetypes of the Unconscious," *C.W.,* IX, part I, 21/45

3. —— *Memories, Dreams, Reflections,* pp. 244–5

4. Ibid., p. 235

5. C. G. Jung, *C.W.,* VIII, 310/588

6. —— *C.W.,* IX, part II, 266/422

7. —— *C.W.,* IX, part I, 20/44

8. Ibid., 123/222

9. C. G. Jung, *C.W.,* IX, part II, 9/17

10. Ibid., 10/19

11. J. G. Frazer, *The Golden Bough. A Study in Magic and Religion.* Abridged edition (London, Macmillan & Co., Ltd., 1963, first published 1922) p. 250

12. C. G. Jung, *C.W.,* VIII, 309/585

13. —— *C.W.,* XIV, 417/602

14. —— *C.W.,* XI, 78/134

15. Harold C. Goddard, *The Meaning of Shakespeare,* vol. II, p. 44

16. See W. W. Lawrence, *Shakespeare's Problem Comedies,* p. 68 ff.

17. Emile Legouis, "La Comtesse de Rousillon," *English,* I (1936–7) 399–404

18. See H. B. Charlton, *Shakespearian Comedy,* pp. 261–2

19. *All's Well That Ends Well,* Arden edition (Methuen, 1959), Introduction by G. K. Hunter, p. xlviii

20. E. M. W. Tillyard, *Shakespeare's Problem Plays,* p. 109

21. C. G. Jung, *C.W.,* XI, 197/292

22. —— *C.W.,* VIII, 393/766. For a specifically Jungian interpretation of the play see Barbara Hannah, *"All's Well That Ends Well,* Studien zur analytischen Psychologie C. G. Jungs," *Festschrift zum 80. Geburtstag von C. G. Jung.* (Zurich 1955) II, 344–363

23. See J. I. M. Stewart, *Character and Motive in Shakespeare*, p. 102
24. Bernard Spivack, *Shakespeare and the Allegory of Evil. The History of a Metaphor in relation to his Villains*, p. 31
25. W. H. Auden, *Selected Essays*, "The Joker in the Pack," p. 102
26. Robert B. Heilman, *Magic in the Web. Action and Language in 'Othello,'* p. 58
27. C. G. Jung, *C.W.*, XV, 90/141
28. Erich Neumann, *The Origins and History of Consciousness*, vol. II, p. 352
29. Ibid., p. 353
30. C. G. Jung, *C.W.*, VIII, 370/712
31. Contemporary psychological research, for instance W.I.D. Scott, in his *Shakespeare's Melancholics* (p. 47 ff.), calls Don John a "morally defective" or simply a "pyschopathic personality." Such an approach in terms of "character" turns Don John into an individual with pronounced personal traits. He is, says Scott, "incapable of affection" and has "no moral basis for [his] behaviour." All this may, of course, be found in Shakespeare's text but appears somewhat irrelevant when Don John is considered as an archetypal emanation of evil embodied in the figure of the hostile brother. His various activities, then, need no longer be subjected to psychological analysis which—however true as part of Don John's medical case-history (of no concern at all to Shakespeare)— does not explain his presence in the play.
32. Previous commentators on the theme of the hostile brothers have emphasized its dramatic significance. The following is a characteristic example: "The basic purpose [of brother-hate in Shakespeare's plays] is to create a dramatic situation necessary in the development of the plot and character. . . . On the other hand [Shakespeare] showed how, despite the existence of such evil in human nature, man may overcome grave passions and find happiness." (Joseph T. McCullen, Jr., "Brother Hate and Fratricide in Shakespeare," *Shakespeare Quarterly*, III 4 (1952) 339–340). The theme of brother-hate and fratricide is of considerable interest to psychoanalysts in their studies of literature and the drama. However, they have to admit that too little is known about Shakespeare's childhood to draw any valid conclusions. For some revealing remarks on the limitations inherent in the biographical approach see Otto Rank, *The Myth of the Birth of the Hero* (New York, Vintage Books, 1959), pp. 233–4. Anthropological research, on the other hand, reports at least one instance where, in primitive society, the "Cain-jealousy" is effectively disposed of: "The Central Australian mother eats every second child, sharing it with the older baby." This unusual solution to the problem of the hostile brother is mentioned in Ian D. Suttie, *The Origins of Love and Hate*, p. 112.
33. C. G. Jung, *Memories, Dreams, Reflections*, p. 335

4 / *The Inner Voice*

1. C. G. Jung, *Mysterium Coniunctionis, C.W.,* XIV, 496/706
2. ——— "The Meaning of Psychology for Modern Man," *C.W.,* X, 155/332
3. ——— "The Development of Personality," *C.W.,* XVII, 173/292
4. Some of the following observations dealing with Angelo as a man more sinned against than sinning may illustrate my argument:
"If we don't see ourselves in Angelo, we have taken the play very imperfectly. Authority, in spite of his protest, was forced upon him, and there are grounds for regarding him as the major victim of the experiment." (F. R. Leavis, *"Measure for Measure."* In: *The Common Pursuit,* London, Chatto & Windus, 1952, p. 172).
"Angelo, indeed, does not know himself. . . . He is no hypocrite. . . . Angelo is the symbol of a false intellectualised ethic divorced from the deeper springs of human instinct." (G. Wilson Knight, *"Measure for Measure* and the Gospels." In: *The Wheel of Fire,* 1930, p. 85).
"The attempt to enforce the law by delegating authority to Angelo fails. It fails ultimately because of the Deputy's lack of self-knowledge" (D. A. Traversi, *"Measure for Measure."* In: *An Approach to Shakespeare,* p. 112).
5. C. G. Jung, *C.W.,* XVII, 185/319
6. Ibid., p. 200/341
7. William Empson, " 'Sense' in *Measure for Measure."* In: *The Structure of Complex Words,* p. 272
Literary comment on the bed-trick as dramatic convention dismisses it as a purely mechanical device to make the villain of the piece repent: "Such old tricks as the substitution of one woman for another . . . had no moral valency at all" (M. C. Bradbrooke, *Themes and Conventions of Elizabethan Tragedy).* Similarly Helen's role at the end of *All's Well* is described as pertaining to Elizabethan dramatic convention and of no symbolic significance: "When, with a moral reflection upon his [Bertram's] lack of moral sense, she strips off her pilgrim's weed to catch her runaway husband by a trick more worthy of him than her, she has become the puppet figure of an overworked craftsman" (M. C. Bradbrooke, *The Growth and Structure of Elizabethan Comedy,* p. 80). The historical approach to the bed-trick in *Measure for Measure* and *All's Well* explains it in terms of the different moral standards by which such conduct was judged in the past. In the opinion of the editor of the Arden edition of *All's Well* "There was little sense among Shakespeare's contemporaries that this was a degrading and unsatisfactory way of getting a husband either in real life or on the stage" (p. XLIV). The spectator who wishes to interpret the bed-trick (in either play) as an action fraught with religious symbolism may find the following

observation helpful: "The substitution motif . . . provides an analogue to the ransom paid by Christ for man . . . for love of man Christ descended from the state of pure spirit, much to the horror of the neo-platonist, to that of the flesh, and assumed the sufferings of that flesh to redeem man. Does not Helena, in a sense, do the same thing?" (William B. Toole, *Shakespeare's Problem Plays. Studies in Form and Meaning,* p. 150). In Freudian perspective, finally, the bed-trick constitutes a rearranged incest situation, the substituted girl standing for the tabooed mother whom the son has himself dishonored, his own birth proving the fact that she has had intercourse with a man. (Cf. Otto Rank, *Das Inzest-Motif in Dichtung und Sage,* 1912.)

8. Erich Neumann, *Amor and Psyche. The Psychic Development of the Feminine. A Commentary on the Tale of Apuleius.* Translated from the German by Ralph Manheim, p. 63.

9. Ibid., p. 19

10. Ibid., pp. 78–79

11. C. G. Jung, *Mysterium Coniunctionis, C.W.,* XIV, 207/271

12. The close relation between lust and blindness was, of course, a commonplace in Elizabethan philosophy, psychology, and medicine. The following quotations may help to place Gloucester's blindness in a historical perspective. In James Ferrand's *Erotomania,* the full title of which is *Or a Treatise Discoursing of the Essence, Causes, Symptoms, Prognostics, and Cure of Love, or Erotique Melancholy,* the eye is called "the most spermatical part about the Head" (Oxford, 1640, chapter XXII, p. 171); elsewhere Francis Bacon assures the reader that "much use of Venus doth dim the sight" and that the causes of this dimness is "the expense of the spirits" (*Sylva Sylvarum,* 1628, Sec. 693). Thus in Bernard Garter's *Tragicall and True Historie* (1563), "the lovers see each other but once, then take to their beds, and require the attention of a physician." (Quoted from Franklin M. Dickey, *Not Wisely But Too Well, Shakespeare's Love Tragedies,* p. 29)

13. C. G. Jung, *Two Essays,* p. 82

14. Ibid., pp. 204–5

15. Ibid., p. 226

16. Ibid., p. 252

5 / Logos—Fathers and Daughters

1. C. G. Jung, *Two Essays,* p. 220

2. —— *Aion, C.W.,* IX, part II, 14/28–29

3. —— *Contributions to Analytical Psychology,* translated by H. G. and Cary F. Baynes, p. 180

4. —— *Two Essays,* p. 199

5. —— *Contributions to Analytical Psychology*, p. 164

6. Ibid., p. 180

7. In a contemporary stage-production of *Twelfth Night* any undue emphasis on the relative masculinity or feminity of the actress who plays the part of Viola posing as a young man, may prove a serious handicap. Too much of either may turn the comedy into farce, and the archetypal situation into a transvestite game. The following description of how one of the key-scenes should be acted, given by one who himself frequently played the part of Orsino, may illustrate the danger of personalizing the archetype. Orsino and Viola-Cesario are listening to Feste's song, "Viola deeply in love with Orsino, Orsino not yet aware that he is already deeply in love with Cesario. He has an arm around the boy, holds his hands, listening to the love-poignancy of Feste's wavering melody, Olivia all but forgotten; for it is a nameless love only that rules, Cesario by his side." (G. Wilson Knight, *Principles of Shakespearian Production*, p. 61)

8. In this sense Helena's love for Bertram, in *All's Well* symbolizes an equal challenge to her Logos. To achieve integration of her own self, she has to confront and, ultimately, give shape to Bertram's incomplete and wavering anima. Her own conscious ego neither asks any questions nor hesitates: to be able to guide Bertram she must, at the very outset, "bury" her father. When she mourns, at the beginning of the play, it is not for a lost paternal image, but for Bertram's unresponsive anima. She hardly remembers her father:

> What was he like?
> I have forgotten him, my imagination
> Carries no favour in't but Bertram's. (I, *1, 78*)

9. Symbolically, now that Rosalind and Orlando are "one," they have outgrown the merely personal aspect of their encounter and marriage. Jung calls this union "a royal game played out between the active, masculine side of the woman (the animus) and the passive, feminine side of the man (the anima). . . ." And significantly he adds, "The personal protagonists in the royal game should steadfastly bear in mind that at bottom it represents the 'trans-subjective' union of archetypal figures, and it should never be forgotten that it is a symbolic relationship whose goal is complete individuation." ("The Practice of Psychotherapy," *C.W.*, XVI, 259/469)

10. Quoted in G. Gordon, *Shakespearian Comedy and Other Studies*, p. 24

11. E. C. Pettet, *Shakespeare and the Romance Tradition*, p. 132

12. Geoffrey Bullough, *Narrative and Dramatic Sources of Shakespeare*, vol. III: The Comedies, p. 77

13. Walter N. King, "Much Ado About Something," *Shakespeare Quarterly*, XV/3 (Summer 1964) 146

14. H. Granville Barker, "From Henry V to Hamlet," in *Studies in Shakespeare, British Academy Lectures,* p. 82.
15. Richard David, "Shakespeare and the Players," ibid., p. 51
16. J. G. Frazer, *The Golden Bough,* p. 555
17. C. Kerényi, "Kore," in *Essays on a Science of Mythology. The Myth of the Divine Child and the Divine Maiden,* p. 105
18. Ibid., p. 108
19. Ibid., p. 123
20. Ibid., p. 129
21. Ibid., p. 139
22. Geoffrey Bulloughs, *Narrative and Dramatic Sources of Shakespeare,* vol. III, p. 81
23. Robert Graves in his Introduction to his Translation of Apuleius' *Golden Ass,* p. 18
24. Erich Neumann, *Amor and Psyche,* p. 7
25. Ibid., p. 23
26. Ibid., p. 25
27. Ibid., p. 89
28. Ibid., p. 138
29. Sigmund Freud, "A Special Type of Choice of Object made by Men," first published in *Jahrbuch,* vol. II, 1910, translated by Joan Riviere. Reprinted in *On Creativity and the Unconscious. Papers on the Psychology of Art, Literature, Love, Religion and the Unconscious,* p. 162 ff.
30. C. G. Jung, *Aion, C.W.,* IX, part II, 16/31
31. Ibid., 21/41. (Hermes is supposed to have evolved as a god from the stone phalli which were local centers of a pre-Hellenic fertility cult; he was also worshipped under the name of Priapus. Cf. Robert Graves, *The Greek Myths,* pp. 58 and 66.)
32. C. G. Jung, *Aion, C.W.,* IX, part II, p. 22/42
33. C. G. Jung, *Two Essays,* p. 137 ff.
34. See Edith Sitwell, *A Notebook on William Shakespeare,* pp. 90–91
35. Mrs Jameson, *Characteristics of Women* (London, 1833) as quoted in *A New Variorum Edition of Hamlet* (New York, Dover Publications, 1963) p. 160 ff.
36. Ulrici, as quoted in John F. Danby, *Shakespeare's Doctrine of Nature. A Study in "King Lear,"* p. 115
37. A. C. Bradley, *Shakespearian Tragedy. Lectures on Hamlet, Othello, King Lear, Macbeth,* p. 323
38. Sigmund Freud, "The Theme of the Three Caskets," first published in 1913. In *On Creativity and the Unconscious,* p. 63 ff.
39. In a letter, written some twenty years later, Freud revised his previous view on *King Lear.* According to it "the secret meaning of the tragedy" can be found in Lear's "repressed incestuous claims on

the daughters' love." He elaborates this point further in the course of a letter: "Your supposition illuminates the riddle of Cordelia as well as that of Lear. The older sisters have already overcome the fateful love for the father and become hostile to him: to speak analytically, they are resentful at the disappointment in their early love. Cordelia still clings to him; her love for him is her holy secret. . . . In an early essay 'The Theme of the Three Caskets' I have another interpretation of the Lear story which only appears to contradict yours. . . . With the insertion of this feature, the saga gains a psychological interest which puts the earlier one in the background." (Letter of S. Freud to James S. H. Bransom, March 25, 1935, as quoted in Ernest Jones, *Sigmund Freud, Life and Works,* vol. III, p. 487)

40. Maud Bodkin, *Archetypal Patterns in Poetry. Psychological Studies in Imagination,* p. 15

41. C. G. Jung, *Aion, C.W.,* IX, part II, pp. 21/41

42. G. Wilson Knight, "The Lear Universe," *The Wheel of Fire,* p. 202

43. L. C. Knights, *Some Shakespearean Themes,* p. 114

6 / *Eros—Sons and Mothers*

1. C. G. Jung, *C.W.,* IX, part I, 85/162

2. —— *Symbols of Transformation. An analysis of a Case of Schizophrenia, C.W.,* V, 283/431

3. —— *C.W.,* IX, part I, 69/141

4. —— *C.W.,* V, 329/508

5. Timon who considers all mankind to be his enemy asks the earth to

Ensear thy fertile and conceptious womb:
Let it no more bring out ingrateful man. (IV, *3, 178*)

6. C. G. Jung, *C.W.,* IX, part I, 83/158

7. Erich Neumann, *The Origin and History of Consciousness,* II, 157

8. C. G. Jung, *C.W.,* IX, part I, 263/472
The more conventional "literary" approach looks upon Puck from the outside, not as part of the lovers' unconscious risen to the surface, but merely as a traditional dramatic device used by Shakespeare to make the lovers look even more foolish than they would otherwise have done. According to this view Puck, then, is the only one in the wood who possesses "consciousness"; for "it is he who knows 'which way goes the game'; therefore a festive confidence that things will ultimately go right supports the perfect gaiety and detachment with which Puck relishes

the preposterous course [the lovers] take . . ." (C. L. Barber, *Shakespeare's Festive Comedy,* Cleveland, Ohio, A Meridian Book, World Publishing Company, 1963, pp. 130–1). The text does not altogether bear out such an interpretation: surely, it is Oberon's "consciousness" rather than Puck's that makes him act the way he does. And the mischief he commits is a result of his "unrelatedness" and not due to any knowledge he might have of the intricacies of human nature.

9. C. G. Jung, "The Spirit Mercurius," *C.W.,* XIII, 194/241

10. —— *Symbols of Transformation, C.W.,* V, 221/324–5

11. —— *The Structure and Dynamics of the Psyche, C.W.,* VIII, 155/332

12. Ian Kott is, to the best of my knowledge, the first to have given a Freudian interpretation to this scene. Though the parallel with Goya's *Caprichos* with its obsessive naked asses, hairy apes, and repulsively sexualized bats appears far-fetched, some of his remarks are welcome corrections to Mendelssohn's falsely romantic musical version: "Chagall has depicted Titania caressing the ass. On that picture the ass is sad, white and affectionate. To my mind, Shakespeare's Titania, caressing the monster with head of an ass, ought to be closer to the fearful vision of Bosch and to the grotesque of the surrealists. . . . Titania has embraced the ass's head and traces his hairy hooves with her fingers. She is strikingly white. . . . The ass's hooves are entwining her more and more strongly. He has put his hand on her breasts. The ass's head is heavy and hairy. . . . Titania has closed her eyes: she is dreaming of pure animality." (Ian Kott, *Shakespeare Our Contemporary,* p. 82 ff.)

13. C. G. Jung, *Psychology and Alchemy, C.W.,* XII, 437–8/537–9. Shakespeare's sources for Bottom's metamorphosis tell a variety of stories having only one element in common, man's transformation into an ass in order to gratify either his or his beloved's sexual passion. Thus in Thomas Mouffet's poem "Of the Silkwormes, and their Flies," the manuscript of which Shakespeare is supposed to have read, and in which the story of Pyramus and Thisbe occurs, Venus's advice to Saturn on how to woo the disdainful Phyllis is described in terms of such a transformation, though with the express purpose of making the maid yield to the god's will:

> Transforme thy selfe into a Courses braue,
> (What cannot loue transforme it selfe into?)
> Feede in her walkes; and in a moment haue
> What thou hast woo'd to haue with much adooe:
> Whereto, consent the auncient Suter Gaue,
> In courses clothes, learning a maide to wooe,
>   Filling ech wood with neighs and wihyes shrill,
>   Whilst he possesst his loue against her will.

(Quoted in Kenneth Muir, *Shakespeare's Sources,* vol. I, p. 45)

In Apuleius's *Golden Ass* this change from man to beast is actually encouraged by the girl, Fotis, though with rather unexpected results. Their love-making, which is described in considerable detail, proves more exhausting than young Lucius has bargained for. He therefore asks the girl to provide him with an ointment that may transform him into a bird—"I want to be able to fly. I want to hover around you like a winged Cupid in attendance on his goddess." By mischance or perhaps because of the girl's unconscious preference, it is the wrong ointment that she supplies him with. The effect is astounding and humiliating: ". . . Then my face swelled, my mouth widened, my nostrils dilated, my lips hung flabbily down, and my ears shot up long and hairy. The only consoling part of this miserable transformation was the enormous increase in the size of a certain organ of mine: because I was by this time finding it increasingly difficult to meet all Fotis' demands upon it" (Apuleius, *The Golden Ass*, pp. 90–91). It is hard to say which of his possible sources Shakespeare remembered when he put Bottom translated on the stage: nowhere in the play does Bottom ever see himself as Titania sees him. He always remains human and remarkably reasonable though he might have been easily forgiven had he taken a less civilized attitude to Titania's provocative ardor. All that Shakespeare permits himself to say is that after her passionate embrace they fell asleep.

14. C. G. Jung, *C.W.*, IX, part I, 135/240
15. —— *C.W.*, V, 374/580
16. —— ibid., 373/579
17. —— ibid., 369–370/577
18. Tolstoy as quoted in William James, *Varieties of Religious Experience*, p. 185 (Cf: G. Wilson Knight, *The Wheel of Fire*, p. 246)
19. G. Wilson Knight, ibid., p. 246 ff.
20. J. G. Frazer, *The Golden Bough*, p. 475 ff.
21. Ibid., p. 460.
22. Eric Partridge, *Shakespeare's Bawdy. A Literary and Psychological Essay and a Comprehensive Glossary*, p. 153
23. J. G. Frazer, *The Golden Bough*, p. 10. (Italics mine)
24. Erich Neumann, *The Origins and History of Consciousness*, vol. I, p. 70
25. Ibid., p. 229
26. Ibid., p. 250
27. C. G. Jung, *Mysterium Coniunctionis*, *C.W.*, XIV, 442/634
28. As quoted in Edith Sitwell, *A Notebook on William Shakespeare*, p. 48
29. Ibid., p. 49. This legend is corroborated in Frazer's *Golden Bough* (p. 513) though with a revealing emphasis on rebirth. In his chapter on Dionysus Frazer tells of "a different form of myth of the death and resurrection of Dionysus" who, like Nero, is supposed to

have "descended into Hades to bring up his mother Semele from the dead. The local Argive tradition was that he went down through the Alcyonian lake; and his return from the lower world, in other words his resurrection, was annually celebrated on the spot by the Argives, who summoned him from the water by trumpet blasts, while they threw a lamb into the lake as an offering to the warder of the dead."

30. *King Lear,* Arden edition, ed. Kenneth Muir, p. 85, footnote to II, 4, 56–7

7 / Hecate

1. Cf. Kenneth Muir's Introduction to the new Arden Edition of *Macbeth* (London, Methuen and Co., Ltd., 1957), p. xxix

2. G. Wilson Knight, *The Shakespearean Tempest,* Appendix B, p. 332

3. Ernest Jones, *Hamlet and Oedipus,* p. 97

4. Ibid., p. 100

5. Erich Neumann, *The Origins and History of Consciousness,* vol. I, pp. 48–9

6. Ibid., p. 181

7. Cf: James Kirsch, *Shakespeare's Royal Self,* p. 367: "For Macbeth the snake is definitely feminine, which of course agrees wifth his whole psychology. The unconscious is not dead for him. It still has the same poison it always had, its numinosity combined with its power to over-whelm consciousness; briefly, its capacity for making man crazy."

8. Erich Neumann, *The Origins and History of Consciousness,* vol. I, p. 42

9. Ibid., p. 63

10. G. Kerényi, *The Gods of the Greeks,* pp. 42 ff.

11. Ibid., p. 48

12. Ibid., p. 51. Jung's comment on Echidna can be found in volume V of his *Collected Works* (182/265): "The double being corresponds to the mother-image: above, the lovely and attractive human half; below, the horrible animal half, changed into a fear-animal by the incest prohibition. Echidna was born of the All-Mother, Mother Earth, Gaia, who conceived her with Tartarus, the personification of the under-world. Echidna herself was the mother of all terrors, of the Chimera, Scylla, the Gorgon, of frightful Cerberus, of the Nemean lion, and of the eagle that devoured the liver of Prometheus. One of her sons was Orthrus, the dog of the monster Geryon, who was slain by Heracles. With this dog, her own son, Echidna incestuously begat the Sphinx."

13. Quoted in William Farnham, *Shakespeare's Tragic Frontier, The World of his Final Tragedies,* p. 95. See also the following: "Both the lamia and the fury of the fairy mythology harmed children, but the

lamia, by assuming an aspect of beauty, might also 'allure young men to company carnally' with her and then devour them." (Definition of "Lamie" in Sir Thomas Eliot, *Bibliotheca Eliotae,* 1548)

14. Ibid., p. 98

15. Ovid, *Metamorphoses,* translated by Rolphe Humphries, Book VII, ll. 74 ff.

16. Ibid., ll. 192 ff.

17. C. G. Jung, *Commentary on "The Secret of the Golden Flower,"* first published in 1931, *C.W.,* XIII, 23–24/34–35

18. Ovid, *Metamorphoses,* Book VII, ll. 40 ff.

19. Ibid., ll. 322 ff.

20. Ibid., Book XIV, ll. 402 ff. (Italics mine)

21. Apuleius, *The Golden Ass,* p. 269

22. G. Kerényi, *The Gods of the Greeks,* p. 35 ff.

23. Robert Graves, *The Greek Myths,* vol. I, p. 125

24. Jane Harrison, *Prolegomena to the Study of Greek Religion,* first publ. 1903 (New York, Noonday Press, 1955) p. 288

25. G. Kerényi, *The Gods of the Greeks,* p. 36

26. Robert Graves, *The Greek Myths,* vol. I, p. 122

27. Ibid.

28. Robert Graves, *The White Goddess—A Historical Grammar of Poetic Myth,* p. 173

29. Appolonius Rhodius, III, 1029 ff. quoted in Guthrie, *The Greeks and their Gods,* p. 218

30. Erich Neumann, *The Origins and History of Consciousness,* vol. I, p. 83

31. Hastings, *Encyclopaedia of Religion and Ethics,* quoted in Erich Neumann, *The Origins and History of Consciousness,* vol. I, p. 86

32. Freudian readers may consider the witches to be symbolic personifications of Macbeth's unconscious. They may then stand for "his deep feeling of castration at the hands of his wife" according to the Oedipal premise that "she who covets her father's power (phallus) will castrate her husband (deny him children) and use him as a tool" (Daniel E. Schneider, *The Psychoanalyst and the Artist,* p. 213 ff.). Although the play is full of hints at the "unsexing" of both wife and husband, Hecate and her three servants fulfill a more significant function in the psychological setting of the play. For if one looks upon them as a living content of the collective unconscious—as indeed Shakespeare's treatment of them seems to imply—they confuse and frighten the minds of almost all the figures in the play, although in Macbeth alone do they actually invade his consciousness: "What happens as a result of this invasion depends on the attitude of the individual. He might become a sayashant, a prophet, a poet, a neurotic, a psychotic, a tyrant or a criminal. It is this individual victim who then suffers most, who carries the burden of the collective guilt or becomes the speaker for

a new knowledge and new attitudes." (James Kirsch, *Shakespeare's Royal Self*, pp. 324–5)

33. Gilbert Murray, *Five Stages of Greek Religion*, p. 80
34. C. G. Jung, *C.W.*, XV, 82/129
35. Erich Neumann, *The Origins and History of Consciousness*, vol. I, p. 161 ff.

8 / Prometheus

1. C. G. Jung, *Two Essays*, p. 250
2. Ibid., p. 252
3. Ibid., p. 318n.
4. C. G. Jung, "The Secret of the Golden Flower," *C.W.*, XIII, 12/13
5. —— *Psychological Types*, p. 220
6. C. Kerényi, *The Gods of the Greeks*, p. 213
7. —— *Prometheus. Archetypal Image of Human Existence*, p. 55
8. C. G. Jung, *C.W.*, IX, part I, 216/396
9. Ibid., 253/455
10. C. Kerényi, *Prometheus*, p. 17
11. Introduction to the Arden Edition, 1903
12. C. G. Jung, *Two Essays*, p. 240
13. Ibid., p. 247
14. J. G. Frazer, *The Golden Bough*, p. 14
15. C. G. Jung, *C.W.*, IX, part I, 220/404
16. Ibid., 222/406

9 / Orpheus

1. Ovid, *Metamorphoses*, Book XI, ll. 17 ff.
2. G. Wilson Knight, *The Shakespearean Tempest*, p. 292
3. Ernest Buonaiuti, "Ecclesia Spiritualis," in *Spirit and Nature, Papers from the Eranos Yearbooks*, p. 224 (Bollingen Series XXX, 1, 1954)
4. C. G. Jung, *C.W.*, XVI, 116/239

10 / Asklepios

1. C. G. Jung, *C.W.*, XVI, 81/185 ("Practice of Psychotherapy" 1954)
2. C. Kerényi, *Asklepios, Archetypal Image of the Physician's Existence*, p. 50
3. Ibid., p. 22, quoted from P. Wolters, "Darstellungen des Asklepios," *Athenische Mitteilungen* (Athens), XVII (1892) 1–15

4. Ibid., p. 41
5. Ibid., p. 69
6. Ibid., p. 100
7. C. G. Jung, *C.W.*, XVI, 116/239 ff.
8. Ibid., p. 78/179
9. C. Kerényi, *Asklepios*, p. 84
10. Ibid., p. 26
11. These are Kent's words addressed to Lear (I, 1, 163). Compare this with Timon's contemptuous reference to doctors:

> Trust not thy physician,
> His antidotes are poison, and he slays
> More than you [thieves] rob. (IV, *3, 434*)

12. Quoted in the Arden edition of *Macbeth*, p. 335
13. J. G. Frazer, *The Golden Bough*, p. 118
14. C. G. Jung, *C.W.*, XVI, 83/190
15. C. Kerényi, *Asklepios*, p. XX
16. C. G. Jung, *C.W.*, IX, part I, 251/453
17. —— *C.W.*, VIII, 277/526
18. —— *C.W.*, XIV, 308/424 and 355/498
19. Cf. especially: E. M. W. Tillyard, *Shakespeare's Problem Plays,* 1950; J. A. Bryant, Jr., *Hippolyta's View, Some Christian Aspects of Shakespeare's Plays,* 1961; Robert Grams Hunter, *Shakespeare and the Comedy of Forgiveness,* 1965; William B. Toole, *Shakespeare's Problem Plays, Studies in Form and Meaning,* 1966.
20. Hesiod, *Theogony,* 590, and *Works and Days,* 53
21. Dora and Erwin Panofsky, *Pandora's Box. The Changing Aspects of a Mythical Symbol,* pp. 7–8
22. Jane Harrison, *Prolegomena to the Study of Greek Religion,* p. 285
23. C. Kerényi, *The Gods of the Greeks,* p. 219
24. Tzetzes, about 1250, from a commentary to Hesiod's *Works and Days,* quoted in Panofsky, *Pandora's Box,* p. 129
25. Goethe, *Prometheus,* 11.173, as quoted in Panofsky, *Pandora's Box,* p. 12
26. Robert Graves, *The Greek Myths,* vol. I, p. 208

Index